THE
DEAD SEA SCROLLS
AND THE
CHRISTIAN MYTH

JOHN M. ALLEGRO

THE

DEAD SEA SCROLLS

AND THE

CHRISTIAN MYTH

First American Edition

Published 1984 by
Prometheus Books
700 E. Amherst Street, Buffalo, New York 14215

Copyright ©1984 by John M. Allegro

First published in Great Britain in 1979 by Westbridge Books (a division of David & Charles).

ISBN 0-87975-241-6
Library of Congress Catalog Card No. 83-63566

Contents

List of Maps

Acknowledgements

The rendering of biblical passages in this book mainly follows
that of the Revised Standard Version (1952, 1956) by permission of the publishers, with such variations as necessary by
reference to the original tongues. Translations of extra-canonical
literature are similarly based upon the editions in R. H. Charles,
Apocrypha and Pseudepigrapha of the Old Testament, Oxford, 1913,
while the works of Josephus and Pliny are quoted by permission
from the editions of the Loeb Classical Library. Citations from
the Dead Sea Scrolls are made by the author from the published
editions of the texts and from the original manuscripts. The
newly-dicovered letter of Clement of Alexandria is reproduced
by permission from Professor Morton Smith's book *The Secret
Gospel*, Gollancz, 1974.

The infra-red photograph of 4Q Therapeia is reproduced by
arrangement with the Palestine Archaeological Museum (ref.
PAM 218/25 viii 65), while all other photographs used in this
book and on the jacket are the copyright of the author.

Preface

I am glad of the opportunity to welcome this edition of my book. When it first appeared in 1979, the English publishers demanded that the recently discovered letter from the second-century Church Father, Clement of Alexandria, should be removed from my manuscript. It had been found by Professor Morton Smith in the library of the ancient monastery of Mar Saba in the Judaean Wilderness and published by him in popular form in his book *The Secret Gospel* (1974). The letter appears to confirm the existence of an original sequence to the story of the young rich man in the New Testament (Mark 10:17–23), and involves a nocturnal initiation ceremony of a homosexual nature. The Church authorities, represented by Clement, were apparently much embarrassed by this "secret gospel," whose circulation was restricted strictly to those "who had been initiated into the great mysteries," for, as the worthy Father admitted, "not everything that is true needs necessarily to be divulged to all men." My own publishers felt similarly inhibited, claiming that their lawyers had warned of the possibility that by publishing the text in my book the publishing house could lay itself open to the charge of blasphemy in a twentieth-century English court of law!

Happily my American publishers are less fearful of litigation and more concerned for the integrity of authors' manuscripts. In this edition of my book the text is complete. (See Appendix 2.)

As far as the Dead Sea Scrolls in general are concerned a more serious and continuing cause for concern is the apparent reluctance

5

of my colleagues of the International Editing Team to publish the texts in their charge. It is now more than thirty years since we began to gather in Jerusalem to piece together, edit, and publish the contents of a newly discovered cache in the Dead Sea area. Some four hundred different documents had been ripped apart and thrown into a subterranean chamber a stone's throw from the Essene monastery at Qumran, probably during its siege by the Romans in AD 68. When the cave was discovered two thousand years later, its precious contents faced us with the task of reassembling some tens of thousands of parchment and papyrus fragments. Some of the tiniest pieces will probably never find a home in their original documents, but the bulk of our work was completed a score or so years ago. In fact, I am still the only member of that original team to have published all of his section of the work in definitive form (1968), and from the beginning had made known the more important of my texts provisionally in the learned journals, as we had been urged to do at the outset of our labours. Despite all the impatient murmurings of fellow-academics over the years, my colleagues have managed to retain their exclusive control over these important manuscripts.

More generally, discussion of the Dead Sea Scrolls in lay as well as academic circles has waned since the sixties for a number of reasons. Popular curiosity, which played such an important part in the original stimulation of interest, has been stifled by a combination of academic professionalism, not to say obscurantism, and the desire of some clerical authorities to deter too great an emphasis upon the Jewish sectarian background of the supposed "unique" revelation of the Christian Founder. Many wished the Dead Sea Scrolls would go away; one learned professor expressed the fervent wish in my presence that they had never been found, indeed, that they had remained "at the bottom of the Dead Sea"! Popular attention was diverted into such harmless trivia as the Turin Shroud. The great questions about Christian origins that have hammered on the door of critical scholarship for centuries have remained unanswered, and the potentiality of the Dead Sea Scrolls for illuminating a hitherto obscure area of first-century sectarian Judaism has remained virtually unexploited. The first desideratum of any piece of honest research is the wish to know the answer, even though its revelation might be at the cost of long-cherished but insufficiently founded dogma. This book is directed to those

6

who are willing to consider fresh lines of approach to these old questions in the light of new evidence from the Dead Sea caves.

As a modest contribution to breaking the seal of silence about the unpublished scrolls, and injecting new blood into discussions about the Essenes, I have included in Appendix 1 to this book a hitherto unpublished document from the Fourth Cave cache, 4Q Therapeia. It seems to me to be a clinical report on some aspects of Essene therapy as practiced at Qumran, and confirms the traditional interpretation of their name as "Healers" (Aramaic 'asayya'). It also gives us a clue to the nature of those highly secret doctrines which, we are told, were on no account to be passed on to anyone outside the inner circle of the Elect. The possession of this "divine Knowledge" puts them in a direct line of tradition with the "heretical" Gnostics who were so troublesome to the so-called Great Church in the early centuries, but whose individualistic ideas of a personal faith and spiritual power have re-emerged so markedly throughout the history of the Church, and not least in claims to possess the ability to exorcize demons and effect miraculous cures. If nothing else, the publication here of this small document lifts the curtain and reveals some of the treasures that are still to be displayed when a handful of privileged scholars can be persuaded to find the will and energy to share "their" jealously guarded manuscripts with less fortunate colleagues and the world at large.

Introduction

For a large part of the year a mist broods low over the waters of the Dead Sea. From early morning till late in the afternoon the sun beats directly into this natural oven of the Palestinian Rift Valley. Limestone cliffs bordering the western shore intensify the heat and in their steep hostility add to the isolation of this desert of the damned. The sins of Sodom and Gomorrah, committed, as it is said, upon the shores of this unholy lake, were avenged by no single catastrophe of fire and brimstone; the curse of God was more perpetual and devastating. The air is heavy with the smell of dank decay.

Yet it was to this bleached wilderness that pious men came two thousand years ago to seek sanctuary, and to await the coming of the Lord. They brought their high expectations, their prayers, and their books, and when at length they departed, hopes unfulfilled, prayers unanswered, they left their writings as a silent witness to their faith. This was the home of the people of the Dead Sea Scrolls.

In 1947, an Arab shepherd chanced upon a cache of these documents in a cave, high in the cliffs at the north-western end of the Dead Sea. He and his friends knew nothing of the real nature of their strange find, and it was some eighteen months before the news broke upon the outside world. Initial incredulity gave way to increasing excitement as the full significance of the discovery was borne upon scholars and laymen alike. Here, at last, it seemed was the treasure religious historians and biblical critics had long been seeking in the Land of the Book, and had despaired of ever finding. Archaeologists had declared the soil of Palestine an unlikely repository for such perishable materials as parchment and papyrus; the climate of the country, particularly the Judaean uplands, was too wet to allow their preservation. Indeed, one venerable explorer of the nineteenth century had roundly pronounced all the caves of that land far too damp to permit the survival of anything so delicate as written documents; largely as a result of his unquestioned dogmaticism at least one early discovery of manuscripts from this comparatively dry Dead Sea area had been declared a shameless forgery and its luckless purveyor hounded to a lonely and desperate suicide. By 1949, scholars and archaeologists were prepared to admit the authenticity of the Arab shepherd's find, and subsequent excavation of the sites concerned verified his story. Religious historians seized upon this fresh evidence for the development of sectarian Judaism in the crucial centuries over the turn of the era, BC to AD; biblical specialists hoped to find in these ancient manuscripts textual variations from the standard versions of the sacred books whose earliest exemplars had hitherto come only from the ninth and tenth centuries.

Most scholars agreed that the owners of the scrolls had been Essenes, known previously only by repute. Early historians, like Josephus, Philo Judaeus, and Pliny the Elder, writing in the first century, had spoken admiringly of this strange Jewish community by the Dead Sea. They were said to have separated themselves from their religious contemporaries to live a more 'holy' life in the wilderness, spurning worldly comforts and even, for some, the company of women. They were clearly an important element of Jewish religious life, ranking with Pharisees and Sadducees, but so secretive about their doctrines and practices that only those who had penetrated to their innermost counsels could know their mysteries.

The ascetic exclusiveness of the Essenes meant that their

10

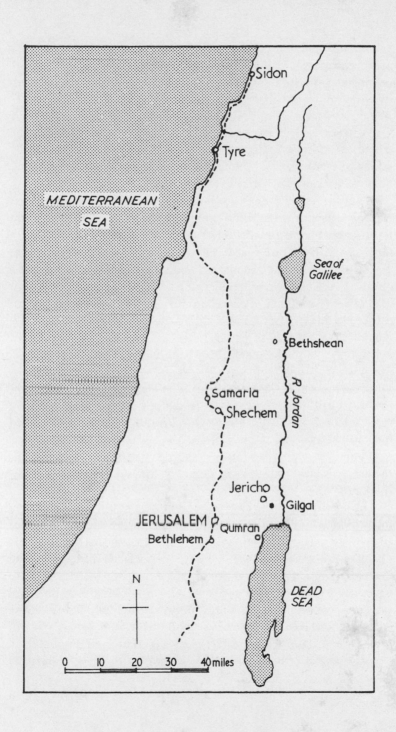

internal discipline needed to be very strict indeed, and their oaths of secrecy were binding on initiates beyond life itself. They were organised into orders of seniority, based upon degrees of training and self-dedication, and their material possessions were held in common. In such closely knit communities, mutual love and respect were of paramount importance, particularly in the desperate living conditions they must have experienced in the Judaean Wilderness. 'Loving one's neighbour' was not so much a moral goal as a necessity for survival.

What gave the Essenes their peculiar interest to religious historians was the possibility that their kind of Judaism might have served as the matrix for that even more unorthodox Jewish faith we call Christianity. Of all the recorded varieties of Judaism, that of the Essenes, as far as it was known, seemed the closest to the religion of the New Testament. The early Church also observed a form of communism, was at loggerheads with established Jewry as represented by the Jerusalem cultus, practised a ritual meal of some kind, baptised its initiates, and paid special regard to the teachings of the biblical prophets, whose every word was thought to offer insight into the future of mankind. Although the name 'Essene' was known only in its transliterated Greek forms, *Essenoi*, or *Essaioi*, there seemed good reason to believe it represented an Aramaic, ie Semitic, word meaning 'Physician' ('*asa*', plural '*asayya*'), and reflected the popular idea that these pious people, like Jesus and his followers, exercised power over demons, an essential part of folk-medicine.

The scrolls from the caves confirmed much of the earlier information about the Essenes, but added a most important feature of their teaching concerning the expected Messiah. This charismatic leader of the future, born of the lineage of the famous King David, would establish a new world order where the will of God reigned supreme. Such a blessed state could only come about after wars and bloody revolution, in which the 'Anointed' (Hebrew *Mashiah*), in his role of warrior prince, would personally lead the forces of Light in their apocalyptic struggle against the powers of Darkness under the arch-fiend

12

Belial, the devil. When the divine kingdom had been established, this Davidic leader would control its administration, while its spiritual direction would be undertaken by another Anointed, a priest, acting as intermediary between God and man in all matters relating to law and doctrine.

Whatever the differences between the Scrolls and the New Testament in their understanding of the messianic office, they clearly share a common Jewish background, and find their support in the same prophetic texts of the Old Testament. If, as it seems on the face of it, the communities interpreted those passages differently and stand at different points in their estimation of their place in the eschatological timescale, that is, their run-up to the 'last days' (Greek *eschatos*), at least both groups began from a common base. All in all, the first eager perusals of the new material supported the idea that in Essenism we might expect to find clues to the conception of Christian ideas.

Attention was now focused upon the essential differences between the Scrolls and the New Testament. While, admittedly, much of the incentive for the early, somewhat frantic, studies in this direction was occasioned by pious fears that the uniqueness of Christianity was being drastically undermined and the Faith set at peril, a more detached scholarship found in these differences the most intriguing aspect of the new finds. However, the comparative process poses a number of special problems.

In the first place, side-by-side comparison of the two sets of records, Essene and Christian, is hindered by the incompatibility of their respective languages. The Scrolls are for the most part written in Hebrew or Aramaic, the Semitic tongues used in contemporary Palestine; the New Testament is in Greek, meaning that underlying Jewish conceptions have been translated out of their native forms of expression into the language of the majority of the Church's non-Palestinian, and largely non-Jewish, adherents. To make adequate comparison, the scholar must try to reconstruct the underlying word or phrase in its original Semitic form, and thus assess its likely meaning in the original context. In other words, insofar as New Testament ideas are of Jewish origin, their form as presented by

13

a gentile Church is second-hand, and possibly distorted.

Again, apart from the obvious difference in chronological standpoint—the Scrolls were written mainly between the beginning of the first century BC and the first half of the first century AD—nothing in Essene literature anticipates a Messiah who would be a professed wine-bibber and companion of rogues and whores, or one so apparently well-disposed towards the hated imperialist enemies of his own people, the Romans. In fact, there is an air of unreality about the whole social and historical context of the New Testament story which has puzzled knowledgeable observers from the very beginnings of critical research into New Testament traditions.

Not least among the difficulties facing the inquirer is that of knowing what the first Jewish believers really thought about their Master's role, or, indeed, how he saw himself. If Jesus really was acting out the part of God's long-awaited Anointed (Greek *Christos*, 'Christ'), his idea of that office was, to say the least, unusual. The low-profile stance he adopted, even to the point at times of enjoining complete secrecy on those who wished to acknowledge his mission publicly, ill-accorded with current ideas about the Davidic Prince who would restore the glories of Israel's past. His disciples were themselves not a little confused by his, and their, situation, and appear to have been completely dumbfounded by his almost inevitable execution at the hands of the occupying power.

On the other hand, the view of Jesus's mission and person as represented by the letters of St Paul, the earliest of the New Testament records, and dating, supposedly, to within a decade or two of the Crucifixion, is completely different again. If we had only this correspondence to go on, we should know practically nothing about the Teacher's public ministry, his sayings, or any details, including the date, of his shameful death. But then, without the book of Acts, we should know very little about St Paul himself, or about the early years of the Church. The nearest we approach to St Paul's 'mystical', other-worldly assessment of Jesus's messianic mission is in the Fourth Gospel and associated Johannine writings, the letters of John and the Apo-

14

calypse (the book of Revelation), which are reckoned the latest of the New Testament books. John seems almost as little interested in the details and chronology of Jesus's mortal life as St Paul, but uses the received traditions as a framework for his more philosophical speculations on the witness of the Logos, the Word, the emanation of the Godhead on earth.

Significantly, it is just here, in the earliest and the latest of the New Testament writings, that we come closest to the Scrolls. One important fruit of recent comparative researches has been to bring the Johannine writings back into the fold of Jewish ideas, and to resist previous inclinations to assign them to sources on the very fringe of extra-Palestinian Judaism. So, in terms of a continuum of religious tradition, we must now count the Pauline and Johannine writings more 'authentic' witnesses to the earliest beliefs of the Church, and the first three so-called synoptic 'single-viewed' Gospels, for all their easier reading and seemingly realistic portraits of the man Jesus and his friends, will command less confidence as factual records.

Nevertheless, there are still serious differences between the Christian Redeemer and the Essene Messiah. The latter seems to be primarily a political figure whose function is related to the liberation of Israel and the establishment of a theocratic kingdom on earth. The Church's Christ, or Messiah, has a more spiritual function: his aim is to save individual souls rather than to establish a national independence, and his enemies are the demonic forces in the universe that hinder man's communion with God, rather than the armies of an imperialist power. There are suggestions in the Scrolls that the Essenes saw in their Teacher a type of the Messiah to come, possibly, some believe, a preliminary manifestation on earth of the Anointed himself, who would one day reappear in glory to lead his saintly cohorts against the forces of evil; but there is nothing there that matches the divine Saviour whose kingdom is not of this world.

So far, therefore, scholars have found the new discoveries by the Dead Sea, if quite as exciting as they anticipated, nevertheless somewhat frustrating. It must be confessed that what little of the material that has so far been published poses more

15

questions than it answers. The distance between the Essene documents and the New Testament is still greater than might be accounted for in the number of years separating them. Yet in some areas their ideas come close enough to warrant assumptions of direct dependence, and one is left with the uneasy feeling that if we understood more of the secret doctrines of the Essenes and of the early Christian 'heresies' which the Church was at such pains to suppress, we should discover a more continuous line of religious development between the two communities. Furthermore, the extraordinarily rapid spread of the nascent Church, if we are to believe the traditional chronology, complete with a well-developed system of intercommunicating cells around the Mediterranean area, highly organised funding arrangements, and an accepted structure of authority, demands a longer period of growth than can be accounted for between the supposed date of the Crucifixion, around AD 30, and the earliest of the Pauline letters. The Essene order possessed such an organisation, certainly, centred on their monastic community by the Dead Sea, but extending far out to the towns and villages of Judaea and very possibly beyond, into Egypt, Asia Minor, and to Rome. But if, as has been suggested, they were Essenes who so swelled the number of converts to Christianity in the first years of the Church, then we might reasonably suppose that their doctrines, and particularly their messianic expectations, were very much closer to those of their Christian mentors than anything that appears on the surface in the Scrolls. Otherwise, they would hardly have been so quickly converted to a faith in a Messiah who had failed so signally to transform the world in his three-year public ministry, and who had ended his life so ingloriously on a felon's gallows; it was not for this unpromising Gospel that the first Christians faced ignominy and death at the hands of their fellow-countrymen and their Roman overlords.

The relationship of the Scrolls and the early Church is, then, the subject of this book. Its elucidation will present us with a better understanding of the genius of Jewish sectarianism and its culmination in a no less 'heretical' form of Christianity.

16

1

The Essene Library

The first finds brought little profit to their finder. Back in camp, the Arab shepherd showed his strange treasures to his companions, but they could make little of the musty rolls of parchment. They were amazed by the length of the largest of the scrolls. Unrolled, it stretched the length of one of their goat-hair tents, some twenty-four feet. The light-brown surface was inscribed with a black, square lettering very different from the more flowing Arabic script to which they were accustomed. They wondered if their companion's find might bring a few much-needed dinars to ease the lot of their marginal living, but otherwise they shrugged off the event as of little consequence.

In fact, the scroll they had unrolled was priceless; it was one of two copies of the book of Isaiah older by a thousand years or more than any previously known manuscript of the Hebrew Bible. Our versions of the Old Testament are for the most part based upon translations of a medieval text, no older than the ninth or tenth centuries, and hope had long since been abandoned of ever finding some earlier witness to the sacred writings. Now, suddenly, out of the deserts of Judaea had appeared biblical manuscripts of much greater antiquity, with the promise of more to come. As it turned out, the biblical scrolls among the Dead Sea writings were the least important of the discoveries. For although they have rightly excited the interest of

17

textual critics whose task it is to try to restore the original words of the biblical writers, those copies of Isaiah served only to confirm the extraordinary accuracy that attended the work of the Jewish scribes over a thousand years of painstaking copying. They are virtually the same as the medieval versions we already had. The mistakes that had already crept into the text in the first or second century BC had been transmitted as faithfully by the copyists of the intervening period as the sound material. To penetrate behind those early corruptions will need copies of the Bible even older than those among the Scrolls.

Of greater general interest was the possibility that in the non-biblical writings were ideas, even personalities, which anticipate the Christian story. In view of the earlier date of the Essene documents, the latest of which could not be after AD 68, and most were of the century over the turn of the era, any borrowing involved must have been by the Church from Essenism, and not vice versa. Thus, of the first seven scrolls recovered from the Arab's cave, the ones that have come in for most discussion have included a commentary on the book of Habakkuk which refers to the sect's leader, the so-called Teacher of Righteousness, and his persecution at the hands of his arch-enemy, the Wicked Priest; a collection of thanksgiving hymns, many of which are of an intensely personal nature, giving reason for thinking they come from the hand of the Teacher himself; and, above all, an almost complete work calling itself the Rule of the Community, containing priceless information on such important matters as the spiritual influences that affect the lives of men for good and evil, and on the ordering and discipline of the sectarians in the harshness of their self-imposed exile. We learn of the regulations controlling the entry, training, and initiation of neophytes, the functions and titles of the chief administrative and spiritual officers of the sect, and we have excerpts from their liturgical ceremonies. Similar regulative manifestos are known from Church circles of the second to fourth centuries, but nothing like this had ever been seen in Jewish sources. Even ecclesiastical offices like those of bishops and presbyters have been found to have their counterparts, if not their source, in Essene administration.

The enthusiasm with which the Scrolls were first greeted became somewhat chilled as their potentiality for undermining the uniqueness and originality of Christianity dawned upon Christians, scholars and laymen alike. The late Edmund Wilson sensed this disquiet and suggested in a series of articles written for the *New Yorker* magazine, later reprinted in his book *Scrolls from the Dead Sea* (1955), that there might be some reluctance on the part of committed biblical scholars to draw out the full implications of the finds, perhaps even to delay their publication. Such reticence was hotly denied at the time, but it must be counted strange, nevertheless, that the bulk of the inscribed material recovered from subsequent discoveries in that area has still to be published in a definitive form.

The Arab's chance find in 1947 proved to be only the beginning of the Scrolls story. In the first place, locally based archaeologists were obliged to focus their attention for the first time upon this barren stretch of Palestine around the western shores of the Dead Sea. It had never hitherto attracted much interest, if only because of its inaccessibility and general inhospitality. There are, after all, enough potentially rewarding sites for excavation in that exciting country without having to endure the unbearable heat of the Rift Valley amid such scenes of desolation, or to limit one's working season to the few cooler months of the year. But now interested parties were demanding confirmation of the palaeographers' dating of the Scrolls; with the originality of the Christian Faith in dispute, it was essential to determine that the Scrolls really did pre-date the Church's records. Some scholars were throwing doubts upon the antiquity of the deposit, even proposing a medieval date for the find since there were some aspects of later sectarian Judaism which could also be paralleled in the Scrolls; not a few earnest Christians were wondering if that might not prove a most acceptable solution to the dilemma facing some of the faithful. It has to be acknowledged that the average western churchman is lamentably ignorant about the Jewish background of his faith, and would silently applaud the sentiment expressed in W. N. Ewer's quip,

19

'How odd of God to choose the Jews'. He finds their Scriptures, if not completely incomprehensible, and at times even repugnant, at best acceptable only as an unfortunate preliminary dispensation whose chief merit is to point up the contrasting excellence of the later Covenant.

The remains of a nearby settlement on a plateau overlooking the Dead Sea, a mile or so from the shepherd's cave, proved to be directly linked by similar archaeological deposits, and coins recovered from the ruins gave a dating to the main occupation of around 100 BC or earlier, to AD 68, the second year of the great Jewish revolt against the Romans, which began in Caesarea in AD 66 and ended in effect with the destruction of the Jerusalem Temple in August AD 70. The generally pre-New Testament dating of the documents was thus confirmed.

The Essene settlement itself was no architectural monument. Its most notable feature was a tower in the north-western corner, from which, when complete, it must have been possible to command a view from the head of the Dead Sea, some three or four miles to the north, southwards to the point where the cliffs shelve steeply down into the waters. The various rooms seem to have served more for the administration of the community than as dwellings. One large room, oriented towards Jerusalem, some twenty miles to the west, had clearly been used as a Hall of Congregation and as the community's refectory. A smaller room at the side was found to contain a thousand platters and similar utensils neatly stacked according to type along the walls; a fall of roof had preserved many intact for posterity. Not far away is a kiln used for making the community's pottery, including the characteristic tall storage jars in which the first scrolls to be discovered had been stored.

Another, two-storeyed building had contained in the upper chamber long plaster tables and benches, and their function was clearly demonstrated when the archaeologists came upon three inkwells in the vicinity, still containing the dried remains of the carbon-and-gum ink with which the Essene scribes had written many of the Scrolls. This must have been the Scriptorium of the 'monastery', as we may now begin to describe this religious establishment. Indeed, many scholars believe that it is here that we find the origins of Christian monasticism.

Water in such a barren area as the Rift Valley must have been a continual problem, for the average rainfall is barely two inches a year, and there is no evidence that the climate has radically changed over these past two millennia. It was, of course, the prevailing dryness of the western side of the Dead Sea basin, in the shadow of the rain-bearing winds from the Mediterranean, that had made the caves such excellent archaeological repositories. The Essenes had taken what steps they could to counter the climatic disadvantage of their sanctuary by digging out a number of large water cisterns and connecting them by canal and conduit with dams constructed in the cliffs behind. When it rains heavily in the Judaean hills some of the precious water flows eastwards from the watershed, and even reaches the cliffs bordering the Dead Sea. On these few occasions, the dams captured the streams before they fell to waste on the marly plateau, and led their waters to the cisterns.

Water was important to the Essenes not only for domestic purposes, but for their religious rituals. Baptism and lustrations played an important part in their purificatory ceremonials, accompanied by liturgies emphasising the need for spiritual cleanliness.

The keynotes of the whole establishment were simplicity and self-sufficiency. A couple of miles to the south of the monastery there is a freshwater spring, the only source of usable water nearer than Jericho, to the north. The remains of further Essene buildings and other installations in its vicinity clearly demonstrate the spring's existence at that time, and its use by the sectarians for growing crops and watering their small cattle. Enough food had to be supplied from their kitchen gardens and meagre pasturing to provide for the needs of the small community, for its members were not allowed to eat food apart from that grown and prepared according to their own very strict dietary laws. Their communal meals were, indeed, sacramental occasions, accompanied by blessings and prayers.

The excavation of the monastery took five seasons, beginning in November 1951, with a sixth concentrated on the installations grouped near the spring. Local archaeological talent in the wilderness is, to say the least, limited, and the work's directors, based in Jerusalem and Amman, were glad enough to use the services of the local Bedouin, fellow tribesmen of the initial discoverer of the Scrolls. They worked well and willingly, and were not deterred by the privations of the place and its climate. Their wages were a welcome supplement to a herdsman's sparse living, and since one of their number had sparked off the whole operation, they probably felt some proprietary claim to the place and its unexpected treasures.

It was therefore with some particular interest that these newly-enthusiastic antiquarians listened one evening to one of their elders describing an event that had befallen him long before, when, as a young man, he had been out shooting partridge in the very area of the monastery. It seemed he had winged a bird which fell on the plateau close to the dust-covered ruins. He had seen the bird flap its wounded way along the edge of the plateau and disappear down a hole. Being then young and agile, the hunter had squeezed his way through the cavity and, to his amazement, had found himself in an underground chamber, hollowed from the soft limestone of the plateau. He could see on the walls the tool-marks made by its excavators, and in one of several niches carved into the sides he found a small pear-shaped pottery lamp of an antique kind such as he had seen for sale in tourist shops. He had been somewhat frightened by this mysterious man-made refuge in the wilderness, and he had been glad enough to rescue his prey and escape to the sunlight and a more familiar world.

His younger companions listening to the story needed no further inducement to return to the site of their archaeological labours. The digging season had come to an end with the onset of the stifling heat of late spring and summer, so the Bedouin were able to work unhindered, searching for the old man's partridge chamber. It was not long before they located the hole in the edge of a dry wady that carves its way down to the sea alongside the ruins. They followed the sheikh's example, squeezed

22

through the aperture, and found themselves in the subterranean chamber he had described. Now, however, they were not looking for wounded birds; a cave so near the site of the former discovery and within a stone's throw of the ruins they had been excavating promised a rich reward, if the stories they had heard about the fate of those first musty parchments were true. It was said that four of the scrolls had been sold in America for a quarter of a million dollars.

The Arabs set to work scrabbling in the dust of the floor. They were soon successful. Under the hitherto undisturbed dust of two millennia their fingers encountered the frail leaf-like texture of parchment fragments, layer upon layer of them, in their tens of thousands. Here were no carefully rolled scrolls, wrapped about in linen cloths, and stored in jars, as in the first cave, but the torn remains of hundreds of documents, debris of what must have been the major part of the Essene library.

However inexperienced the Bedouin excavators may have been before in the gentler arts of archaeology and archivism, they had learnt much during their short apprenticeship; artifacts, however unprepossessing, were apparently considered of great value by the archaeologists, and their recovery unharmed and carefully preserved was rewarded generously. Very gently, then, this team of illicit cave-explorers worked through several days and nights, lifting the tiny fragments from the dust and placing them in empty cigarette cartons or any other containers that came to hand. By the time news reached official quarters that a new find had been made, the Bedouin had retrieved practically everything of value from the Partridge Chamber.

Then began the long and frustrating process of buying the precious fragments back from the Arabs. No one who has worked in the Dead Sea caves, and been subjected to the intolerable heat and the fine dust that fills the eyes, nose, and mouth, will begrudge the tribesmen a penny of their just reward. One merely wished that those who had been in charge of the operations during the previous months had used a little more imagination in searching the ground in the immediate vicinity of the monastery, and had not assumed from the first

23

find that any further documents would be discovered similarly in caves situated in the cliffs. Certainly some of the scroll fragments from the Partridge Chamber, officially numbered Cave Four in subsequent documentation, have been lost to mankind for ever, through illicit sales to unauthorised persons, or worse, destroyed in the less careful hands of intermediaries. Some, although smuggled illegally from Jordan, the country of their origin, have been photographed by their proud owners and copies made available to the scholars entrusted with the editing of the scrolls. However, most of this fabulous, if fragmentary, library was retrieved through purchase from the Bedouin (at a dollar or so a square centimetre!), although the raising of the necessary funds, some sixty thousand dollars, took more than three years to accomplish.

It is this collection which remains largely still unpublished, although its contents are well enough known to those of us privileged to form the small international team brought together in 1953 onwards to reconstruct and edit the documents. At the outset of our work, we divided the literature among us according to our various scholarly interests and abilities, and each specialist is responsible under a general editor for the publication of his section. The present writer alone of the team has so far published the whole of his allotted group in its final form (1968), with earlier provisional publication of the more important documents during the intervening years.

When eventually the embarrassed officials of the Antiquities Department reached the scene of the Arabs' illicit operations, they set to work to scour the immediate area for similar underground chambers. Several more were found adjacent to the Partridge Chamber, but they had mostly collapsed in antiquity and their contents had long since been strewn down the sides of the wady and lost for ever. However, a small deposit still remained in the Partridge Chamber to authenticate the source of the Bedouin's hoard.

A renewed search of the cliffs behind the monastery brought forth no more scrolls at first, but produced evidence to show that many caves had been used by the sectarians as living-

24

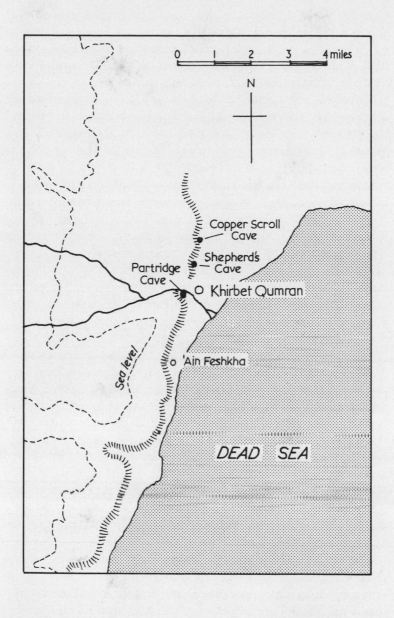

0   1   2   3   4 miles

N

Copper Scroll
Cave

Shepherd's
Cave

Partridge
Cave

O Khirbet Qumran

Sea level

o 'Ain Feshkha

DEAD SEA

quarters, for it seemed that the monastery itself was only their administrative headquarters and communal centre. The cliff caves would, indeed, have been cooler places for sleeping in the heat of the summer, and are reminiscent of anchorites' cells similarly attached to desert monasteries elsewhere.

However, one partly collapsed cave, to the north of all the others in the settlement area, produced inscribed material and the greatest surprise of the whole search. Its existence was betrayed by the presence of pieces of broken pottery among the rock debris. The rubble was hurriedly cleared, and the cave entrance revealed. The front part of the roof had fallen in long ago, but under some of the stones were found tiny pieces of parchment that raised the excavators' hopes. This was the first undisturbed cache that the official archaeologists had themselves discovered in the cliffs, and expectations ran high. Then, lying against an inner wall, covered with dust but otherwise apparently unharmed, they saw two cylindrical objects, placed one on top of the other, and quite unprotected. The searchers began gently to brush away the dust, fearful lest they disturb the rolls or that they should disintegrate to the state of those slight wisps of parchment and papyrus that have so taxed the patience of finder and editor alike. But the two rolls maintained their form and substance and were gently lifted from their resting-place and carried in triumph to Jerusalem. It was only after they had been thoroughly cleaned and examined that the whole frustrating truth was revealed. These were not, like the first discoveries, parchment scrolls, but rolls of copper, inscribed certainly, but with a stylus and not a pen, and the sheets of metal had been riveted together instead of being sewn with gut. They had once constituted a single scroll, certainly, or at least an imitation of a normal parchment scroll, but, for the moment at least, were unreadable.

The copper had long since completely oxidised; it was no longer flexible but just a brittle representation of the original. Any manipulation of the outer skin resulted in the piece breaking away. Yet the outer surface of the rolls showed clearly that letters had been indented on the inner face, and even a word or

26

two could be read, including some numerals and the Hebrew words for 'gold' and 'silver'. It had to be presumed that the whole face of the copper sheets had been similarly engraved, and that it had been part of the Essene library, since a close examination of the other, more normal, scroll fragments found in the same cave showed that they were clearly related to the Essene literature from other caves.

For three years, the copper rolls lay in a showcase in the Jerusalem museum, tantalisingly retaining their secret. A visiting wag suggested their message may have been a stern warning to the pious sectarians to refrain from spitting on the mosaic; most of us felt the use of a fairly precious metal—almost pure copper—warranted some more significant text.

A German professor named K. G. Kuhn was allowed limited access to the precious rolls, too delicate it seemed even for the gentlest handling. His tentative studies of the marks visible on the outer surfaces resulted in conclusions which evoked little more than amused dismissal in some academic quarters, whose experience of the Essene writings so far published had been limited to the biblical, liturgical, and doctrinal literatures. Kuhn had suggested that this strange copper document was an inventory of buried treasure, perhaps a record of the personal wealth which each full initiate was required to surrender to the Order's common fund, lest his concern be diverted by material possessions from his spiritual life.

The long frustration of all concerned ended eventually when the Jordanian authorities were prevailed upon to allow the precious rolls to be taken from the museum for expert examination in an English laboratory, with a view to finding a means of cutting them open. In 1955 and 1956 they were sawn open under the present writer's supervision and their message lay revealed to the world for the first time in two thousand years. Professor Kuhn had been right.

Copper sheets had been joined together to form a scroll of about eight feet long and eleven inches deep. The Hebrew writing, engraved somewhat inexpertly over its surface, did indeed record an inventory of buried treasure. However, it was almost

27

certainly not the pooled resources of the Essene community, but rather the long-lost wealth of the Temple itself in Jerusalem, destroyed by the Romans in AD 70. In August of that year, the legionaries had set fire to the sacred edifice after pillaging what precious objects they could find in use at the time. Josephus, the contemporary historian, also records that some of the soldiers forced ministering priests to show them where the long-famed Temple treasuries lay. We are told that Romans could be seen staggering away from the doomed building bearing gold and silver vessels, the sacred deposits of pious Jews from all over the Mediterranean for many centuries.

But they did not take everything. This copper scroll lists deposits of such treasures, and of gold and silver bullion, which the city's last defenders, the Zealots, had earlier salted away, not only within the confines of the Temple and city environs, in underground installations, secret passageways and cisterns, but outside in the countryside, in fortresses and hideouts in those areas where the rebels still had control, to the east and south of the city.

As the scroll was cut open, it was deciphered piece by piece, and its contents communicated to the authorities back in Jordan. But the success of the operation met with a strangely cool reception. Not until six months later was the world allowed to know what the copper scroll contained, and even then the news was strangely released in a manner and form intended to throw considerable doubt upon its authenticity as a genuine record of the Temple's sacred wealth. It was suggested that it belonged to a well-known genre of Jewish fables concerning the miraculous disposal of the treasures of King Solomon's Temple, destroyed by the Babylonians in the sixth century BC. In fact, of course, the text of the copper scroll bears little or no relation to such legends in style or content. Its detailed references to objects and their hiding-places are much more realistic and localised. No likely explanation was ever advanced by the authorities responsible for the press release for the painstaking engraving of the inventory upon precious sheets of copper, or for their being so carefully placed in the cave along with other

28

documents from the Essene library.

The secrecy and delay attending this official disclosure of the contents of the copper scroll was probably motivated by no more sinister intent than the reluctance on the part of the field archaeologists to over-dramatise the discovery of an ancient document giving details of buried treasure. It has always been difficult to persuade local inhabitants of areas of great archaeological interest that official excavators are only interested in unearthing crumbling walls and potsherds, or that *objets d'art* and other valuables encountered in the course of this worthy exercise are more of an embarrassment than a source of delight. It is usually very difficult also to patrol potentially rich archaeological sites or actual excavations to safeguard them from treasure-hunters. One can understand, then, that the publication of such a list of buried gold and silver from a long-lost cave in the wilderness might make local scepticism of archaeological intentions even more pronounced, and endanger even further sites in the vicinity. Nevertheless, this slanting of information for public consumption was not a happy precedent in the treatment of such sensitive issues as are raised by the Dead Sea Scrolls. Furthermore, the resultant neglect of this important text failed to give due weight to several aspects of the attitude of its authors to the topography of the area around the monastery, even to the identification of the ancient name of the site of the Essene establishment itself.

Today the place is known as Qumran, pronounced *koomrahn*, an Arabic name of uncertain meaning. When the archaeologists began working on the ruins they soon realised that the sectarians had built upon a site which was already ancient. It was probably one of the so-called 'cities of the wilderness' mentioned in the book of Joshua (15⁶¹), a series of fortresses located in the desert province of Judah. The fact that the copper scroll repeatedly mentions one of them, Secacah, and that a treasure hoard of over three hundred silver tetradrachmae was actually discovered hidden under the plaster floor of one of the monastery rooms, suggests that to the list's compilers, at least, this place was to be identified with ancient Secacah. They had then purposely sited their sanctuary upon an earlier Israelite foundation, just as they based their appreciation of their own present and future position in history upon biblical precedent, as we shall see. In other respects also the copper scroll's topography gives us an important insight into Essene motivation and understanding of their relationship to Israel's past.

In 1956, news reached the authorities in Jerusalem and Amman that the ever-active Bedouin had found another cave in the vicinity of the first, and that, unlike the Partridge Chamber, this had produced complete scrolls, like those of the shepherd lad's initial discovery in 1947. Several large fragments were acquired from their finders, but the two scrolls were seen only fleetingly in the hands of an Arab in Jerusalem, and then disappeared. Following the six-day war, the Israelis entered areas previously under Jordanian administration and set about ferreting out scrolls believed to be in the custody of Arabs in Jerusalem and Bethlehem, using rather more forceful methods than had been employed hitherto. The result was to bring one of the lost scrolls into the open, certainly, but not surprisingly to scare off the holders of any other documents from that cache. They may well have been lost for ever, since, whatever their present hiding-place, it is unlikely to be as dry and undisturbed as the caves by the monastery. Unfortunately, such forthright tactics, however successful in international politics and territorial expansion, rarely pay off in such delicate matters as the retrieval of archaeological remains, least of all those so delicate and precious as two thousand year old scrolls.

2
The Lion of Wrath

What we knew of the Essenes before their writings were discovered had led us to expect a highly motivated and exclusive
organisation. Early descriptions had stressed their asceticism
and piety. They appear not to have been very numerous (Pliny
estimates their number as about 4,000), but they were widespread, living in their own communities on the outskirts of
towns and villages throughout Palestine. The Essenes themselves spoke of these settlements as 'camps', consciously recalling the desert encampments of their forefathers under Moses.
They were a secretive and closely knit society, with a well-
arranged system of intercommunication, offering hospitality
and facilities to brethren whose business took them around the
country. This secrecy and ease of movement can hardly have
endeared them to the Roman colonial administration, always
on the lookout in this rebellious corner of the empire for signs of
subversion through underground channels of communication.
The Essenes' rejection of the Jewish hierarchy in Jerusalem
would have made them no less obnoxious in orthodox circles at
a time when the Jews had to be careful not to offend their
Roman masters for fear of their religion losing its favoured
status as a permitted faith with its own independent cultus.

Essenism may have been a quietist movement, prepared to
await with patience God's time for the inauguration of His

31

Kingdom, without actively provoking the war that would herald the event, but one of its scrolls deals in detail with the order and events of that awful cataclysm. Then, as the Sons of Light under their princely Messiah, the Essenes would assume a leading role in the struggle against the Children of Darkness led by the Archon of Evil, the devil, or Belial. In the meantime, from at least the beginning of the first century, a more activist group was working behind the scenes with the intention of bringing about that war. These Zealots, as they were called, had identified the cosmic forces of evil with the Roman occupying army, and were preparing an armed insurrection against that mighty Colossus in the expectation that their puny numbers would be supplemented with angelic hosts from on high. It was largely owing to Zealot activities that the disastrous revolt took place, beginning in Caesarea in AD 66, and spreading like wildfire throughout the country. Its end, with the destruction of the Temple in AD 70, turned the tide of human history certainly, but not in the way its instigators intended or could have foreseen.

The precise relationship between the Essenes and their more vigorous and ruthless contemporaries is difficult to determine, since both groups were highly secretive, and no documents specifically related to the Zealot faction have come to light. Both movements had some historical precedent in the Maccabean uprisings of the second century BC, when a comparatively few courageous men had managed to wrest a short-lived independence from a weakened Greek administration. Even then, however, the activities of the militants were challenged by a pious section of the community who grew increasingly alarmed at the degree to which the exigencies of war were allowed to conflict with and override religious principles long established among a theocratic people.

Pious Jews looked back to biblical prophecies proclaimed during the Babylonian exile of the sixth century BC, which declared that Israel's mission in the world was that of a Chosen People, ordained to be spiritual leaders of mankind. Upon this rock of faithful piety, God would found His Kingdom on earth, and restore the world to its primeval state of innocence and glory. Just how this promise was to be fulfilled was variously understood by a succession of charismatic leaders, depending largely on the political conditions obtaining at their time and on their own social status. This constant interplay in Jewish history between religious, social, and political forces was always important, but never more so than during the events leading to the first great revolt of AD 66–70, and in the moulding of Essene–Christian ideas over the turn of the era.

After the Scrolls were discovered and began to be studied in depth, scholars spilt much ink and generated a good deal of heated debate about whether their authors were Essenes or Zealots. In fact, the division between these two parties was probably never so clear-cut. Much the same ideas were cherished by both factions; it was in their interpretation and implementation that they differed most. Their underlying community of purpose would have been increasingly manifested when news of the great revolt reached the Essene communities. Such an act of heroic madness must be the long-awaited sign of the end-time, the necessary preliminary to Armageddon and the inception of the messianic rule on earth. At such a time one might well expect the Essenes to doff their traditional white robes of peace and to don the trappings of the Holy War, to lay aside their quills and march to join the angelic forces of the Lord of Hosts. In any case, as far as their monastery by the Dead Sea was concerned, the appearance of a Roman legion in Jericho in the spring of AD 68 would have left any remaining doubters no option but to fight for their little home, or leave its defence to their more militant cousins. Only such an amalgamation of interests could account for the deposit of a Zealot inventory of Temple treasures in an Essene cave along with sectarian documents.

The Essenes were not strangers to political activism. Their scrolls speak of sharp divisions of opinion with other Jews and even, apparently, within their own movement. Certainly these differences would have been religious in origin, but it has to be remembered that our modern tendency to segregate

33

the religious life from secular affairs had never any counterpart in the Jewish world, and even today complicates vital decision-taking in Israel's international relations.

The Essene separatist movement within Judaism was motivated by a concern for the purity of the Faith, but it had political overtones: the pietists believed that in the Jewish Establishment's anxiety to accommodate the cultus and city administration to Roman colonial requirements, it had betrayed its sacred trust. In one respect in particular the quarrel was deep-seated. It is clear from the Scrolls and certain apocryphal works like the books of Jubilees and Enoch, long known but now recognised as having emanated from Essene circles, that the sectarians observed their religious festivals according to a solar-based calendar, whereas the official Temple cultus was regulated according to lunar observations. It has been shown that, in fact, the Essene system was the more ancient and traditional, traceable in literature to the time of the Exile at least, and, as with so much of Essene thinking, having its roots in the very heart of the old agricultural life of ancient Israel. The official adoption of a 'new-fangled' lunar reckoning may have been no older than the later Maccabean leadership, when it seemed more important to integrate Judaism closer into the Hellenistic world than to adhere to outmoded and indeed less exact forms of reckoning time.

If some form of dual-calendar compromise had ever been tried, the Hellenistic lunar arrangement being followed for diplomatic and commercial purposes, and the traditional solar reckoning being maintained for cultic use, it did not apparently satisfy the purist inclinations of the Essenes. Their only alternative was to separate themselves entirely from the Temple rituals and to follow their calling as best they could in a self-imposed exile. In their eyes, such a drastic step could only be a temporary measure until such time as the messianic 'Interpreter of the Law', as they called the expected priestly Anointed (Hebrew *Mashiah*), should come and clarify all matters of faith and conduct. In any case, it is easy to see that the motivation for their withdrawal could be reckoned as much political as religious; when the Kingdom of Heaven had been established on earth there would be no more disputes about the closer integration of the secular with the religious, for all would be one, with God ruling every aspect of life for all mankind.

From our point of view, it is a pity that the Essene writers follow a custom shared by the author of the book of Daniel in referring to persons and events cryptically by pseudonym rather than by their real names. In the eleventh chapter of that book, for example, the various Ptolemaic and Seleucid rulers of the Greek kingdoms are called simply 'kings of the north' and 'kings of the south', and the Romans are known as the 'Kittim', a term properly applied to the inhabitants of Cyprus. Similarly, the Scrolls call their revered leader the 'Teacher of Righteousness', or 'Righteous Teacher', his arch-enemy the 'Wicked Priest', along with similar designations of reproach, like 'Man of Lies', 'Scoffer', 'Spouter of Lies', and they refer to one major faction of the opposition as 'Seekers-after-Smooth-Things'. They never refer to themselves by what must have been their popular title, 'Essenes', but as 'Men of the Covenant', 'Men of the Community', the 'Children of Light', and so on.

Only in one document do the Essene writers allow themselves to identify by name characters otherwise known in Jewish history, in a context which shows clearly that the event had some particular relevance for the history of their own movement and the fate of their own people. It is reasonable to assume that this break with custom was intended to convey information deemed of paramount importance to the Essene cause, and which it was essential for all future generations of Covenanters to recall accurately. The names of the sect's enemies were not of lasting importance; there had doubtless been many in the course of their rebellious rejection of the official Jewish hierarchy, and there would be others before they were finally justified before God. But the work and vicarious suffering of their Teacher of Righteousness was of another order, marking a significant development in the history of mankind. According to one of their oldest writings, God had raised him up 'to guide

35

them in the way of His heart', to lead them into a New Covenant in 'the land of Damascus', and they look forward to the coming of a Messiah who bears his titles of 'Priest' and 'Teacher of Righteousness'. If they were not anticipating their own Teacher's return in the flesh, as some commentators believe, at least they had no doubt that the coming 'Interpreter of the Law' would be modelled after their martyred leader, as he himself had been in his day a later counterpart to one who expounded the Law to Israel (see below, Chapter Five).

The historical references occur in a fragmentary commentary on the biblical book of Nahum, reconstructed from scroll fragments recovered from the Partridge Cave, and first published by the present writer in 1956. The crucial lines of text run as follows, the biblical source being printed in italics, and reconstructions of broken passages placed within square brackets, as elsewhere in citations of defective texts:

Whither the lion, the lioness went, there is the lion's cub [with none to disturb it (2¹¹). Interpreted, this concerns Deme]trius, king of Greece, who sought to enter Jerusalem through the counsel of the Seekers-after-Smooth-Things. [But God did not permit the city to be delivered] into the hands of the kings of Greece, from the time of Antiochus to the appearance of the rulers of the Kittim. But then she will be trodden down [. . .]

The lion tears enough for his cubs, and strangles prey for his lionesses (2¹²). [Its interpretation] concerns the Lion of Wrath who smites by means of his nobles and the men of his council.

[And strangles prey for his lionesses; and he fills] his caves [with prey] and his den with torn flesh (2¹²). Its interpretation concerns the Lion of Wrath [who executes ven]geance upon the Seekers-after-Smooth-Things when he hangs men up alive, [a thing never done] in Israel before, for it is in respect of a man crucified upon a tree that it goes on: *Behold, I am against [you, says the Lord of Hosts. I will burn up in smoke your abundance], and the sword shall devour your young lions. I will [cut off] your prey from the earth [, and] the voice of your messengers shall no [more be heard]* (2¹³). Its interpretation: *your abundance*—they are his warrior bands [who are in Jerusa]lem; and *his young lions*—they are his nobles [. . .] and *his prey*—it is the wealth which the priests of Jerusalem have amassed, which . . .

36

Despite the strangeness of the sect's methods of biblical exposition, taking passages out of context and even changing them to suit the occasion, the historic references of this commentary are clear. The Jewish king-priests who later represented the Maccabean line on the throne of Israel were more political warlords than leaders of the nation's religious life. Their policy was one of conquest and plunder of their neighbours, and they undoubtedly 'amassed great riches' in the process. But in fairness it has to be appreciated that, however idealistic may be the aims of all holy wars such as those waged by the Maccabees, political independence needs thereafter to be sustained through the same military means that achieved it. The pietists of that age, the so-called Hasidim, from whose stock both Essenes and Pharisees probably derived, saw the danger and urged the men of war to call a halt when it seemed they had secured the nation's religious freedom. However, war is rarely an isolated event; even if the original enemy is defeated, there are usually more antagonists waiting in the wings to seize the fruits of victory, or through envy or sense of deprivation to harass the infant state before it can grow dangerously powerful. So it was with the later Maccabean kingdom and its rulers, of whom the most infamous was Alexander Jannaeus (103–76 BC).

There was no doubt of Jannaeus's prowess as a military leader, and his entire reign was spent in almost ceaseless warfare against his Arab neighbours. But it is one thing having a successful general fight your battles, particularly if, as with Jannaeus, he employs foreign mercenaries to do the actual fighting; it is another having this same person return from the wars, his hands still stained with blood, and proceed to perform the sacred duties of High Priest in the Temple. Josephus tells us how, on one such occasion, on the Feast of Tabernacles, outraged pietists screamed abuse at the king, denying his legal right to the office he desecrated, since he was the son of a slave woman and not of pure descent. They began pelting him with the citron fruits they were carrying as part of the celebrations. Jannaeus was not the sort of person to take these insults lightly, and he set his mercenary troops on his own people, massacring several thousands. Perhaps we should see the hands of the Essenes behind this rallying of the faithful, for one of their documents speaks of the time when 'bastards and sons of strangers' should never again set foot in the Temple. In any case, it has seemed to many scholars that it was about this time that the Teacher of Righteousness gathered together some of the faithful priests and fled into the desert to begin their exile from Israel's spiritual centre in Jerusalem until such time as God should see fit to vindicate His sons and inaugurate the Kingdom of Heaven on earth.

It is certainly to this Alexander Jannaeus that the Nahum commentary refers under the pseudonym of the 'Lion of Wrath' seeking vengeance upon his foes. He was a terrible enemy, hated and feared by all men. We are told by Josephus that he was known by the nickname 'Thracian'. Many of his mercenaries came from Asia Minor (Thrace), and one suspects that they taught their Jewish master not only the art of ruthless warfare, but something of their own Dionysiac religion, the worship of the god Bacchus, or Dionysus. The divine hero they served, 'the Thracian' *par excellence*, was famed above all for the strange power he wielded over his devotees, particularly women. These Maenads, or Bacchantes (*Bacchae*), as they are called, were said to run berserk through the coniferous forests, calling on their god and demonstrating a superhuman strength and blinding blood-lust. They seized any animal that crossed their path and tore its living body to pieces, as a 'lion tears its prey'. Whatever their source of religious inspiration, there is little doubt that they owed much of their frenzied strength to some other form of intoxication, including the use of drugs.

The most famous story concerning the Maenads is that which forms the climax of the Euripidean play *The Bacchae*. Pentheus, king of Thebes, aroused the god's disfavour by declaring him an impostor and his votaries mere dupes. The king tried his best to stop their secret revels, but to no avail. The Maenads escaped his restraint and went raging up the sacred Mount Cithaeron, tearing calves to pieces with their

38

bare hands. Dionysus, in disguise, suggested to Pentheus that he should dress himself as a woman and spy on their revels from a tree. This he did, but the frenzied females saw him watching them, spreadeagled upon the branches and helpless, and pulled him down. His own mother, Agave, leading the screaming horde, was the first to lay hands on her son, and, blinded to his identity by her divine madness, tore off his head.

In the terrible sequel to the demonstration by the Jewish dissidents, Alexander Jannaeus showed himself a true follower of 'the Thracian'. After the butchery in Jerusalem, he led his mercenaries off to fight more wars with his neighbours, but this time was heavily defeated by the Arab king Obedas. He barely escaped with his life, and just managed to struggle back to Jerusalem, only to find that the Pharisees had taken this opportunity to make open rebellion against him. So far they might have expected to have had the moral, if not active support of the exiled Teacher and his friends. But after six years of civil war, the rebels took the unwise step of 'seeking the Smooth Thing', in this case calling in outside help in the shape of the Greek king Demetrius III, Euchaerus. This will be the Demetrius referred to in the Nahum commentary which, incidentally, contributes a new piece of information on the course of events at that time.

Demetrius arrived with his army and met the malcontents at Shechem. Together they dealt a crushing defeat on Alexander, but then Josephus tells us that for some reason many of the rebels changed sides and joined Jannaeus's defeated army. The explanation for this apparent change of heart is now evident from the Essene commentator's note that Demetrius 'had tried to enter Jerusalem'. Naturally enough, the Greek ruler intended to secure the fruits of victory and take over the country. But while it was expedient for the Pharisees having a foreign army help settle their differences with a native tyrant, it was quite intolerable for an alien to assume the vacant throne and tread the sacred courts of the Holy City. So many of Demetrius's supporters deserted him, choosing the lesser of the two evils, and the Greek general was obliged to retire northwards.

Alexander was not one to forget his humiliation, however. Inflamed with lust for revenge no less frenzied and terrible than that which characterised the votaries of the Thracian god, he set about rounding up those who had betrayed him to a foreign enemy. He dragged forth from their places of refuge all who had challenged his priestly legitimacy, and in that state of mind he would have cared little whether they had supported the call to Demetrius or drawn back from that 'Smooth Thing'. It was enough that they should be among those who had deplored his kingship and denied his sacerdotal authority. He determined once for all to make an example of his opponents, whatever their motivation. As many as he could capture he turned over to his Thracian mercenaries to be 'hanged alive upon a tree', that is, crucified. We are told that the stakes were erected on the terrace below the palace in Jerusalem, so that this Jewish king, High Priest of the Israelite God, could enjoy the spectacle of people of his own race being crucified while he caroused with women from his harem. To add further savour to the horrific feast, he had the wives and children of the wretched victims massacred before their dying eyes.

This manner of execution was a foreign punishment, originating in Persia. The Nahum commentary expresses the wave of horror that must have swept through Jewry at the news of Jannaeus's terrible vengeance: 'it was never done before in Israel', that is, a Jew crucifying Jews, for the Law of Moses states that 'a hanged man is accursed of God' (Deuteronomy 21^{22}). The punishment, extending even to estrangement from God, inflicted upon pious men whose only fault had been zeal for the proper conduct of Israel's most sacred office, merited the Essene commentator's applying against its instigator, the Lion of Wrath, the biblical imprecation that follows in the Nahum text: 'Behold, I am against thee, says the Lord of Hosts.'

This awful event of about 88 BC must have had some particular significance for the Essenes, or their commentary on Nahum would not have made so pointed a reference to the crucifixion of the faithful, nor gone so far as to name the chief foreign characters in the drama and thus to set the scene firmly into history.

Looking back years later, the Essene commentators must have seen the infamous act as marking a turning-point in the affairs of man, a sign of the dawn of that eschatological period they call 'the End of Days'. It cannot be stressed too strongly in our appreciation of the sectarians' point of view of historical events that their importance lay not in any ordered sequence of cause and effect, or in their immediate outcome, nor even in the details of persons and places involved, but in their eschatological significance, that is, in their value as markers to point the way to the end of the present world order. That is why we have found the Scrolls so disappointing as records of history of the sect and its chief personalities; there are no 'gospels' in the New Testament sense of a collection of stories and sayings of an inspired teacher and his friends and kinsfolk. We should not expect to read in the manuscripts descriptions of individuals, the way they looked and spoke, their dress and manner of speech, nor accounts of conjuring tricks performed on water that changed into wine, or fig trees withering at a word, or tales of mouldering corpses springing to life. Indeed, were such to appear we should be rightly suspicious of their purpose and wonder why, in such a serious and esoteric society, their writers should be so free to divulge names and places with such abandon, or to dwell so lovingly on the kind of day-to-day minutiae which so enliven the New Testament narratives, and assure their perennial popularity. The Essene, living in this crucial period of the end-time, was not concerned with such trivia; he looked for 'signs of the times', the better to estimate the approach of the end of his age's agony, and the manifestation of God's new order. Of such signs, the Essene must have counted the crucifixion of the eight hundred as of the greatest significance, and particularly if among the victims he numbered his own beloved Teacher of Righteousness.

For if their own leader had not been involved in the tragic sequel to the folly of the Seekers-after-Smooth-Things, the events would not have been recalled so pointedly in the Essene commentary. There had been other attacks upon dissident religious groups in that turbulent period; the relationship between the Maccabean house and the nation's spiritual leaders had always been strained. Even the bestiality of Jannaeus in his treatment of his own subjects was sadly not unparalleled in the post-Maccabean era; yet nowhere else in the Scrolls so far recovered is there such deliberate reference to an identifiable act of vicious tyranny.

Another Essene biblical commentary refers to the onslaught upon the Teacher of Righteousness in 'the place of his exile'. It comes in a similar treatment—or mistreatment—of passages in the book of Habakkuk:

Traitors! Why do you merely look on and remain silent when a wicked person attacks one who is more righteous than he? (1¹³). Its interpretation concerns the House of Absalom and the men of their council who remained dumb when the Teacher of Righteousness was chastised, and gave him no help against the Man of Lies who flouted the Law in the midst of the whole congregation . . .

Woe to him who makes his companions drink the outpouring of his venom, intoxicating them so that he may gaze upon their solemnities! (2¹⁵). Its interpretation concerns the Wicked Priest who pursued after the Teacher of Righteousness to the place of his exile, to make him drink of the cup of his venom. And at the time appointed for rest, the Day of Atonement, he appeared suddenly before them to attack them, and make them stumble on the Day of Fasting, their Sabbath of rest.

Yet another reference to the Teacher's persecution appears in a commentary on Psalm 37, first published by the present writer in 1954 and 1956:

The wicked watches for the righteous and seeks [to slay him. The Lord will not abandon him in his hand and will not] condemn him when he is tried. (vv 32–33). Its interpretation concerns the Wicked Priest who [rose up against the Teacher of Righteousness] to put him to death [. . .] and the teaching he delivered to him. But God will not abandon him and will not [condemn him when] he is brought to Judgement. But [God will] pay [him, (ie the Wicked

42

Priest)] his due when he gives him into the power of terrible nations for the execution upon him [of judgement].

This theme of the Teacher's passion and of his betrayal has a corollary that those who believe in him and suffer on his account may hope to reap the reward of the righteous. Like the Teacher himself, they will not be abandoned by God on the Day of Judgement that must face all men. Thus another passage in the Habakkuk commentary reads:

[*But the righteous shall live by faith* (2⁴)]. Its interpretation concerns all who observe the Law in the House of Judah, whom God will deliver from the Hall of Judgement because of their suffering and because of their faith in the Teacher of Righteousness.

(See also Chapter Ten.)

43

3

Secacah in Galilee

On one occasion, during the filming for a television programme on the Dead Sea Scrolls, one of our cameramen was being driven down the road from Jerusalem to Jericho. He was making his first acquaintance with the Rift Valley, and as the journey progressed and the road plunged ever deeper into the wilderness, he became unusually silent and morose. At length, with all the heartfelt disillusion of an exiled Englishman, he exclaimed, 'Lord, what a god-forsaken hole!'

One could see his point. In the parched heat of summer this desert scene has a certain grandeur, certainly, and in the past it has inspired prophets of doom, but it is not a pretty sight. Nevertheless, the pious sojourner of the Essene settlement would not have echoed our friend's sentiments in quite those terms. He had, after all, come to this scene of desolation specifically to seek his God, and to await His further revelation. But why there, of all places, in the Holy Land?

We have already seen that the Essenes built their monastery upon a much earlier structure, probably identifiable with one of the biblical 'cities of the wilderness', Secacah. While the name is reminiscent of the Hebrew word for 'tabernacle' (*sukkah*), the desert sanctuary of God during the Exodus, and thus of some special interest to these latter-day pilgrims, this alone would not have persuaded them to site their temporal dwelling on this

44

spot. The reason for their choice must lie, as with almost every other aspect of Essene thought and practice, in their philosophy of history.

Pious Jews believed that everything that had befallen their people was part of God's master-plan for mankind. He had chosen Israel to serve Him before even the world had been made. She was to be the instrument of His salvation. In the beginning the world had been created in perfect harmony, but the disobedience of Adam and Eve had brought sin and suffering into Eden. Feeding upon itself, this first disobedience had bred more corruption until at length it became necessary to destroy nearly all human life and start afresh with the one remaining nucleus of righteous piety that remained, Noah and his immediate family. When, alas, this new brave world also strayed into rebellion and depravity, God called forth Abraham from Mesopotamia to found a more faithful lineage. Thereafter He nurtured the patriarchal ancestors of Israel with love and discipline through a series of vicissitudes and victories until He could reveal to them the nature of their divine calling and responsibilities.

During the desert wandering under Moses, following their providential escape from Egypt, the Israelites were welded into a nation, allowed to know the secret name of God, and given the inestimable gift of the *Torah*, or Law. During those forty years they were made aware of the duties and privileges that must accompany their status of a Chosen People. Israel had been favoured above all other nations with knowledge of the Law, since through this self-revelation on the part of God she alone could know His will perfectly, and in obedience to its demands could achieve a harmony with the divine master-plan hidden from lesser men. At the same time, more was required of her than could be expected from less enlightened peoples. Disobedience would be punished more harshly, and, above all, to serve other gods would estrange her from the love and protection of her God, leaving her open to the envy and hostility of stronger nations.

The desert wandering was thus a school of discipline to

prepare Israel for her entry into the Promised Land, when she would fulfil her missionising role of bringing all mankind to the throne of the one true God. Her first great leader Moses was not himself to see that day, but she was granted another law-giver, no less favoured in wisdom and miraculous power, Joshua, son of Nun.

This pattern of events—election, recurrent rebellion, chastisement, repentance, and salvation—was to be repeated throughout the following centuries of Israel's history. In every age, her people would go astray and reject their high calling, only to be called back to their responsibilities by a new charismatic leader, priest, king, or prophet. The message was always the same: a reminder of Israel's election to divine favour, her past apostasies, her punishment, and her restoration through unmerited grace. As God spoke once through Moses, so He speaks again; as He punished the nation's sins by withdrawing His love and protection, and condemning her to further periods of enslavement and humiliation, so He will do again. But repentance will be met with renewed promise and a restoration to the fold of His exclusive service.

In the fulness of time, this repeated pattern of apostasy and restoration would reach a climax in the final holocaust which would engulf all mankind, grown too corrupt to respond to Israel's evangelistic mission. As in the days of Noah and the Flood, the wicked would be swept from the face of the earth, renegade Jew and gentile alike, leaving only the Sons of Light under their messianic leadership to inaugurate the new order and usher in the Kingdom of God. There would then follow the millennium, a thousand-year period of peace and harmony with the divine will, until the final dissolution of all things.

There was, then, in Essene understanding a repetitiveness in human history which was basic to their philosophy. What had happened before would happen again, not through some automatic process triggered by a mindless fate, but through the fluctuating nature of man's response to God. Given that Adam had been granted—or had recklessly seized—the gift of knowledge and self-determination, God could only effect His plan through

46

persuasion and correction. It was therefore inevitable that the record of human affairs should be marked by successive periods of waywardness and reconciliation, of rebellion and repentance, and that the ideal state of grace and harmony should at times be disrupted by wars and natural disasters.

The record of these cycles in human affairs could be seen in the Scriptures, and their interpretation in the words of the prophets. The Essenes paid more attention to these prophetic books of the Bible than was customary among more orthodox Jews of their time, for they sought there clues to the course of future events. These prophecies were not the vague predictions of a fortune-teller peering into a crystal ball, but the inspired utterances of men of God, well versed in the Law. They could estimate Israel's future by measuring the quality of her previous responses to God's demands. The art of prognostication lay in understanding the past.

We have already noted a few examples of biblical exegesis in the Scrolls, and may have wondered at the freedom with which the commentators manipulated the text to suit their purpose, and at the strained, even at times bizarre, meaning they wrested from the plain words of Scripture. But it has to be remembered that the Essene exegete considered himself as inspired by the spirit of prophecy as the original writer, and thus had been granted no less a divine authority for his interpretation. We shall only understand these strange people and their ways if we try to enter into their time and place, suspend our more 'scientific' approach to documentary traditions, and above all free ourselves from our insistence upon a logical progression of events and an exact chronology.

We must adopt the Essene cyclical view of history and pore with those extreme 'fundamentalists' over the sacred text, word for word, letter for letter, seeking with them some clue to their expectations of the future and appreciation of the past. With them we must regard every syllable of Scripture as inspired, and every meaning we can extract from each word, however offensive the process to our philological training, must be accepted if it seems to help in the task of discerning with the

47

Essene prognosticators the 'signs of the times'.

The Covenanters were, then, a People of the Book, studying the Law and the Prophets day and night. But they were not just observers; they believed they were required to play an active role in the establishment of the new Kingdom, and had thus to use their predictive powers to fit themselves for their special calling. It was not enough that they should be able to apprehend the divine plan; they must conform to its design in all that they thought, said, and did. They must become the perfect instruments of God, completely at one with the divine purpose, and totally dedicated to His cause. Only by appreciating this high resolve can we begin to enter into the Essene mind, or to comprehend the nature and purpose of their existence by the barren shores of the Dead Sea.

Going back, then, to our search for the answer to 'why Qumran/Secacah?', we shall expect to find the clue in the history of Israel and in biblical prophecy concerning the last Days.

As to the past, we need look no further than a few miles to the north, to Jericho and the fords across the Jordan. It was there that Joshua, son of Nun, in his role of Moses's successor, led the Israelites across to the Promised Land (Joshua 3). As the Red Sea had parted before Moses and the tribes fleeing from their Egyptian oppressors, so now the waters of the Jordan piled themselves in a heap upstream to leave the river-bed dry to the feet of priests and people (v 14ff). In this repetition of history was a sure sign of God's intentions towards Israel, and of His confirmation of Joshua's prophetic office. Before the Israelites lay many generations of continual struggle against the inhabitants of the land they had come to possess, and of even more perilous contacts with the seductive cults of local gods. It was fitting, therefore, that Joshua should immediately lead the people into a renewal of their covenant with their God, in preparation for the times of trial that awaited them and their descendants.

So now, a millennium and a half later, when the Essenes faced the most exacting challenge of all time, they gathered in the vicinity of the first crossing to renew their vows before God.

48

They called themselves the 'men of the New Covenant, or New Testament', and prepared themselves under their Teacher, another 'Joshua' (in its Greek form, Jesus), to enter the Promised Land of the new era. They speak of their exile as a token 'forty years' of trial, or temptation, in the desert. It was for them, as for their forefathers, a time of great privation and self-imposed discipline, to fit them for their glorious mission and high office in the messianic Kingdom. Later we shall look at other associations of the Jericho area which seemed to the Essenes to confirm their belief that they were following in the footsteps of history.

As to their fulfilling biblical prophecy in their choice of home, we need to bear in mind one important feature of the messianic age. It was to be marked by a restoration of harmony in nature, lost, as it was believed, since the expulsion of man's first parents from Paradise. We see this hope expressed in a number of very familiar passages in the Bible. For example, Isaiah's description of the future rule of the Messiah, a scion of the house of David, includes this highly idealistic, if improbable, ecological situation:

> The wolf shall dwell with the lamb,
>   and the leopard shall lie down with the kid,
> and the calf and the lion and the fatling together,
>   and a little child shall lead them.
> The cow and the bear shall feed,
>   their young shall lie down together;
> and the lion shall eat straw like the ox.
> The sucking child shall play over the hole of the asp,
>   and the weaned child shall put his hand on the adder's den.
> They shall not hurt or destroy
>   in all my holy mountain;
> for the earth shall be full of the knowledge of the Lord
>   as the waters cover the sea.
>
> (Isaiah 11⁶⁻⁹)

A similar transformation would take place in the distribution of natural resources, bringing water to the desert, and fertility where all had previously been barren:

When the poor and needy seek water,
  and there is none,
  and their tongue is parched with thirst,
I, the Lord, will answer them,
  I, the God of Israel, will not forsake them.
I will open rivers on the bare heights,
  and fountains in the midst of the valleys;
I will make the wilderness a pool of water,
  and the dry land springs of water.
I will put in the wilderness the cedar,
  the acacia, the myrtle, and the olive;
I will set in the desert the cypress,
  the plane and the pine together;
that men may see and know,
  may consider and understand together,
that the hand of the Lord has done this,
  the Holy One of Israel has created it.

(Isaiah 41$^{17-20}$)

Among such miraculous manifestations of God's healing power, bringing life where there was none, was the transformation of the Dead Sea to a lake teeming with fish, where fishermen might fill their nets to bursting. Furthermore, on its shores there would grow many kinds of trees bearing continual crops of fruit. The stream of life-giving water that would bring about this wonderful change would spring from the threshold of the Temple in Jerusalem and flow into the eastern 'Galilee', or 'region', in the Arabah, the name given to the Rift Valley. This was the vision recorded by the prophet Ezekiel in far-off Babylon during the Exile:

Then he brought me back to the door of the Temple; and behold, water was issuing from beneath the threshold of the Temple toward the east (for the Temple faced east); and the water was flowing down from below the south end of the threshold of the Temple, south of the altar . . .
    And he said to me, 'This water flows towards eastern Galilee and goes down into the Arabah; and when it enters the stagnant waters of the Sea, the water will become fresh. And wherever the

50

river goes every living creature which swarms will live, and there will be very many fish; for this water goes there, that the waters of the Sea may become fresh; so everything will live where the river goes. Fishermen will stand beside the Sea; from En-gedi to En-eglaim it will be a place for the spreading of nets; its fish will be of very many kinds, like the fish of the Mediterranean. But its swamps and marshes will not become fresh; they are to be left for salt. And on the banks, on both sides of the river, there will grow all kinds of trees for food. Their leaves will not wither nor their fruit fail, but they will bear fresh fruit every month, because the water for them flows from the Sanctuary. Their fruit will be for food, and their leaves for healing . . .'

(Ezekiel 47[1-12])

Another prophet of the Exile, Zechariah, whose words seem to have had a very special significance for the Essenes in the formulation of their messianic ideas, writes similarly of the miraculous stream of living water:

On that day, living waters shall flow out from Jerusalem, half of them to the eastern Sea [ie the Dead Sea] and half of them to the western Sea [ie the Mediterranean]; it shall continue in summer as in winter.

(14[8])

It seems reasonable to assume that whatever freshwater spring Ezekiel had in mind when he set the northern limit of the new Galilean fishing grounds at 'En-eglaim', the Essenes would have interpreted it as referring to the little freshwater stream to the south of their monastery, called today by the Arabic name of 'Ain Feshkha. They made much of its welcome waters for their plantations and small cattle, as we know from excavated traces of their installations in the area around the spring, but it must have needed all their faith to conceive of this comparative trickle as growing suddenly to a mighty river 'deep enough to swim in, a river that could not be crossed' (Ezekiel 14[5]).

Zechariah's vision extended to the means by which this life-giving stream should be able to flow unhindered from the

Temple eastward to the Dead Sea. Blocking its way, beyond the Kidron valley outside the eastern wall of the Sanctuary, stands the Mount of Olives. But on the Day of Judgement God would stand upon the Mount, 'and the Mount of Olives shall be split in two from east to west by a very wide valley; so that one half of the Mount shall withdraw northward, and the other half southward' (14⁴).

Among the apocryphal works that have come down to us in Jewish–Christian literature, but which never achieved canonical status, are those attributed to the patriarch Enoch, recording a series of visions he was supposed to have experienced after his translation to heaven. Many fragmentary copies of these works have been found among the Scrolls, indicating at least a strong Essene interest in the Enoch traditions, if not actual Essene origin. It is therefore of particular significance that Enoch also refers to the miraculous stream running eastward from the Temple (26³), changing the desert into a plantation of 'aromatic trees, exhaling the fragrance of frankincense and myrrh' (29¹).

In such prophetic visions the Essenes clearly recognised not only references to their own place of exile, in the 'eastern Galilee', one day to be so marvellously transformed into a veritable Garden of Eden, but to themselves as the 'fishers of men', spreading their nets upon the waters. Thus writes the author of their Thanksgiving Hymns, probably their own Teacher of Righteousness:

> Thou hast given me a dwelling with many fishers
> who spread a net upon the face of the waters,
>   and with those who hunt down children of iniquity;
> there Thou hast established me for judgement.
>
> (Hymns, Col. V)

> I [thank Thee, O Lord, for] Thou hast lodged me beside
> a fountain of running waters in a waterless land,
>   and by a spring in a parched land,
>   and by channels that irrigate a garden [of delight in the
>   wilderness].
>
> (Col. VIII: see below, Chapter Eleven, p 175)

This idea of a holy stream as a fount of inspiration, bringing life and healing into the souls of men, found particular favour among these ascetics for whom the parched heat of the desert was no mere figure of speech. The desolate landscape of the Dead Sea shores must have made them more than ever aware of the contrasts between their exile and the luxuriant herbage of more favoured areas. The only trees they saw were gnarled branches lying bleached by the sun on the salt-encrusted shores, whence they had been swept from ravines on the other side of the Dead Sea. On the far shore there were, indeed, palm trees and groves surrounding the famous hot springs; but they merely accentuated the desolation of this western shore whose only sign of verdure, south of Jerico, would have been in the Essenes' own kitchen gardens about the spring of En-eglaim. Thus, the prophets' visions of fruit and aromatic trees, whose leaves were 'for healing', would have had particular appeal. Hear again the words of the psalmist Teacher:

[that they may grow] together, a plantation
of cypress, pine, and cedar, for Thy glory,
trees of life beside a fountain of mystery,
    hidden among all the other trees by the water's edge;
so that they may put forth a Shoot
    for an eternal Planting;
And before that, establish their own roots,
    extending them to the watercourse,
that its cutting might be open to the living waters
    and refresh them from the everlasting spring . . .

And the Shoot of holiness grows up
into a Planting of truth, hidden and not esteemed;
and being unrecognized,
    its mystery remained sealed.
Thou didst hedge about its fruit, [O God],
    with the mystery of the warrior Hosts,
    and the Spirits of holiness,
    and the whirling flame of fire;
that no [man should approach] the fountain of life
    or drink the waters of holiness
    with the everlasting trees,

or swell his fruit through [the bounty] of clouds,
   who, seeing, has not recognized,
   and, considering, has not believed
in the fountain of life;
who has put [his hand against] the everlasting [Shoot].
(Col. VIII)

The Teacher identified himself with this 'fountain of living waters' in whom his followers might find the secrets of eternal life:

But Thou, O my God, hast put into my mouth
   as showers of early rain for all [those who thirst]
   and a spring of living waters . . .
Suddenly they shall gush forth
   from the secret hiding places . . .

But the fruitful Planting
   [by the] everlasting [spring
shall be] an Eden of glory . . .
(Col. VIII; see also below, Chapter Eleven, p 176)

The 'trees' that were nourished from this life-giving source were, of course, the Essenes themselves. This figure of the Elect as trees is common enough elsewhere in Jewish thought. Thus, for instance, Isaiah cites God's promise to His people:

You people shall all be righteous;
   they shall possess the land for ever,
the shoot of my Planting,
the work of my hands,
   that I might be glorified . . .
(60^{21})

and in the prophet's gospel of 'good tidings to the afflicted':

to grant to those who mourn in Zion,
   to give them a garland instead of ashes,
the oil of gladness instead of mourning,
   the mantle of praise instead of a faint spirit;

54

that they may be called oaks of righteousness,
    the Planting of the Lord,
    that He may be glorified . . .

(61³)

But the Essenes of Secacah could make an even closer identification with themselves of the visionary trees by the sacred
stream. Among the varieties mentioned by Isaiah was the
myrtle (41¹⁹), and of the unidentified fruit trees he says that
their leaves will be 'for healing'. The most probable Semitic
origin for the name 'Essenes' is, as we have said earlier, the Aramaic word *'asayya'*, 'healers', of the root *'sy*, 'heal'. The Aramaic
word for 'myrtles' is almost exactly similar, *'asayya*. The cura-
tive powers of this aromatic tree were well known and widely
applied in ancient pharmacy, and the myrtle wreath has a
special place in many religions, not least in Judaism. It is speci-
fied among the branches required to make booths in the Féast
of Tabernacles (Nehemiah 8¹⁵), with all the relevance for that
word for the name of the Essenes' home, Secacah, already
noted (p 44).
Furthermore, they were able to apply to themselves one of
those enigmatic visions so beloved of biblical apocalyptists,
vivid in their imagery, but darkly mysterious and pregnant with
esoteric meaning for those inspired to interpret them. It
appears at the beginning of the prophecy of Zechariah:

I saw in the night, and behold, a man riding upon a red horse! He
was standing among the myrtle trees in the Shady Place [so the
Greek version, reading the Hebrew word as *mesillah*; the traditional reading, 'glen, deep place', Hebrew *mesullah*, prefers a
slightly different vowelling]; and behind him were red, sorrel,
and white horses. Then I said, 'What are these, my lord?' The
angel who talked with me said to me, 'I will show you what they
are.' So the man who was standing among the myrtle trees answered, 'These are they whom the Lord has sent to patrol the
earth.'

(1⁸⁻¹⁰)

55

Elsewhere in Jewish tradition, the 'myrtle trees' of this passage are identified as the Righteous Ones, or Saints, so the Essenes were not alone in interpreting the visionary's trees as men, and themselves in particular.

Of greater interest and significance is the Hebrew name of the place where these 'myrtles' were located, Mesillah, the Shady Place, similar in meaning to Secacah, and philologically not very different from the place *'Asel*, to which the same prophet's miraculously opened valley through the Mount of Olives was to extend. That is, he saw the end of the gorge from Jerusalem reaching the Dead Sea at Secacah/Mesillah.

If, then, ancient Secacah was known later also by the synonymous Mesillah, 'Shady Place', we may locate with fair certainty the place to which Alexander Jannaeus pursued the rebels who had so humiliated him before King Demetrius. It will be remembered that in 88 BC, following the change of heart of many of the Jewish dissidents, leaving Demetrius and the 'Seekers-after-Smooth-Things' to face Jannaeus alone, the Jewish priest-king was able to drive the alien from his territory and turn his attention to teaching the rebels a lesson Jewry would never forget. Josephus, in one account, says that the fugitives were driven to take refuge in 'the city of Bemeselis', a Greek approximation to the Hebrew *Beth* ('House of') *Mesillah* ('Shade'). From that place of concealment Jannaeus dragged them forth to be crucified.

That the worsted rebels should have sought sanctuary in the Essene stronghold by the shores of the Dead Sea is reasonable enough; they had, after all, received earlier support from the Teacher and his friends. However, they could hardly have expected the settlement to offer a safe hiding-place for long, although the watch-tower would have given them an advance warning of the approach of the enemy from the north. Perhaps the fugitives hoped to move on when occasion offered, crossing the Dead Sea and landing on the other side in Transjordan. There they might have hoped to seek help from Jannaeus's Arab enemies, the Nabateans based in Petra, and found a safe passage onward to Egypt.

Plate 1 (above) Qumran Monastery with the Dead Sea beyond. At the edge of the plateau on the right is the Partridge Cave in which scrolls were found

Plate 2 (below) The Partridge Cave (four) seen from the monastery

Plate 3 (above left) Inside the
"partridge" cave

Plate 4 (above right) Arab with a
typical scroll jar in the same cave

Plate 5 (left) The first Scroll cave,
discovered by an Arab shepherd in
1947

Plate 6 (above) A Qumran manuscript of Exodus, inscribed in proto-hebraic writing, 1st or 2nd century BC

Plate 7 (below) Examining a scroll of Psalms found in a cave near Qumran in 1956

Plate 8 (above) Sorting scroll fragments

Plate 9 (below) The "Scrollery", Palestine Archaeological Museum, Jerusalem

In any event, the terse references in the Essene commentaries already noted, recalling the attack upon the Teacher 'in the place of his exile' by the Wicked Priest, the 'lion of Wrath', who 'tears enough for his cubs, and strangles prey for his lionesses', begins now to make excellent sense, and to throw the Essene involvement in the terrible events of those days in a new light. The first reaction of the monastery's survivors must have been one of numbed shock. It was, perhaps, only later when they contemplated the death of their revered leader, and particularly the dreadful curse of estrangement from God that befell 'him who is hanged upon a tree', that the propitiatory nature of the sacrifice that had been made on their behalf would have been borne upon them. For the time being, at least, the crucifixion of the Master was not a matter for mystical speculation, but rather of hushed and fearful whispers, and a sense of disillusionment that God should have allowed such a tragedy to overtake His servant, the spiritual mentor and guide of His Elect.

However, before we pursue this line of inquiry, and the likely course of theological speculation as later Essene thinkers contemplated the fateful Tree as a symbol of God's redeeming love for His people, we should look for other aspects of Jericho's topography which would have directed the Teacher to lead his followers to this area.

4

Judgement and Hell-fire

In one respect at least the television film-cameraman was right: the Rift Valley had been cursed, if not completely abandoned, by God. Even if one were unaware of the biblical traditions that associated the shores of the Dead Sea with divine judgement, the most religiously insensitive visitor to the barren scene could hardly fail to sense an air of doom pervading the place.

The story of Sodom and Gomorrah and their fate reflects the sinister melancholy of the Dead Sea basin, literally, as well as metaphorically, the lowest place on the surface of the planet. It will be remembered that Abraham's nephew Lot had offered hospitality to two angels sent specifically by God to test the truth of the evil reputation surrounding the two cities. However, no sooner had the travellers responded to Lot's traditional invitation to enter his dwelling for the night, than the house was beset by ruffians of Sodom demanding that the good man produce his guests for their perverted amusement. Lot offered them his virgin daughters to satisfy their lust, but local male preferences lay in another direction, and they threatened to break down the doors. At this, the angels struck the men of Sodom with blindness and urged Lot to escape while there was yet time. The rumours having been fully substantiated, nothing could now prevent the Lord from inflicting a terrible punishment on the cities of the Plain. Once Lot and his family were out of the way, God rained fire and brimstone down from heaven, and soon nothing was left but a pall of smoke and a strong smell of burning sulphur. Of Lot's presence the only memento was a pillar of salt; his wife, with characteristic feminine curiosity, had dared to look back and had been thus transformed as a perpetual warning against marital disobedience (Genesis 19).

But it was not merely the populations of Sodom and Gomorrah who lay buried under the reeking debris of the Plain. Long before, in remote antiquity, a group of angels under their leader Azazel had dared to challenge the sovereignty of God and go their own way. It led to that traditional meeting-place of gods and men, Mount Hermon, in the north of Palestine. There the angels took to themselves mortal women as wives, and taught them the arts of enchantments and various skills. Among the heavenly secrets then betrayed were the arts of self-adornment and cosmetics, and 'the cutting of roots and acquaintance with plants' (Enoch 7^{1ff}), that is, the mysteries of pharmacy and healing.

A brief reference to this age-old myth of the fallen angels and the havoc they wrought appears in the Bible:

> When men began to multiply on the face of the ground, and daughters were born to them, the sons of God [ie the angels] saw that the daughters of men were fair; and they took to wife such of them as they chose . . .
>
> (Genesis 6$^{1-2}$)

Of that unnatural union was born, as might have been expected, a race of supermen, or giants, called variously Nephilim or Rephaim, both names meaning in origin 'Fallen Ones (from Heaven)'. It was the corruption that their special knowledge introduced into the world that brought mankind to the state when God had no option but to sweep away all life in the Flood and start again with Noah and those he had saved with him in the Ark.

The Bible makes only a passing reference to the story of the fallen angels, or Watchers, as they are elsewhere called, but the theme is developed at length in apocryphal literature, and

63

particularly in the books of Enoch, whose Essene affinities, if not origin, have already been noted. It is clear that the sectarians believed that they had some special connection with these Rephaim and their heavenly knowledge. They probably interpreted their name as 'Healers', from the Hebrew verb *rapha'*, 'heal', and thus associated it with their own popular designation Essenes, 'Healers, Physicians'. The special skills attributed to the Rephaim, particularly their knowledge of herbalism and enchantments, were just those accredited to the Essenes in our historical sources. In that they would have believed themselves similarly entrusted with these mysteries, they were the spiritual descendants of this super-race.

It was fitting, then, that the Essenes should take up their residence down by the Dead Sea, for it was just there that the fallen angels lay imprisoned, as we learn from the visions of Enoch. He tells us that the archangel Raphael ('God heals') was told to 'bind Azazel hand and foot and cast him into the darkness, and make an opening in the desert . . . and place upon him rough and jagged rocks, and cover his face that he may not see the light. And on the day of great judgement he shall be cast into the fire.' Along with their chief, most of the other rebellious angels were locked into this abyss of judgement in the Rift Valley and left to languish there until arraigned with all mankind before the seat of judgement.

A few were allowed to rove freely about the world, doing mischief, for it was essential to God's purpose that man's eventual salvation should be tempered in the furnace of temptation, the 'time of trial, or testing' as the Scrolls and the Lord's Prayer call it. In another account of the Watchers story, found in the apocryphal work called Jubilees, another favourite of the Essenes to judge from the copies found in the Scrolls, Noah is made to pray to God:

> And Thou knowest how Thy Watchers, the fathers of these spirits, acted in my day; and as for these spirits which are living, imprison them and hold them fast in the prison of condemnation, and let them not bring destruction on the sons of Thy servant, my God; for these are malignant and created in order to destroy.

64

And let them not rule over the spirits of the living; for Thou alone canst exercise dominion over them. And let them not have power over the sons of the righteous from henceforth and evermore.

God accordingly had the evil spirits bound. But their chief, here called Mastema ('Enmity'), that is, Satan, protested:

Lord, Creator, let some of them remain before me, and let them hearken to my voice, and do all that I shall say unto them; for if some of them are not left to me, I shall not be able to execute the power of my will upon the sons of men; for these are for corruption and leading astray before my judgement, for great is the wickedness of the sons of men.

Obligingly, God permitted a tenth of the condemned spirits to remain unbound:

all the malignant evil ones we bound in the place of condemnation, and a tenth part of them we left that they might be subject to Satan on earth.

However, lest God's favoured sons should be exposed to the mischief of the liberated demons, He allowed Noah to know

. . . all the medicines of their diseases, together with their seductions, how he might heal them with herbs of the earth. And Noah wrote down all the things in a book as we instructed him concerning every kind of medicine. Thus the evil spirits were precluded from hurting the sons of Noah. And he gave all he had written to Shem, his eldest son, for he loved him exceedingly above all his sons.

(Jubilees 10$^{5-14}$)

These precious secrets were subsequently passed on to Jacob from Abraham in his blessing:

Jacob, my beloved son, whom my soul loveth, may God bless thee from above the firmament, and may He give thee all the blessings wherewith He blessed Adam, and Enoch, and Noah, and Shem; and all the things of which He told me, and all the things which He promised to give me, may He cause to cleave to thee and to thy seed for ever . . . And the spirits of Mastema shall not rule over thee or over thy seed to turn thee from the Lord . . .

(Jubilees 19²⁷⁻²⁸)

From Jacob this protective knowledge was passed to his son Levi in

all his books and the books of his fathers . . . that he might preserve them and renew them for his children.

(45¹⁶)

They thus entered the protective custody of the Levitical priesthood of the Jews, or, as the Essenes would maintain, into that faithful remnant of the priesthood which remained true to their high calling. It has been shown that one of the most powerful officials of the Essene establishment, the Overseer, or Guardian, whose functions are so strongly reminiscent of the Church's Bishop, was chosen from the order of Levites. He may thus have claimed his authority as a spiritual healer from this special knowledge, derived ultimately from the Rephaim, 'Healers', of antiquity, through Shem, Noah's favourite son.

Thus protected with angelic knowledge of healing, the Essenes were able to take up their station above the 'cleft in the desert' where the fallen sons of God lay imprisoned. Lesser men also sought cures for their diseases in this area, but for them it was a dangerous undertaking since it meant exposing oneself to the malign influence of the demons under the ground. Nevertheless, proof of the place's healing efficacy and of its demonic associations was manifested in the hot springs which bubbled then, as now, out of the ground on the eastern shores of the Dead Sea. They were much patronised by those rich enough to avail themselves of their powers, and of the services of doctors who professionally administered the cure. Josephus vividly describes the treatment meted out to the dying king Herod; one almost feels sorry for the tyrant:

His condition led diviners to pronounce his maladies a judgement on him for his treatment of the sophists. Yet, struggling as he was with such numerous sufferings [the list given earlier reads like a medical student's nightmare; it includes dropsy, gangrene of the genitals, worms, asthma, and convulsions], he clung to life in the hope of recovery, and devised one remedy after another. Thus he crossed the Jordan to take the warm baths at Callirrhoe, the waters of which descend into the Lake Asphaltitis [so named from the lumps of bitumen which could sometimes be seen floating on the surface], and from their sweetness are also fit to drink. There, the physicians decided to raise the temperature of his whole body with hot oil, so he was lowered into a bath full of that liquid. He thereupon fainted and turned up his eyes as though he were dead . . .

(*War* I, xxiii, 5 § 657ff;
cp. *Antiquities* XVII, vi, 5 § 171ff)

As late as the last century, popular local belief held that the hot water of the springs was released from the lower regions by evil spirits merely to stop it being available to assuage the pains of the damned in hell. Another legend had it that King Solomon sent a servant to open the springs when he discovered how thin was the crust of the earth at this point. However, lest the threats of the subterranean demons should deter his messenger, the kindly monarch had his eardrums pierced so that the man should not be distressed by their continual wailing.

The royal patronage of the hot springs finds another reference in the books of Enoch:

And I saw that valley in which there was a great convulsion and disturbance of the waters. And when all this took place, from their fiery molten metal, and from the convulsion thereof in that place, there was produced a smell of sulphur, and it was associated with those waters and that valley of the angels who had led mankind astray where a fire burned underground. And through its gorges run streams of fire where these angels are punished who led earth-dwellers astray.

But those waters shall in those days serve for the kings and the mighty and the exalted, and for those who dwell on the earth, for

67

the healing of the body but the punishment of the spirit; now their spirit is full of lust, that they may be punished in their body, for they have denied the Lord of Spirits and see their punishment daily, and yet believe not in His name. And in proportion to the severity of the burning of their bodies, a corresponding change shall take place in their spirit for ever and ever; for before the Lord of Spirits none shall utter an idle word. For the judgement shall come upon them, because they believe in the lust of their body but deny the Spirit of the Lord.

(Enoch 67$^{5-10}$)

Interestingly, the writer believed that when the punishment of the fallen angels had been completed, the waters would cool down and lose their therapeutic efficacy. Nevertheless, the fires would go on burning down below, and what once cured men's ills would then serve to punish their sins for eternity.

This idea of the Dead Sea valley as a place of trial and preliminary judgement finds a number of echoes in biblical and post-biblical literature. The prophet of the Exile, Ezekiel, looks to a time when God would bring His scattered peoples from all parts of the world and purge them of their sins in 'the Desert of the Peoples':

As I live, says the Lord God, surely with a mighty hand and an outstretched arm, and with wrath poured out, I will be king over you. I will bring you out from the peoples and gather you out of the countries where you are scattered, with a mighty hand and an outstretched arm, and with wrath poured out; and I will bring you into the Desert of the Peoples, and there I will enter into judgement with you face to face. As I entered into judgement with your fathers in the desert of the land of Egypt, so I will enter into judgement with you, says the Lord God. I will make you pass under the rod, and I will bring you into the bond of the covenant. I will purge out the rebels from among you, and those who transgress against me; I will bring them out of the land where they sojourn, but they shall not enter the land of Israel.

(Ezekiel 20$^{33-38}$)

The scroll from the first cave, which describes in idealistic

68

terms the apocalyptic war between the Elect and the Sons of Darkness, also speaks of this 'Desert of the Peoples' as their own furnace of affliction and place of testing:

> The sons of Levi, Judah, and Benjamin, exiles in the desert, shall battle against them . . . when the exiled Sons of Light return from the Desert of the Peoples to camp in the Desert of Jerusalem . . .
>
> (War Scroll, Col. I 2–3)

The enigmatic fourteenth chapter of Genesis refers to a running battle which was fought in the Rift Valley about the Dead Sea. No one has ever been able satisfactorily to identify the non-Israelite characters involved, nor the historical circumstances of the incident, but it has served to provide an abundance of legend in post-biblical literature, as well as material for hundreds of academic papers and hours of inconclusive speculation. What makes the story of particular interest is that at its conclusion there appears a mysterious king of Salem called Melchizedek, 'King of Righteousness', to whom even the patriarch Abraham does obeisance and pays tithes. He is said to be a priest of *El Elyon*, 'God Most High', although he is nowhere else mentioned in biblical history. Behind the scenes of canonical tradition, however. Melchizedek was vested with considerable prestige, for in Psalm 110 he appears as chief representative of the priestly order to which even the Messiah may aspire:

> Thou art a priest for ever after the order of Melchizedek.
>
> (v 4)

Among the Essenes, also, this theological speculation finds considerable development and, of course, the writer of the Epistle to the Hebrews in the New Testament plays on a similar messianic tradition in glorifying Christ:

> So also Christ did not exalt himself to be made a high priest, but was appointed by him who said to him,
>   'Thou art my Son,
>   today I have begotten thee';

as he says also in another place,

'Thou art a priest for ever
after the order of Melchizedek.'

(Hebrews 5^{5–6})

We have this as a sure and steadfast anchor of the soul, a hope that enters into the inner shrine behind the curtain, where Jesus has gone as a forerunner on our behalf, having become a high priest for ever after the order of Melchizedek.

For this Melchizedek, king of Salem, priest of the most high God, met Abraham returning from the slaughter of the kings and blessed him; and to him Abraham apportioned a tenth part of everything. He is first, by translation of his name, King of Righteousness, and then he is also king of Salem, that is, king of peace. He is without father or mother or genealogy, and has neither beginning of days nor end of life, but resembling the Son of God he continues a priest for ever . . .

(Hebrews 6¹⁹⊤7³)

The Genesis story relates how, following a rebellion on the part of the cities of the Valley against their Mesopotamian overlords, the feudal kings formed an alliance to resist the inevitable punitive incursion from the east. The battle was fought in the 'Valley of Siddim (that is, the Salt Sea)'. Unhappily, the eastern generals routed the allies, and the kings of Sodom and Gomorrah were hindered in their flight by falling into bitumen pits with which the valley abounded, leaving their undefended cities to be plundered by the victors. Lot was still at that time a resident of Sodom, and he and his family were also taken and had to be rescued by his uncle Abraham, who made a special expedition to cut off the retiring enemy columns. The triumphal return of the patriarch and his restoration of the plunder was honoured by a royal reception from Melchizedek, who brought out from Salem, his capital city, sacramental bread and wine and pronounced a solemn blessing on Abraham (Genesis 14^{19–20}).

Jewish traditions created a number of legends about Melchizedek to account for his precedence, among them that he was a kinsman of Noah; some even said his son Shem. This, together

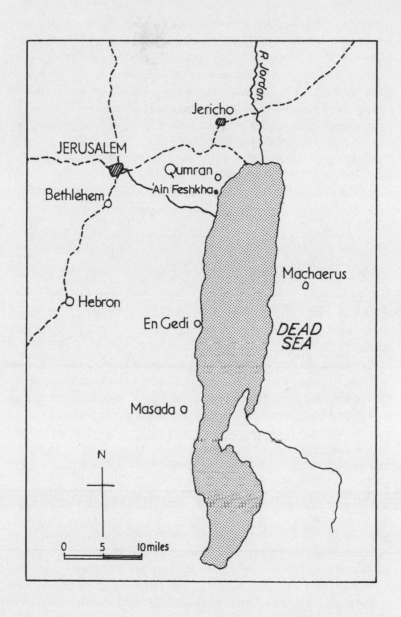

Jericho

R. Jordan

JERUSALEM

Qumran o

'Ain Feshkha •

Bethlehem o

Machaerus
o

o Hebron

En Gedi o

DEAD
SEA

Masada o

N

0   5   10 miles

with the location of the events of the Genesis story, would certainly have enhanced Melchizedek's reputation in Essene eyes, believing as they did that they were the spiritual heirs of Shem in their possession of the secrets of healing. Furthermore, in Melchizedek's city of Salem the Essenes may have found a further contact with their own geographical situation.

Orthodox Jewish opinion identified Salem with Jerusalem, the one name being merely an abbreviation of the other. Even in the Scrolls, in an Aramaic elaboration of the book of Genesis, this interpretation is reproduced with a note appended to the place-name Salem. But in fact this was by no means generally accepted, and certainly the topography of the Genesis narrative would imply a location nearer the scene of the battles fought by the kings of the Valley. Jerome sought an identification with a place called Salumias in the Jordan valley, eight miles south of Scythopolis (biblical Bethshean), where, in his time in the fourth–fifth centuries, the palace ruins of Melchizedek were shown to the faithful. The Fourth Gospel similarly locates a Salim in the Jordan valley, near the scene of John the Baptist's activities at Aenon, 'where there was much water' (John 3[23]).

A much stronger tradition places Melchizedek's Salem in Samaritan territory, in central Palestine. The biblical justification for this identification is to be found in a reading of the passage in Genesis describing Jacob's travels in Canaan on his way from Paddan-aram. In the thirty-third chapter, the word which our English versions translate 'in safety' (Hebrew *shalem*) was read by the early Greek translators as a place-name, Salem, 'a city of Shechem', which lay by Mount Gerizim. The fourth-century Church historian Eusebius preserves a similar tradition that the meeting of Abraham with Melchizedek took place near Mount Gerizim, and more recently, Samaritans have pointed to a place called Salim, east of modern Nablus, ancient Shechem, for the site of Jacob's encampment.

So much for what we may call the 'realities' of biblical topography. But we have at this point to remind ourselves that where the Essenes are concerned we are not dealing so much with locational actualities, based upon physical geography,

72

comparative weight of rival traditions, similarities between modern place-names and their ancient counterparts, archaeological soundings, and all the rest of the modern topographer's apparatus for locating biblical sites, but with religious symbolism and typology. We are in a shadowy half-world, where hard facts of history fade off into mythology, and where the clear dividing line we like to draw between fact and fiction has no place in religious speculation. If a sacred site can be shown from the Bible to have been located in a certain place, and its main features identified with some natural, or unnatural, formation on the ground, then that is sufficient to warrant its acceptance in such circles, no matter how much better support could be advanced on rational grounds for alternative locations.

Of such was the siting of Mount Gerizim by some early

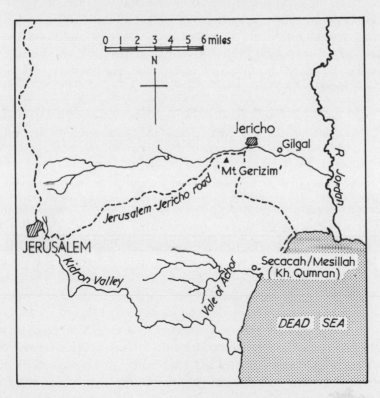

authorities around the turn of the era; there is no doubt where the sacred mounts of Gerizim and Ebal were actually located, some thirty miles north of Jerusalem, on either side of an important pass crossing the mountain range of central Palestine. They overlook the main road running north and south through the country, and between them nestled the key city of Shechem, later the Roman Neapolis (modern Nablus). Since the fifth century BC, Gerizim has been a Samaritan sanctuary, and long before that it had a profound strategic and religious importance in ancient Israel. The Samaritan temple erected on Gerizim in about 412 BC was destroyed in about 110 BC by the priest-king John Hyrcanus.

However, there is a text in the book of Deuteronomy which, read literally in its present form, seems to offer an alternative location for Mount Gerizim, and one that is much nearer the site of the Israelites' crossing-place into the Promised Land, by ancient Jericho. Moses directed the people to pronounce a blessing and a curse on Mount Gerizim and Mount Ebal after they had entered the country, and he describes the positions of these landmarks as follows:

> Are they not beyond the Jordan, west of the road, towards the going down of the sun, in the land of the Canaanites who live in the Arabah [ie the Plain, used of the Jordan valley], over against Gilgal, beside the Teacher's Oak [or Oak of Moreh]?
>
> (11^{26-30})

The plain meaning of this passage can only be that Mount Gerizim lay just across the fords of the Jordan, near Gilgal, which lay between Jericho and the river, and in the Arabah, the Jordan depression. This, anyway, is how Eusebius and other early commentators saw it. The famous sixth-century map at Madeba in Transjordan shows Gerizim and Ebal above Elisha's fountain in ancient Jericho. A certain Rabbi Eleazar of the second century affirmed that the biblical text referred not to the mountains above Shechem but to two artificial mounds called by the same names but erected by the Israelites themselves. Above all, for our immediate interest, the treasure inven-

74

tory in the copper scroll (see Chapter One) places one important deposit of the sacred hoard in a hiding-place on Mount Gerizim, which would be highly unlikely if the reference were to the Samaritan sanctuary in central Palestine which by then was almost certainly firmly under Roman control.

Following Rabbi Eleazar's clue, we can see exactly what these later traditionalists had in mind. Behind Jericho, where the great gorge of the Wady Kelt debouches on to the open plain, stand two mounds, in their final form almost certainly artificial constructions. They rise on either side of the old Jericho–Jerusalem road, scene of the New Testament 'Good Samaritan' parable, and their position and general aspect, apart from the obvious difference in size, are not dissimilar from those of the true Gerizim and Ebal of the north (see the present writer's *Treasure of the Copper Scroll*, p 76ff). They are, in fact, the sites of two fortresses built by Herod the Great (37–4 BC) as part of a series of military posts defending the eastern approaches to Jerusalem. Even before Herod's time, the hills, although less prominent, would nevertheless have been sufficiently noteworthy to have borne the interpretation required by the Deuteronomic topography.

If, anyway, this was the understanding of the Essenes at Secacah, a number of very important considerations follow. For, in this case, not only do Gerizim and Ebal lie here in the vicinity of Jericho and the old sanctuary of Gilgal, but so also does Shechem, with all its associations for the history of Israel, from the time of Joshua onwards. Religiously, it brings Samaritan territory into the sphere of Essene eschatological geography, and this is particularly interesting since, on a number of counts, Samaritan influences are elsewhere apparent in the Scrolls and, as we shall see, play a significant part in the further development of Essene theology. We should do well now to look more closely at the persons and events that attended the Israelites' entry into the Promised Land, bearing in mind that the Essenes of Secacah imagined that they were following in their forefathers' footsteps, and reliving the past in their anticipation of the future.

5

Joshua, Son of Nun, and the Teacher of Righteousness

While Moses lived, Joshua's star burned less brightly. It was only after the death of the Prophet of the Exodus that this other great figure of the desert wandering came into his own, and proved himself no less favoured of God, or less gifted as a leader of men. As Josephus says of him, calling him by the Greek form of the name, Jesus, son of Naue: 'a man of extreme courage, valiant in endurance of toil, highly gifted in intellect and speech, and withal one who worshipped God with a singular piety which he had learnt from Moses, and who was held in esteem by the Hebrews' (*Antiquities* III ii 3 § 49).

Moses's commission to Joshua, signified by the laying on of hands (Deuteronomy 34⁹), was confirmed by Yahweh himself:

> This day will I begin to exalt you in the sight of all Israel, so that they may know that as I was with Moses, so will I be with you.
>
> (Joshua 3⁷)

As the people prepared for their first great battle for possession of the land, 'they stood in awe of Joshua, as they had stood in awe of Moses' (Joshua 4¹⁴). Events fully justified their confidence. Not only did he prove himself an inspired general in the field, but the miracles that attended his campaigns, from the drying up of the Jordan's waters, and the collapse of Jericho's walls, to the arrest of even the sun and moon in their courses, spoke of his divine patronage:

> There has been no day like it, before or since, when Yahweh hearkened to the voice of man.
>
> (Joshua 10¹⁴)

Joshua's authority over the people extended even to the priests who bore the Ark of the Covenant (Joshua 3⁸), and, as Moses's successor, he became the nation's Lawgiver and Teacher. His combined prophetic and administrative duties began when, at the site of Israel's first encampment in the Promised Land, at Gilgal, he led them in a renewal of their covenant with God, symbolised by the circumcision of all males born during the forty years' desert journey.

Following the army's complete destruction of Ai, in the foot-hills bordering the Jordan valley, the biblical record speaks immediately of Joshua's building an altar on Mount Ebal, and of his pronouncing the blessing and curse on the mountains of Gerizim and Ebal as Moses had commanded before his death. Furthermore, as if to set the seal upon his authority as Lawgiver, Joshua made a copy of the Law of Moses and recited its provisions before the whole people (Joshua 8³⁰⁻³⁵).

There was a tradition among the Essenes that Joshua had sealed the Torah, the book of the Law, inside the Ark of the Covenant, and that it was not revealed again until the days of the pious king Josiah, who instituted cultic reforms at Jerusalem in the seventh century BC. The story in the Old Testament tells how, during the course of some repairs to the fabric of the Temple, the 'book of the Law' was rediscovered, and its reading before the king provoked him to a show of great contrition that 'our forefathers have not obeyed the words of this book' (II Kings 22). An Essene document says:

> David had not read in the sealed book of the Law which was inside the Ark, because it had not been opened in Israel since the day when Eleazar and Joshua and the elders died . . .
>
> (Damascus Document V 2–4)

77

This idea that Joshua had salted away the original words of Moses receives further support in an old tradition recorded in the apocryphal Assumption of Moses, dating to around the first century of our era. There we read:

> And he [Moses] called to him Joshua, son of Nun, a man approved of the Lord, that he might be the minister of the people, and of the Tabernacle of the Testimony with all its holy things . . .
>
> (1 [6ff])

Moses then commits his words to Joshua:

> And receive thou this writing that thou mayest know how to preserve the books [ie the Pentateuch, the first five books of the Bible, traditionally ascribed to Moses] which I shall deliver unto thee: and thou shalt set these in order and anoint them with oil of cedar, and put them away in earthen vessels in the place which He made from the beginning of the creation of the world, that His name should be called upon until the day of repentance in the visitation wherewith the Lord will visit them in the consummation of the End of Days.
>
> (1 [16ff])

In this passage we have the answer to a problem which beset scholars when the Dead Sea Scrolls were first found in the caves: why were they so carefully wrapped in linen cloths and stored away in 'earthen vessels', the tall scroll jars with which we have become so familiar? Was it intended that the goatherd's cave should be a permanent storage centre for the priceless scrolls, or was it a temporary sanctuary until they could be moved elsewhere? Clearly, in obedience to the supposed directive issued to the first Joshua/Jesus, the second 'Joshua' had ordered his followers to seal the manuscripts ready for their eventual return to 'the place which God had made from the beginning of the creation' (that is, Jerusalem) at the End of Days, when they would all return to the Holy City to celebrate the visitation of the Lord. Doubtless the Teacher of

78

Righteousness also had in mind that he was fulfilling the words of God transmitted through His prophet Isaiah:

Bind up the testimony, seal the teaching among my disciples . . .
(8^{16}; see also below, Chapter Fourteen, p 209)

The Teacher's own interpretations of the Law for his time are called in one of the Scrolls, 'the second Torah' again in fulfilment of his role as the second 'Joshua', Interpreter of the Law.

To return to the first Joshua, son of Nun, nothing in the Bible text describing his recital of the provisions of the Law and the blessing and curse of Gerizim and Ebal (Joshua 8$^{30-35}$) indicates the long journey inland which would have been required before reaching the true site of these sanctuaries; so those authorities who sought the sacred mountains nearer Jericho would have found here further support for their strange topography.

A single parchment sheet from the Partridge Cave, published by the present writer first in 1956, contains a collection of prophetic blessings culled from the Bible, relating to the coming Messiah in his capacity as Prophet, King, and Priest. The blessings are ascribed to Joshua, and followed by a curse against 'the man who rebuilds this city [Jericho]' (Joshua 6^{26}), with an appended expansion which is as cryptic in its references to historic characters as most of the Essene Bible commentaries, but which we may assume was directed against the Teacher's archenemy, the Wicked Priest. It appears, therefore, that the Essenes believed that when Joshua pronounced the blessings and curses on the slopes of Gerizim and Ebal, as his master had commanded, he directed them prophetically towards the sect's own situation: the benediction upon their Teacher, as the prefiguration of the Messiah, and the malediction upon the Wicked Priest, as the epitome of evil in their time, and precursor of the satanic opposition to the establishment of the Kingdom of God in the Last Days.

Furthermore, the involvement of the Wicked Priest in the Jericho curse must make us look again at the place and circumstances of the dramatic confrontation between the Teacher and his arch-enemy, so often alluded to in the Scrolls. First, it is worth recalling that the city overlooked by the twin mountains, Shechem, was one of the 'cities of refuge' appointed by Joshua to serve as temporary sanctuaries for those who had unwittingly shed blood and were being pursued by the victim's avenger. The fugitive could find refuge in one of these places until his friends had had time to muster support for his defence before the local judges (Joshua 20^7,21^{21}).

Again, Shechem had long been a royal city and credited with special sanctity. It was there, by the so-called 'Teacher's Oak', elsewhere called the 'Diviners' Oak' (Judges 9^{37}), that Abimelech was anointed king (Judges 9^6). The similarly named 'Teacher's Oak' by Gilgal, 'near Jericho' (Deuteronomy 11^{30}), where Joshua received his vision of the angel, would doubtless have confirmed to the Essenes their location of Shechem in the Jericho area.

The angelic commander of the Lord's hosts, who confronted Joshua with a drawn sword in his hand, ordered him to remove his shoes, 'for the place where you stand is holy' (Joshua 5^{15}). The Israelites made their first encampment in the Promised Land at Gilgal and there observed the Passover, after which the supply of desert manna ceased and they began to eat the produce of the land 'flowing with milk and honey' (Joshua 5$^{10-12}$).

Thus biblical tradition, as interpreted by the Essenes, linked the miraculous crossing of the Jordan, the establishment of the first shrine in the Promised Land, and the renewal of the covenant, with a 'city of refuge' and a local oracle called the Teacher's Oak. Well might they connect the place and its traditions with their own situation and experience. They had sought refuge in this area from the persecution of the world, and they had been pursued here by their enemies, for Jericho would have certainly been on the route of Alexander Jannaeus's punitive expedition from Jerusalem in his search for the rebels. One wishes that an Essene commentary on the book of Hosea could have been preserved in a less fragmentary form. Some estimate of its possible significance for Essene interpretation of history can however be judged from its inclusion of the verse which reads:

> As robbers lie in wait for a man, a company of priests, on the way to Shechem they murder, they commit villainy
>
> (v 9; see also below, Chapter Thirteen, p 197)

Was the supreme act of 'villainy' committed at the Essene 'Shechem', by Gilgal, upon the Teacher's Tree? The dramatic irony of the situation would not have been lost upon Jannaeus, certainly, as he had his old enemy scourged and crucified upon the sacred 'pillar' (Judges 9⁶). The other rebels who had been more directly responsible for inviting the Greek forces to join their cause he dragged away to Jerusalem to pay the penalty of betrayal before the horrified gaze of its citizens; the broken body of this other 'Joshua/Jesus' he left exposed to humiliation and contempt until his chastened followers could crawl from their cave refuges to retrieve his remains.

We find some echo of the event in another apocryphal work called the Testaments of the Twelve Patriarchs, a collection of oracles supposedly left by the twelve sons of the patriarch Jacob. Again, some fragmentary parts of this work have turned up among the Scrolls, and it appears likely that in their final form they were modelled on the pattern of an Essene composition, the Testament of Levi. There were later interpolations, often assumed to be 'Christian', but, as we shall see, this designation must now be deemed of little value; one should speak rather chronologically, of time, rather than diverse sectarian associations. In any case, the fourteenth chapter of Testament Levi is certainly well represented in extant Essene writings from the caves, and it is in this section of the work that we find the following admonition against the Temple hierarchy, and their Wicked High Priest in particular:

> The offerings of the Lord ye rob, and from His portion shall ye steal choice portions, eating them [contemptuously] with harlots. And out of covetousness ye shall teach the commandments of the Lord, wedded women shall ye pollute, and the virgins of

Jerusalem shall ye defile; and with harlots and adulteresses shall ye be joined, and the daughters of gentiles shall ye take to wife, purifying them with unlawful purification; and your union shall be like unto Sodom and Gomorrah. And ye shall be puffed up because of your priesthood, lifting yourselves up against men, and not only so, but also against the commandments of God. For ye shall contemn the holy things with jests and laughter . . .

(14^{5-8})

And a man who reneweth the Law, in the power of the Most High, ye shall call a deceiver; and at last ye shall rush [upon him] to slay him, not knowing his dignity, taking innocent blood through wickedness upon your heads. And your holy places shall be laid waste because of him . . .

(16^{3-4})

This last passage is strongly reminiscent of the Essene commentary on Psalm 37, referred to earlier:

The wicked watches for the righteous and seeks to slay him . . . This refers to the Wicked Priest who watched for the Teacher of Righteousness and sought to slay him . . .

Even more pointedly, we find among a collection of cryptic oracles called the Sibylline Books, the earliest of which date from about the first or second century BC, a reference which clearly links the Teacher's great predecessor, Joshua, son of Nun, with his own tragic death:

Then there shall come from the sky a certain exalted man who spreads his hands on the many-fruited tree, the noblest of Hebrews, who one day caused the sun to stand still, when he cried with fair speech and pure lips.

(Book V 257–59)

The allusion to the sun standing still is, of course, a reference to the miraculous lengthening of the day in order that Joshua might complete the destruction of Israel's enemies (Joshua 10^{12-14}). There is, therefore, no doubt that in the eyes of the faithful the crucified Teacher, the 'exalted man', was a reincarnation of Joshua, son of Nun, known in the Greek texts as Jesus.

The mention of the 'many-fruited tree' is of particular interest, for it clearly links the Tree of the Master's crucifixion with the life-giving stream which was to flow from the threshold of the Temple and bring life to the Dead Sea at Secacah/ Mesillah:

> And on the banks, on both sides of the river, there will grow all kinds of trees for food. Their leaves will not wither nor their fruit fail, but they will bear fresh fruit every month, because the water for them flows from the sanctuary. Their fruit will be for food, and their leaves for healing.
>
> (Ezekiel 47[12])

This conception of the Tree of the Teacher's sacrifice as being the Tree of Life of the Garden of Eden was capable of considerable theological development, as the New Testament apocalyptist appreciated:

> Then he showed me the river of the water of life, bright as crystal, flowing from the throne of God and of the Lamb, through the middle of the street of the city; also on either side of the river, the Tree of Life with its twelve kinds of fruit, yielding its fruit each month; and the leaves of the tree were for the healing of the nations.
>
> (Revelation 22[1-2])

By then we have come the full circle, linking the Essenes' Tree of Life with the fateful tree in the Garden of Eden by which men fell: 'as in Adam all die, so also in Christ shall all be made alive' (I Corinthians 15[22]). But in those early days, immediately following the chastening shock of the Teacher's martyrdom, the Essene philosophers still had far to go before the Tree, or Cross, of death should seem to them a sign and instrument of divine redemption.

To understand something of the reasoning that must have underlain this doctrine, we should look, as always, for the

83

scriptural models on which the Essenes would have based their appreciation of their present experience. Even before the Israelites entered the Promised Land, they had flirted with local cults encountered on their journey. These usually had strong sexual associations and were blamed for the plagues that beset those who indulged in their rituals. In expiation Moses had the tribal chiefs, as representatives of the nation, executed by exposure to the sun's heat, 'that the fierce anger of the Lord might turn away from Israel' (Numbers 25[4]).

Such 'hanging before the Lord' seems to have been regarded as offering to the deity some propitiation for incurring his displeasure, evident through a natural calamity or otherwise unaccountable affliction. So, at a later date, when in the days of King David the country suffered a prolonged famine, inquiry was made of God for the reasons that had prompted the divine rebuke. On learning that they were suffering because King Saul had treacherously shed the blood of some Gibeonites, then under a treaty of protection, David asked the victims' kinsfolk how the blood-guilt might be lifted. The Gibeonites suggested that Saul's seven sons 'be given to us, so that we may hang them up before the Lord at Gibeon, on the mountain of the Lord'. The myth originally had an agricultural origin, to judge from the detail that 'they were put to death in the first days of the harvest, at the beginning of the barley harvest' (II Samuel 21).

The Hebrew word used in these passages to describe this particularly barbaric form of ritual execution means properly 'dislocate, be torn away', and is variously translated in the ancient versions as 'impale'; 'expose (in the sun)'; 'make an example of, put to shame'; or 'crucify'. Essentially, the limbs were broken in some way to incapacitate the victim, and he was then pegged out on the ground, or hanged from gallows or a tree, so that death was the result of exposure to the elements. It was, of course, a cruel fate, but clearly in its religious context the idea was not so much to inflict suffering in vengeance as to make an act of propitiation to the deity through exposure and

84

public humiliation. The victim was the scapegoat for the people; his alienation and rejection was the means for their redemption.

The Essene commentary on the book of Habakkuk makes the point that it was on the Day of Atonement that the Wicked Priest suddenly appeared at the place of the Teacher's exile in pursuit of his enemy, to make him 'swallow the cup'. Writing probably long after the event, the commentator still shrinks from openly acknowledging the manner of the Lawgiver's death. Even the otherwise surprisingly direct Nahum commentator will go no further than to speak of 'the man hanged alive upon a tree', and to emphasise the gravity of the crime as perpetrated by a Jew against one of his own people. Nevertheless, the sacrificial nature of the Teacher's death is implicit in the Essene writings, and was further developed as the socio-religious situation affecting Judaism, and Essenism in particular, changed.

Looking back on the Teacher's hymns of thanksgiving, it appears that even in his own lifetime his eventual martyrdom was not entirely unexpected. He suffered on more than one occasion from the persecution of his enemies, and even from schismatic groups within his own movement. Some of this sense of disappointment and isolation finds expression in the hymns:

And Thou hast made me a reproach and a derision to traitors,
    but a counsel of truth and insight for the upright of way.
And because of the deviousness of wicked men
    I am become a slander on the lips of the violent,
    and scorners bare their teeth.
Yea, I am become a taunt for rebels,
    and a gathering of the wicked rage against me,
    and roar like storms at sea;
when curling breakers crash, they shower me with mire and
    mud.

But to those who are chosen for righteousness, Thou hast made
    me a banner,
    and an interpreter of knowledge in wonderful mysteries,
    to test [men of] truth
    and to try those who make correction their friend . . .

And I am become a zealous spirit against the Seekers-after-
    Smooth-Things,
  [and all] deceivers roar against me,
  like the sound of mighty waters,
and [all] their thoughts were devilish devices.
They have cast towards the Pit the life of the man
  whose mouth Thou hast confirmed,
and into whose heart Thou hast put teaching and under-
    standing,
  that he might open a fount of knowledge
  to all men of insight . . .

(Col. II)

Violent men have sought my life
  because I have clung to Thy covenant.
For they, a council of deceit,
  and a devil's crew,
know not that my confidence is based on Thee,
and that through Thy pledged love Thou wilt save my soul
  since my steps are directed by Thee.
From Thee it is [permitted]
  that they threaten my life,
that Thou mayest be glorified
  by the judgement of the wicked,
and demonstrate Thy might through me
  in the presence of the sons of men;
for it is by Thy pledged love that I stand.

(Col. II)

I thank Thee, O Lord,
  for Thou hast [fastened] Thine eye upon me,
Thou hast saved me from the zeal of lying interpreters,
  and from the party of Seekers-after-Smooth-Things.
Thou hast redeemed the life of the Poor One
  whom they planned to destroy,
  spilling his blood because he served Thee.
Because [they were unaware]
  that my steps were directed by Thee,
they made me a mockery and an object of shame
  in the mouth of all who seek deceit.

86

But Thou, O my God, hast rescued
    the soul of the oppressed and poor,
    from the power of one stronger than he;
Thou hast redeemed my soul
    from the hand of the powerful.
Thou hast not permitted their insults to dismay me
    so that I forsook Thy service
    for fear of the corrupting influence of the [ungodly],
or exchanged my steadfast resolve for folly . . .

                       (Col. II)

[Teachers of lies] have smoothed Thy people [with words],
    and deceitful interpreters [have led them astray];
they perish without understanding,
    for their works are foolishness.
For I am despised by them,
    and they account me as nothing,
that Thou mayest demonstrate Thy might through me.
They have thrust me from my country
    like a bird from its nest;
all my friends and kinsmen are driven from me,
    and regard me as a broken vessel.
And they, lying interpreters and false prophets,
    have schemed against me a devilry,
to exchange the Law impressed on my heart by Thee
    for the smooth things [they urge on] Thy people.
And they withhold from the thirsty the drink of Knowledge,
    and relieve their thirst with vinegar,
that they may witness the misdirection of their ways,
    their reckless behaviour at their feast-days,
    and their falling foul of their own snares . . .

                       (Col. IV)

As for me, shaking and trembling seize me
    and all my bones are broken;
my heart dissolves like wax before the fire
    and my knees are like a stream
    tumbling down a waterfall.
For I remember my sins and the faithlessness of my forefathers.

When the wicked rose against Thy covenant
and the vicious against Thy word,
I said in my obstinacy,
'I am forsaken by Thy covenant.'
But when I remembered the power of Thy hand
and the many examples of Thy compassion,
I drew myself erect
and my spirit found new strength in the face of the scourge . . .

(Col. IV)

But I have become [. . .] a cause of dispute and quarrelling to
my friends,
indignation and anger to the members of my Covenant,
a growling and grumbling to all my companions.
Even those [who have ea]ten my bread
have lifted their heel against me,
and all those who have bound themselves to my counsel,
have mocked me with perverse speech.
The members of my [Covenant] have rebelled
and have complained on every side;
they have gone about spreading slander
among a brood of mischief-makers
about the mystery which Thou hast hidden in me.
But to demonstrate Thy greatness through me,
and because of their guilt,
Thou hast concealed the fount of understanding
and the counsel of truth.
They consider but the mischief of their hearts;
with devilish [schemings] they unsheathe
a perfidious tongue,
like the periodic injection of a basilisk's poison,
and like serpents which creep in the dust,
so they aim [their poisonous darts],
the [venom] of vipers that are deaf to charming;
and this has brought incurable pain
and a malignant sickness
within the body of Thy servant,
causing [his spirit] to fail
and his strength to falter,
so that he can no longer maintain his confidence . . .

(Col. V)

88

For Thou, O God, didst open wide my heart,
    but they persist in constraining it,
    and surround me about with deep darkness.
I eat the bread of sighing
    and drink tears unceasingly;
truly, my eyes are dimmed with grief
    and my soul with each day's bitterness . . .

(Col. V)

[I am] at home with disease,
    [I am acquainted] with scourges.
I am like a man forsaken in [. . .]
    lacking inner resources.
For my sore breaks out in bitterness,
    and in incurable pain that knows no relief;
[. . .] over me, as upon them that go down to Hell.
My spirit burrows its way below with the dead
    for [my life] has reached the Pit;
my soul suffocates [. . .]
    day and night without rest . . .

And the tongue which Thou didst make
    powerfully unrestrained in my mouth
    can no longer give voice.
[I have no word] for my disciples
    to revive the spirit of those who stumble
    and to offer a word of support to the weary . . .

For the breakers of death [overwhelm me]
    and Hell is upon my bed.
My couch wails in lamentation
    [and my pallet] in sighing.
My eyes burn like a furnace
    and my tears flow like water brooks;
my eyes grow dim for want of rest
    [for my salvation] is yet afar off
    and my life stands apart from me.

(Col. VIII–IX)

Of particular interest in these hymns is the idea that God
achieves His purpose by permitting the persecution of His

faithful servant in order that through his sufferings He may redeem the world:

> From Thee it is [permitted]
>   that they threaten my life,
> that Thou mayest be glorified
>   by the judgement of the wicked,
> and demonstrate Thy might through me . . .

(Col. II)

> For I am despised by them,
>   and they account me as nothing,
> that Thou mayest demonstrate Thy might through me.

(Col. IV)

The theme has good Old Testament precedence, of course, in the idea of Israel personified as the Suffering Servant whose affliction will atone for the sins of the world:

> For he grew before him like a young plant,
>   and like a root out of a dry ground;
> he had no form or comeliness that we should look at him,
>   and no beauty that we should desire him.
> He was despised and rejected of men,
>   a man of sorrows, and acquainted with grief;
> as one from whom men hide their faces,
>   he was despised, and we esteemed him not.
> Surely he has borne our griefs
>   and carried our sorrows;
> yet we esteemed him stricken,
>   smitten by God, and afflicted.
> But he was wounded for our transgressions,
>   he was bruised for our iniquities;
> upon him was the chastisement that made us whole,
>   and with his stripes we are healed.
> All we like sheep have gone astray;
>   we have turned every one to his own way;
> and the Lord has laid on him
>   the iniquity of us all.

He was oppressed, and he was afflicted,
   yet he opened not his mouth;
like a lamb that is led to the slaughter,
   and like a sheep that before its shearers is dumb,
so he opened not his mouth . . .

(Isaiah 53²⁻⁷)

These sentiments, at times even the actual words, find an echo throughout the Teacher's hymns, and we cannot doubt that in his own disappointments and spiritual torment, combined with a strong conviction of his divine calling, he identified himself with this Suffering Servant of the Lord. He cannot have been a young man when he took his followers into the desert; there are allusions in the Scrolls which have seemed to many observers to relate to the time of Jannaeus's predecessor, John Hyrcanus (135–104 BC), who had aroused the opposition of pious Pharisees. By the time of the Teacher's death in about 88 BC he was probably an old man. Some of the hymns breathe a sense of grief and isolation that would welcome a release in death:

For Thou, O God, didst open wide my heart,
   but they persist in constraining it,
   and surround me about with deep darkness.
I eat the bread of sighing
   and drink tears unceasingly;
truly, my eyes are dimmed with grief
   and my soul with each day's bitterness . . .

I have no word for my disciples
   to revive the spirit of those who stumble
   and to offer a word of support to the weary . . .

For the breakers of death overwhelm me
   and Hell is upon my bed . . .
my eyes grow dim for want of rest
   for my salvation is yet afar off
   and my life stands apart from me.

There is also in the hymns a hint of some recognition in messianic terms. The famous prophecy of Isaiah:

> For unto us a child is born,
>   to us a son is given;
> and the government will be upon his shoulder,
>   and his name will be called
> Wonderful Counsellor, Mighty God,
>   Everlasting Father, Prince of Peace . . .

(Isaiah 9⁶)

is conciously recalled in the hymn:

> and she who has conceived a Man-child labours in pain;
>   for amid the breakers of death
>   she shall bring forth a Man-child to life,
> and from the midst of the pains of hell
>   there shall spring forth from her womb
>   a Wonderful Counsellor with his strength,
> and the Man-child shall be delivered from out of the breakers . . .

(Col. III)

Here in this passage the anguish of childbirth is dwelt on at some length as symbolic of the suffering through which the Messiah will pass in order to achieve his redemptive purpose. The context makes it clear that the author portrays his own sufferings in this figure of the travailing woman:

> They made me like a ship in the deeps of the sea,
>   and like a besieged city before the invader,
> and like a woman in labour with her first-born
>   when her pangs come upon her,
>   and anguish in her birth-canal . . .

(Col. III)

There is no reason to suppose that the Teacher's own followers fully appreciated the implications of the nature and likely outcome of his mission while he lived, but a later reconsideration of the Master's words, so carefully preserved in their

Scrolls, would have laid bare their theological significance in the light of his tragic martyrdom. When Josephus speaks of the Essenes' reverence for their 'Lawgiver'—'after God they hold most in awe the name of their Lawgiver, any blasphemer of whom is punished with death' (*War* II viii 9 § 145)—we may reasonably assume that he speaks of their Teacher, the 'Joshua/Jesus' of the Last Days. By the first century, therefore, it seems that he was being accorded semi-divine status, and that his role of Messiah, or Christ, was fully appreciated.

6
Mortal Teacher to Immortal Christ

The years that followed Jannaeus's death in 76 BC were but the chaotic preliminary to the entry of Rome on to the Palestinian scene. For a few years yet, the Maccabean family, in the persons of Alexander's widow, Salome Alexandra, and her two unruly sons, Hyrcanus II and Aristobulus II, might play with intrigue and despotism in the absence of a dominant foreign power, but when proud Pompey strode into Jerusalem in 63 BC Rome showed herself the major force in the area. Local rulers could still swagger and threaten, bribe and coerce, slander each other and fawn upon the colonial governor, but in the end it was the legions of Rome that determined the main course of events. From that time on, all hope of establishing another Maccabean-type independence by force of Jewish arms faded into unreality, or flourished only in the dreams of nationalist fanatics.

That year, then, was decisive for Judaism, and the effect of Roman expansion eastwards cannot be exaggerated for the development of Jewish messianic ideas. Religio-political struggles, like the feuding between Pharisees and royalists, supporting first one, then another of the ruling factions, began to give way before less overt developments. There had, of course, always been a strong individual element in Israelite religion, persisting even into the later politically oriented Judaism of the post-exilic period, but now this became especially pronounced. The Kingdom of God became more a condition of the soul than a political theocracy supported by the panoply of state. It was to be another century before the fall of the Temple spelt the doom of the last remaining aspirations to independence, and the disruption of the cultus upon which the priestly administration of formal religion so largely depended, but already in Pompey's time the shadow of Rome had driven pious men to look inwards for the fulfilment of their hopes of redemption. Where a more militant philosophy still prevailed within Judaism, its eschatology depended more and more upon the direct intervention by God into human history, forcing His will upon men through angelic hosts bearing real weapons and overriding human intransigence with brute force. Among such dissidents were the so-called Zealots, allied religiously, as we have seen, with the Essenes, but adopting a more dangerous policy of underground subversion and political extremism. The fruit of their work was the great revolt of AD 66, culminating in the fall of Jerusalem and the destruction of the Temple. There were other attempts later to fire the patriotism of Jews throughout the Mediterranean area with similar, equally ill-fated actions, but Essenism itself continued and developed along more quietist and personal lines, renouncing the corrupt world altogether and seeking individual salvation through mysticism and the occult.

The seeds of this intensely spiritual religion are already to be seen in the Scrolls, as in the ascetic life adopted by the Essenes in the desert. The Covenanter had not just been born into a Holy People ordained by God to lead mankind back to the throne of grace, but out of all Israel he believed himself chosen before birth to play a special part in the establishment of God's rule. He was foreordained to his great mission, for being born within a certain conjunction of the planets, he had inherited more of the Spirit of Light than other men and was thus more fitted to walk in the ways of truth:

95

From the God of Knowledge comes all that is and shall be. Before they ever existed He established their whole design, and when, as ordained for them, they come into their being, it is in accord with His glorious plan that they fulfil their work. . . . The pattern of everything is unchanging in His hand, and He supplies them with all their delights.

He has created man to govern the world, and has assigned him two spirits in which to walk until the time of His coming: the spirits of truth and falsehood. The generations of truth have their origin in a fountain of Light, but those born of perversity spring from a well of Darkness. All the children of righteousness are ruled by the Prince of Light and walk in the ways of Light; but all the children of perversity are ruled by the Angel of Darkness and walk in the ways of Darkness . . .

(Community Rule, Col. III)

The natural corollary to this pre-election of natural aptitude to the spiritual life was that the Essene depended less than other men on the outward discipline of the cultus. He had renounced even his attachment to the Temple by his self-imposed exile; sacrifice was for him the offerings of prayer and hymns of thanksgiving. Philo says that, being more scrupulous than any in the worship of God, they did not sacrifice animals, but held it right to dedicate their own hearts as a worthy offering. If ritual gifts were made at all in their sanctuary, it was in their communal meals which were for them religious ceremonies; as Josephus says, 'they repair to the refectory as to some sacred shrine' (*War* II viii 5 § 129). Their voluntary separation from the cultic life of Jerusalem had thus prepared the Essenes for the deprivation of the Temple more than for other Jews; their spiritual self-sufficiency led them naturally into contemplative monasticism.

The Light which illumined their spiritual being was the 'Knowledge of God', and through that inner perception they could become the Sons of God. It was a direct revelation from heaven, unlike the kind of book-learning or instruction by rote by which we might understand 'knowledge', that is, facts and figures relating to the laws of nature. In Old Testament terms it

96

was the *Torah*, or Law, revealed to Moses and repeated after the Entry by Joshua. The Law was a means of knowing God's will for man, and obedience to its provisions led the believer into a state of grace. Similarly, among the Essenes, not only was the Mosaic Law a prerequisite to salvation, but it had to be supplemented by teaching revealed to their own Lawgiver, 'Joshua/Jesus', and preserved in the Community Rule. This body of revelation for the Order was a gift from God made through His servant, the Teacher of Righteousness, but the ability to receive and adopt its instruction was no less God-given and a mark of divine election. The technical term for this kind of special revealed 'Knowledge of God' in religious writing is the Greek word *gnosis*, from the verb *gignosko*, 'know', and we shall meet it very often in our inquiry, along with the related 'gnostic', a term used to denote those religionists who claimed to find in such mystically revealed knowledge the path to salvation.

A hymn at the conclusion of the Community Rule expresses this idea of justification by divine grace, and the imparting of the saving knowledge of God to the believer:

From the well of His righteousness
    flows my justification,
and from His marvellous mysteries
    is the light of my heart.
Mine eyes have gazed
    on that which is eternal,
on wisdom concealed from men,
    on knowledge and cunning device
    [hidden] from the sons of men;
on a well of righteousness
    and on a reservoir of strength,
on a spring of glory
    [hidden] from mortal counsel.
To those whom He hath chosen
    God has given them
    as an eternal possession,
and has cast their inheritance
    in the lot of the holy angels.

He has joined their counsel
   with the Sons of Heaven
to be a Council of the Community,
that their conclave dwell in the Abode of Holiness,
an eternal Planting throughout all ages to come.

(Col. XI)

The Teacher speaks often in his hymns of his insight into the wonderful mysteries of God's Knowledge, and there can be no doubt that he, and probably others of the Community, believed themselves specially endowed with the ability to penetrate to the very fount of all wisdom, God Himself. The various procedures of dissociation by which the mystic can enter a trance state and undergo what seems to him to be another dimension of experience are well known. Some use hallucinatory drugs, others employ physical means like over-breathing, monotonous repetition of words and phrases, stamping, whirling in dance, and the like, or simply undergo prolonged fasting which we are told can induce the same bio-chemical effect on the brain.

Shamans, ancient and modern, liken their mystic experiences to long journeys ('trips') into other, fanciful worlds, where sensual impressions are intensified, colours are brighter, sounds are magnified, emotions heightened. The messages they bring back as their *gnosis* are sometimes incomprehensible, or so mysterious as to require interpretation by the visionary himself or an acolyte similarly endowed with spiritual insight.

Jewish mysticism of this kind sought to penetrate the mysteries of God by concentrating upon some biblical theme which was itself imbued with divine mystique. A particular favourite, especially of later, medieval, esotericism, was the 'Chariot' imagery of the book of Ezekiel. From his place of exile in Babylonia, the prophet fancied he saw a divine chariot accompanied by strange winged creatures, the Cherubim, supporting a throne on which sat God Himself, resplendent in glory. From this fiery, flashing vision of the divine presence, the source of heavenly *gnosis*, the prophet received his mission and message to his fellow exiles (Ezekiel 1, 10).

Rabbinic Judaism disliked the kind of unrestrained theological speculation that emerged from circles practising Chariot mysticism, that is, concentrating upon the biblical vision of the heavenly throne and deriving from this transcendental experience inspirational revelations of the nature and purposes of God. The authorities tried at least to forbid the promulgation of such gnostic oracles. However, the discovery in the Essene Scrolls of fragments expounding the glories of the Chariot of God and the vision of the 'Glorious Face' among 'angels of Knowledge' indicates that this kind of mysticism was developed much earlier than has hitherto been thought, and suggests that orthodox Judaism was as much concerned to counter the influence of gnostic Essenism as to restrict religious speculation:

> The Cherubim praise the vision of the Throne-Chariot above the celestial sphere, and they extol the [radiance] of the fiery firmament beneath the throne of His glory. And the Holy Angels come and go between the whirling wheels, like a fiery vision of most holy spirits; and around them stream rivulets of molten fire, like incandescent bronze, a radiance of many brilliant colours, of exquisite hues gloriously mingled.
>
> The Spirits of the living God move in constant accord with the glory of the Wonderful Chariot . . .

Another example of Chariot imagery is to be seen in the New Testament book of Revelation where the apocalyptist is granted the vision of the 'Lamb', a mythical representation of gnostic Wisdom (see below, p 174ff), 'between the throne and the four living creatures and among the elders' (5^6).

In order to reach the throne of heavenly grace and glimpse the radiance of the divine Presence, it was believed that the mystic needed to pass through seven heavens, each guarded by a corps of angels, or demons, intent on delaying or destroying him. St Paul records that he had an acquaintance who had been 'caught up to the third heaven' and 'heard things that cannot be told, which man may not utter' (II Corinthians 12^{3-4}).

Since the processes of dissociation were often arduous and,

indeed, dangerous, failure of the free-flying spirit to return to the visionary's body was attributed to the activities of these guardians of the heavenly spheres.

There is an old Jewish tradition, dating from the second century, which tells of four mystics who 'entered the garden', as the trance state was called. Only one emerged 'in peace'; of the other three, one went mad, another died, and a third took up magic.

Considerable physical and mental preparation was recommended before attempting the exercise, and an essential safeguard was to be able to call upon the guardian spirits by name, since knowing a person's name was considered to place him in one's power. Josephus tells us that among the Essenes' secrets, which they swore never to divulge to anyone outside the Order, were 'the names of the angels' (*War* II viii 7 § 142).

The visions of Enoch, which were of such interest to the Essenes, were similarly revealed to him during his journeying between the heavens, usually in the company of an angelic interpreter of the mysteries he encountered. The patriarch Levi, whose 'Testament' is partly preserved in the Scrolls, recounts that his 'sleep', during which he traversed the seven heavens, took a whole fortnight.

The Essenes, then, were already in a sense prepared for the spiritualising of the messianic Kingdom, from a dream of political independence to the establishment of the rule of God in the hearts of men. They were also able to adapt their ideas of the coming Messiah to fit this new concept. He was now, above all, to be a Teacher, not an army commander, an Interpreter of the Law, not a Prince. As they grew accustomed to think of their own Teacher in messianic terms, his earthly role would have seemed particularly well fitted to this shift of emphasis, even as his biblical pattern Joshua, son of Nun, encompassed both aspects of a leader's duties. He was not only Moses's successor as Lawgiver, but was officer-in-charge of the occupying forces. The 'Joshua/Jesus' of the Essenes similarly led his people as commander of their 'camps', as their communities are called in the Scrolls, but he was also, and essentially, their spiritual

100

mentor, a revealer of God's Word. In the years that followed his death, it was that aspect of his work which would have seemed increasingly important to his followers and through which he would have seemed best equipped to serve a messianic function. While it may have been difficult to imagine the return as a mighty warrior Prince of one last remembered hanging dying on a tree, exposed to the scorn and humiliation of passers-by, it would have seemed entirely appropriate that this aged rabbi should return from the divine Presence, transfigured from his encounter with the Source of Light, to lead his children to the heavenly throne. As on earth he had been for his followers the embodiment of heavenly wisdom, so as Messiah, or Christ, he would be the perfect emanation of the Mind of God, His Word, the Logos of the philosophers.

The fall of the Temple in AD 70, and the disruption of the Jerusalem cultus with all that this terrible event meant for orthodox Judaism, had in a sense already befallen the Essene community by the Dead Sea. Two years before, in the spring of 68, the Tenth Legion under Vespasian had carried out a clearing operation in the vicinity of Jericho in preparation for their final advance on the centre of the revolt in Jerusalem. If, in the event, that mortal blow to Zealot hopes was delayed, the two years' interval gave the soldiers more time to ensure that the last pockets of resistance around their base of operations were cleared. Any Essenes left hiding in the caves would be left in no doubt that, wherever they were destined to rejoin their revered Master, it would not be in Secacah; nor would they proudly march, as once they dreamed, across the biblical Vale of Hope above the cliffs overlooking their settlement, to the foothills of the Holy City. In the years that followed, as they wandered in search of a new home, Essene hopes would have become increasingly centred upon a spiritual reunion in heaven. Separated from the body of his fellow Covenanters and the rigid framework of their communal discipline and doctrinal teaching, the individual Essene would have increasingly sought spiritual solace and illumination through private contemplation. In such times, corporate worship becomes of less importance

101

than personal devotion; ritual makes way for revelation.

If then the saving activity of the Messiah, or Christ, was to reveal to the believer the divine will, the *gnosis*, then his true spiritual home was at the right hand of God, preparing the way for the suppliant and pleading his cause before the Judgement Seat. He could best do this if he had himself shared the temptations and limitations of the flesh, even to the extreme sacrifice of estrangement from his heavenly Father. In the light of that understanding, the Essene would have begun to appreciate the saving work of his revered Teacher on earth, both as Interpreter of the Law and as a sharer in the human condition. Through his earthly witness the Master had been able to inspire his 'children' to follow in 'the Way'. By their 'suffering, and their faith in the Teacher of Righteousness', as the Habukkuk scrolls says, 'they are delivered from the House of Judgement'.

The contemplative Essene would, in retrospect, now be able to put the propitiatory act of the Teacher's martyrdom in a messianic context. Since it was understood that the Teacher's mission had been foreordained by God, even before his birth, then it followed that his death also had been long planned, and had to be understood as part of the divine plan for man's salvation. The 'Cross' or 'Tree' was, then, not a mark of shame and humiliation for the believer, as for the mere observer; it was a glorious mark of God's love that He would not spare even His own son that those who believed in him might be saved.

This sense of close kinship with God and his followers shines through the Teacher's hymns and is explicit in such passages as:

> Until I am old Thou wilt care for me;
>   for my father knew me not
>   and my mother abandoned me to Thee.
> For Thou art a Father
>   to all [the sons] of Thy truth,
> and as a woman who tenderly loves her babe,
>   so dost Thou rejoice in them;
>   and as a foster-father supporting a child in his lap,
>   so carest Thou for all Thy creatures.

(Col. IX)

Even if God had not actually engendered him, He had known him before birth:

> For Thou hast known me from my father's time,
>   [And hast chosen me] from the womb.
> [From the belly of] my mother
>   Thou hast dealt bountifully with me,
> and from the breast of her who conceived me
>   Thy mercies have protected me.
> [. . .] in the lap of her who nursed me,
>   and from my youth Thou hast illumined me
> with an understanding of Thy judgement.
>
>   (Col. IX)

His earthly life had been but a preparation for heaven:

> Thou hast cleansed a perverse spirit of great sin
>   that it may stand with the host of Saints,
> and that it may enter into community
>   with the congregation of the Sons of Heaven.
>
>   (Col. III)

As God had been a father to him, so would the Teacher exercise a parental authority over those committed to his care:

> Thou hast made me a father to the sons of grace,
>   and as a foster-father to men of portent;
> they have opened their mouths to me like sucklings . . .
>
>   (Col. VII)

In this filial relationship between God and the messianic Teacher, the Essene believer could see the fulfilment of the biblical prophecy concerning the scion of the house of David:

> I will be his father, and he shall be my son
>
>   (II Samuel 7[14])

interpreted in the Scrolls as referring to the coming Messiah (see below, p 208). With the writer of the Epistle to the

Hebrews, he would also have found further biblical support for the idea in the Psalm of David:

Thou art my Son, today I have begotten thee
(Psalm 2^7; Hebrews 5^5)

The conception of a divine or semi-divine mediator, seated on God's right hand as the personification of Wisdom, is powerfully evocative, and lent itself to a wealth of mythology in later Judaism. Already the portrayal of Wisdom in human form was part of post-exilic literary convention, and it appears frequently in the biblical book of Proverbs:

Wisdom cries aloud in the street;
   in the markets she raises her voice;
on the top of the walls she cries out;
   at the entrance of the city gates she speaks:
'How long, O simple ones, will you love being simple?
How long will scoffers delight in their scoffing
   and fools hate knowledge' . . .
(Proverbs 1^{20-22})

Wisdom is credited with a primacy in all creation, the first-born of God, companion and help-meet in all His works, and delighting with Him in the fruits of His labours:

The Lord by Wisdom founded the earth;
   by understanding he established the heavens;
by his knowledge the deeps broke forth,
   and the clouds drop down the dew.
(Proverbs 3^{19-20})

The Lord created me at the beginning of his work,
   the first of his acts of old.
Ages ago I was set up,
   at the first, before the beginning of the earth.
When there were no depths I was brought forth,
   when there were no springs abounding with water.

Before the mountains had been shaped,
   before the hills, I was brought forth;
before he had made the earth with its fields,
   or the first of the dust of the world.
When he established the heavens I was there,
   when he drew a circle on the face of the deep,
when he made firm the skies above,
   when he established the fountains of the deep,
when he assigned to the sea its limit,
   so that the waters might not transgress his command,
when he marked out the foundations of the earth,
   then I was beside him, like a master workman;
and I was daily his delight,
   rejoicing before him always,
rejoicing in his inhabited world
   and delighting in the sons of men.

(Proverbs 8^{22-31})

In the apocryphal 'Wisdom of Solomon', dating from about the middle of the first century BC, Wisdom is exalted even higher in her divine attributes; she becomes, in fact, 'the breath of the power of God, and a clear effluence of the glory of the Almighty' (7^{25}). She seeks to know those that are worthy of her, and leads them to bask in the radiance of the divine Presence as immortals:

And love of her is observance of her laws;
   and to give heed to her laws is the assurance of incorruption;
and incorruption bringeth near to God . . .

(Wisdom of Solomon 6^{18-19})

And she, though but one, hath power to do all things;
   and remaining in herself, reneweth all things:
and from generation to generation passing into holy souls
   she maketh them friends of God and prophets.
For nothing doth God love save him that dwelleth in Wisdom.

(Wisdom of Solomon 7^{27-28})

The personification of Wisdom as female lends itself to sexual imagery. Solomon seeks her as his 'bride':

Her I loved and sought her from my youth,
   and I sought to take her for my bride.
And I became enamoured of her beauty . . .

And with thee is Wisdom, which knoweth thy works,
   and was present when thou wast making the world,
and which understandeth what is pleasing in thine eyes,
   and what is right according to thy commandments.

Send her forth out of the holy heavens.
   and from the throne of thy glory bid her come,
that being present with me she may toil with me,
   and that I may learn what is well-pleasing before thee . . .

(Wisdom of Solomon 8^2; 9$^{9-10}$)

Other mythologies portrayed the incarnate Wisdom in a less respectable guise, as we shall see. But for the Jewish 'Messianist', or 'Christian', it needed but the identification of the Anointed One, the Messiah, with this pre-existent Wisdom, as the emanation of God's Word, to produce the incarnate Redeemer theology with which the New Testament has made us all familiar.

7

The Celibate Ideal

The gnostic ('knowing') Essenes reappear on the literary scene as 'gnostic Christians', but from the scenario sketched out in the previous chapters it is clear that there is really no justification for the heavy black dividing line that is customarily drawn across the page of history between them. There is a continuous development of religious thought, influenced by the turn of political events, which is perfectly comprehensible chronologically and doctrinally without the artificial separation of 'Christian' from 'pre-Christian'. We might legitimately speak of 'early messianism' and 'later messianism', although, there again, we should be hard put to it to say where one fades into the other. The fall of Jerusalem in AD 70 was certainly a climactic point in Jewish history, but long before that Essenism had begun to develop along the path of a more pronounced individualism, and a redemption of the soul through an incarnate Messiah, which are the hallmarks of gnostic messianism.

The idea of a Redeemer, foreordained by God, who came to earth to show man the way to salvation, and suffered the extremities of human anguish, lent itself to many different mythologies. Unlike the classical legends of gods and goddesses disporting themselves on earth, and making a mockery of mortals and human values, the gnostic stories of incarnated Wisdom, entering fully into the lives of ordinary people and sharing

107

their cruel lot, evoke a more sympathetic response. Whether portrayed as male or female, the character is essentially human and touchingly fallible, subject to mortal passions and sharing our emotional responses. If, in the course of an earthly existence, the divine Saviour experiences the depths of human degradation and despair, it is the measure of God's love for man that He could require of His own Substance the supreme sacrifice of laying aside the cloak of immortality to don the corruption of the flesh.

For, to the gnostic, the world itself was beyond salvation. We have moved far from the biblical visionary who could look to a time when nature would be renewed, waters would spring forth in the desert, and the lion should lie down with the lamb. As in the days of Noah, when a corrupt world needed to be swept clean with the waters of the Flood, so in the Last Days, the earth would be purged with fire, as a refining furnace, and only the true sons of Noah would survive. The therapeutic arts which the patriarch passed on to Shem and thence to Levi and the priesthood of Israel, would then be used, not for the restoration of the flesh, which was beyond healing, but for the cure of the soul. The divine spark which was in every man must be carefully nurtured and fanned to a glowing flame by the Spirit of God. When the flesh was fully consumed, the soul would be free to join the Sons of Light who had gone before.

By such mystical metaphors and dramatic imagery the gnostics expressed their doctrines, and they enshrined them in myth for their better understanding and easier recounting among the faithful. To the world outside, the stories they told were nonsense and the rites ridiculous, even at times crudely licentious. Misunderstanding and scorn hardened into abuse and persecution which, in turn, drove the gnostics even deeper into themselves and persuaded their detractors that they shunned the light to hide even more sinister practices and perversions.

Thus, when we come to examine the reputed beliefs and conduct of the gnostic sects, we have to bear in mind that in most cases the reports have come down to us from those circles most concerned with their extirpation. To examine their validity, we

108

must measure them against what we know of the origin and development of their doctrines, now clarified as never before by the documents recovered from the Dead Sea caves.

The idea that the world was evil gained ground with the turn of political events and the social ills they engendered. When pious Jews saw their most sacred offices bartered for money and royal favours, the sanctity of their holy places violated by barbarian soldiers, their Temple treasuries robbed to pay for other people's wars, it was natural enough that they should despair of the present order. The asceticism of Essene life in the desert and its reduction to a minimum of material needs, emulated as far as possible by lay communities in the urban areas, laid the ground for a rejection of worldliness altogether. Other men might wonder at their sparse living and their scorn of such material comforts as others would count necessities, but there were not many who would share their way of living. One of their greatest admirers was Philo, writing in the first century of our era, who calls their Egyptian successors *Therapeutae*, 'Healers', a Greek term which encompasses both aspects of the healing art for which the Essenes were famous, the restoration of the soul through the service of God, and of the body through the use of natural remedies and power over the evil spirits of disease:

> Inasmuch as they profess to the art of healing better than that current in towns, which cures only the bodies, they treat also souls oppressed by grievous and well-nigh intolerable diseases
> (*Contemplative Life* i 2; cp. ii 10–11)

The Teacher's own Rule for the Essene community offers these two functions of divine healing as a fruit of possession by the Spirit of Truth:

> The visitation of all who walk by it consists in healing and abundant peace over a long life, bearing seed with everlasting blessings . . .
> (Col. IV)

With the gnostic development, more emphasis was placed

upon the welfare of the soul and less on the care of the body, but the underlying essential of God's service remained paramount.

The particular Essene groups Philo describes were in his day living beside the Mareotic Lake in Egypt, but they had settled in other small communities elsewhere in that part of the world. We may suppose that the sectarians who fled from Secacah when the Roman legions appeared on the doorstep would have joined such communes where possible, and found there already established a way of life not dissimilar from the one they had followed by the Dead Sea. One significant difference, however, points to a great individualism in outlook, in that the Therapeutae each occupied his own quarters, a simple hut set apart from its neighbour, and having a small section reserved as a private prayer-room. Nevertheless, as at Secacah, there was a central edifice which served as a communal meeting-place and refectory, with an area for joint worship. It was a mixed community, although of the women Philo says they were 'mostly aged virgins . . . who have kept their chastity of their own free will in their ardent desire for learning'. They were able to maintain this desirable state since celibacy was the rule and the sexes were in general kept separate; even in the community hall they were divided by a partition so that they could hear but not see each other.

On the Sabbath, all the members came together in the chapel, the women on one side of the partition, the men on the other. They sat there in silence, their hands beneath their white robes which was their common dress on solemn occasions. Senior members most conversant with their teachings arose in turn to give an address, to which the audience would respond silently with glances, nods, and smiles, when they approved, or by pointing a finger of the right hand in disapprobation. Every fiftieth day, however, the sexes joined in a jubilee festival of singing and dancing which went on all night. The men and women ranged themselves in two choruses, under the leadership of their respective cantors. Each of the choirs began by singing and dancing apart, partly in unison, partly in antiphonal measures of various metres, 'as if it were a Bacchic festi-

110

val in which they had drunk deep of the pure wine of divine love'. Their biblical model for this performance they found, like the harpists of the Apocalypse (Revelation 15³), in the choral songs of Miriam and Moses by the Red Sea (Exodus 15).

Despite the reference to the Bacchanalia, it appears to have been a highly respectable celebration, the end of which was 'holiness', as our chronicler records. Doubtless this exhausting performance served a psychological need in releasing the pent-up emotions of their unnatural manner of life over the preceding seven weeks, but their own understanding of the situation was that, as Miriam's songs had celebrated the Israelites' crossing of the Red Sea to freedom, so their all-night service proclaimed the release of their souls from material bondage.

Philo goes on to express surprise that, far from appearing to be drowsy after this ecstatic experience, the Therapeutae 'are more wide awake in the morning than they had been at the beginning of their vigil. They turn to the east, and, as soon as they espy the sun rising, they stretch aloft their hands to heaven and start praying for a fair day, and for truth and for clear judgement in their vision.'

Whether, in fact, the sun itself was the object of their adoration may be doubted (see below, p 183), but certainly the heavenly orb was for them, as for their Palestinian counterparts, the Essenes, a symbol of inner illumination. Josephus reports of the Essenes that each morning they celebrated the rising of the sun 'with certain prayers, which have been handed down from their forefathers' (*War* II viii 5 § 128), and elsewhere stresses the importance they attached to hiding anything that might be offensive to 'the rays of the deity' (*id.* § 148).

In the dualism the Essenes largely inherited from Iranian thought, they identified good with light, and evil with darkness. They called themselves, as we have seen, the Sons of Light, their opponents the Sons of Darkness. At birth, they inherited their spirit of Truth from the House of Light, their tendency to evil from the Pit of Darkness. Their Messiah would be the Prince of Light, and Satan, his cosmic enemy, was the Angel of

111

Darkness, and so on. Thus, in the natural world, the sun was the epitome of Good, driving away the shadows of the night when he arose in glory at the beginning of each day. To a lesser degree, the moon ruled the night as the lesser luminary, and the 'bright morning star', Venus, preceded the sun in the morning, and in the evening held the darkness at bay until the moon should give her light (see below, Chapter Twelve). Thus for the gnostic, as for religionists all over the world, the heavenly bodies were imbued with divinity and honoured as angelic beings.

The contrast between light and darkness, especially marked in eastern countries where light and shade are more clearly defined than in less sunny climes, was similarly drawn between spirit and matter; the one good, the other entirely evil. The gnostics' explanation for the existence of wickedness in the world was that light had become mixed with darkness, spirit with matter. All living beings carried within them the spark of divine light, but its imprisonment in the flesh meant that they could no longer communicate with its source, and were thus condemned to ultimate destruction along with the rest of the corrupt material world. Only the enlightened gnostic who had attained *gnosis*, the revealed Knowledge of God, could be saved, and his aptitude to receive that illumination had been fore-ordained. The revelation, when it came, would not be the fruit of acquired learning, but an instantaneous awareness of himself, where he had come from, the Divine Fire, the First Light, and so on, and where he was going, back to the *Pleroma*, or Fullness, from which he had emanated. To 'know' God, in this special, mystic sense, was to know oneself.

But the way to this recognition was often difficult, since the corruption of the flesh dulled man's spiritual receptiveness. In such cases, the suppliant could be helped to recognise the truth if he were met halfway by the self-revelation of God, in the person of a divinely appointed messenger, or Redeemer. Since he had come directly from the Pleroma, and was thus better endowed with its Light than ordinary mortals, he could lead men to God, for in him they could see the Father. The Essene found in his leader, the Teacher of Righteousness, just such a 'mediator of (divine) knowledge', as he himself claimed in one of his hymns, and whose revelation, according to an Essene commentary on Psalm 37, had been ignored by those led astray by the 'Man of Lies'. Such spiritually blind people cannot receive the vision of Knowledge: 'they say, "It is unsure", and of the way of Thy heart, "It is not the way"' (Hymns, Col. IV).

The Children of Light, on the other hand, were able to recognise the truth, and, given the means and opportunity, could allow the divine element in their constitution to return to God and, if only for one fleeting ecstatic moment, receive the 'vision of Knowledge' and know themselves as sons of God, of one essence with the Father.

As we have already said, their journey through the seven heavens was fraught with danger. They must know the names of the guardian spirits and their secret passwords, and must have prepared themselves with mystic rites, including baptism and anointing.

The various gnostic sects which proliferated in the early centuries of this era apparently used a variety of different rituals to initiate their members, and to prepare suppliants for their shamanistic trances. Like the earlier secrets of the Essenes, these were rarely committed to writing, and our knowledge of what was said and done comes second-hand, and often through antagonistic channels. Nevertheless, where these concur independently in their descriptions, and claim to have received their information from informants who were, or had been, members of the various orders, they may be accorded a certain degree of authenticity.

The doctrines and practices of the followers of a certain Mani, a third-century Persian prophet-mystic from Babylonia, are unusually well attested. They have the support of the Master's own writings, and his religion offers us the fullest systematisation and development of gnosticism. It was immensely successful and widespread, passing quickly from Mesopotamia to Palestine, Syria, Asia Minor, Egypt, and North Africa. In the fourth century it reached Rome, Dalmatia, Southern Gaul, and Spain. Severe repressive measures were directed against the

113

Manichaeans, as they are called, in the old Roman Empire. The religion disappeared in the sixth century in those western territories, but in the East it thrived, passing to Iran and into Chinese Turkestan where, in 762, it became the state religion of the Uigur Empire. It was not until the Mongol invasions of Jenghiz Khan in the thirteenth century that Manichaeism came to an end in Turkestan. In China itself it persisted from the seventh to the fourteenth century.

Manichaean gnosticism, then, was no flash in the pan. It was one of the most powerful religions that have ever commanded the allegiance of men, and, as with its Essene predecessor, it owed much of its strength to a fusion of a variety of beliefs and rites, oriental and occidental. It appealed to the individual worshipper who yearned for a spiritual freedom that more formally regimented faiths had failed to offer, and who was disillusioned with their materialism and lust for temporal power.

The extreme dualism of the gnostic philosophy led to some bizarre practices. Since all matter was ultimately to be destroyed, it was a duty of the believer to refrain from doing anything which encouraged its generation. Furthermore, since all living matter contained within it some particle of the divine Light, the further proliferation of animate beings meant that the Good was being more and more fragmented; only when these particles had all been gathered together again and returned to their source, the Pleroma, could the millennium dawn. It followed that the Elect should eschew marriage, or at least any sexual intercourse which left the sperm in a woman's body.

The tendency to a rigid celibacy is to be seen already in Essenism. Josephus says that there were two groups, those who married with the sole intent of procreating children in order to keep up their numbers, and the remainder who avoided sexual congress altogether. He puts this down to their ascetic mode of life, 'shunning pleasures as a vice and regarding temperance and the control of the passions as a special virtue . . . They do not indeed condemn wedlock and the propagation thereby of the race, but they wish to protect themselves against woman's

114

wantonness, being persuaded that none of the sex keeps her plighted troth to one man.' Where marriage is not permitted, they maintain their numbers by adopting other men's children, 'while yet pliable and docile, and regard them as their kin and mould them in accordance with their own principles' (*War* II viii 2 § 120).

This distrust of the female sex does seem to be evident in the Scrolls, as a fragmentary manuscript, published first by the present writer in 1964, testifies:

> Her garments are the shades of twilight,
>   and her adornments are touched with corruption.
> Her beds are couches of corruption,
>   [. . .] depths of the Pit.
>
> Her lodgings are the beds of darkness,
>   and in the depths of night are her dominions.
> From the foundations of darkness she takes her dwelling,
>   and she lives in the tents of the underworld,
>   in the midst of the everlasting fire,
> and she has no inheritance among all who gird themselves with
>   light.
>
> She is the foremost of all the ways of inquity;
>   Alas! ruin shall be to all who possess her,
> and desolation to all who take hold of her;
>   for her ways are the ways of death,
> and her paths are the roads to sin,
>   her tracks lead astray to iniquity,
>   and her paths are the guilt of transgression.
> Her gates are the gates of death,
>   in the opening of her house it stalks . . .
>
> She lies in wait in secret places, . . .
>
> In the cities' broad places she displays herself,
>   and in the town gates she sets herself . . .
>
> Her eyes glance keenly hither and thither,
>   and she wantonly raises her eyelids
>   to seek out a righteous man to lead him astray,
>   and a perfect man to make him stumble . . .

It must be acknowledged, however, that this dire warning is directed more against the whore than womankind in general, and is similar in tone and substance to other such admonitions in the biblical book of Proverbs. It cannot therefore be adduced as proof that the Essenes distrusted the whole sex, as Josephus affirms, or, necessarily, that they avoided sexual relations because they thought it sinful to give way to the passions of the flesh and the desire for physical pleasure. Doubtless this kind of self-denial was considered spiritually beneficial, foreign though it was to Judaism generally, which took the biblical injunction to 'be fruitful and multiply' (Genesis 1^{28}) as a divine command, and considered bachelordom and barrenness as matters for reproach. We may suspect that the Essene preference for celibacy had some more deep-seated and mystical significance which found its fullest expression in gnostic teachings and practice.

Among the few gnostic texts which have come down to us in their original form, is an apocryphal 'Gospel of Thomas'. It forms part of a collection of Coptic papyri of the fourth century, comprising over fifty treatises in thirteen codices, or books, of 1130 pages. They came to light accidentally in 1945 near Nag Hammadi in Upper Egypt, and their contents have in general served to confirm the picture of the gnostic movement that had been presented by its ecclesiastical detractors, and to offer in some cases earlier recensions of works already known from other sources.

The collection stems from the so-called School of Valentinus, the famous gnostic 'heretic' who flourished between AD 135 and 155. The Gospel of Thomas, containing sayings attributed to the New Testament Jesus, is primarily concerned with the denigration of marriage, which is regarded as a symptom of that great sickness inflicted on mankind by the creation of the material world, when light, the Good, became imprisoned in the body of corrupt flesh. Sex had reared its ugly head at the moment when woman was taken from man's body in the Garden of Eden. Had he been left intact, there would have been no sexual attraction, and no progeny to entrap the particles of light. Until that situation is reversed, and man and woman once more made one—a state which may seem to the casual observer's of today's fashions to be fast approaching—the full revelation of God to man must remain unfulfilled. Thus in the thirty-seventh saying, we read:

> His disciples said, 'When wilt thou be revealed to us and when will we see thee?' Jesus said, 'When you take off your clothing without being ashamed, and take your clothes and, like little children, put them on the ground and tread on them; then [shall ye behold] the Son of the Living (One) and ye shall not fear.'

In other words, that blessed day will dawn when, like the unenlightened Adam and Eve, we shall all be naked and un-ashamed.

The twenty-second saying reads:

> Jesus saw children being suckled and was asked, 'Shall we then, being children, enter the Kingdom of God?' Jesus said, '[. . .] and when you make the male and female into a single unity, so that the male will not be male, and the female will not be female . . .'

Elsewhere in the Gospel of Thomas, the ideal gnostic is called 'The Single One', again probably referring to the original androgynous unity of mankind. In the last saying of the collection, Peter says:

> 'Let Mary go out from among us because women are not worthy of the Life.' Jesus answered, 'See, I shall lead her, so that I will make her male that she, too, may become a living spirit, resembling you males. For every woman who makes herself a male will enter the Kingdom of Heaven.'

Another apocryphal gospel, that attributed to Philip, regards the separation of the sexes as the cause of death, and a work from the same circle urges the faithful to 'pray in the place where there is no woman . . . Destroy the works of femininity' (*Dialogue of the Saviour* III 5).

117

Psychologically, it is not difficult to see that this distrust of the sexual drive in religious circles, by no means confined to Essenism and its messianist successors, gnostic and orthodox, stems from an inner awareness of the close affinity between the two emotions; sex and religion are equally powerful, equally unpredictable, and can thus be equally dangerous. In many parts of the world, sex serves religion overtly in providing an outlet for the repressed emotions which religious disciplines sometimes impose on their adherents. As the Therapeutae came together every seven weeks for their all-night song-and-dance session, so, with less restraint, religious communities elsewhere have found in their joint worship occasions for emotional release, culminating often in genuine, if unpartnered, sexual orgasm.

Whatever the psychological basis for the gnostics' denigratory attitudes to sex and marriage, they rationalised their opposition in terms of discouraging the continued generation of life, and the imprisonment of Light in corrupt matter. Light was, of course, a spiritual force, but it was most concentrated in the substances responsible for procreation, semen and menstrual blood. These were therefore regarded as imbued with special power, and played an important part in the gnostics' rituals.

Again, it is not difficult to see the origin of this idea. In any fertility religion it is the god who is responsible for impregnating Mother Earth and the wombs of women and animals. This life-giving force was then, naturally enough, associated with rain and with sperm, and the god within the thunder-storm also motivated the sexual urge in man and beast. It was thought that menstrual blood had a similar potency to that of seminal fluid, and that it was the combination of the two in the womb that produced offspring.

It is important to appreciate that Essenism and its later developments in the gnostic movement had roots deep in the folk-beliefs of the ancient Near East, however abstruse and sophisticated their later philosophies, and however esoteric their doctrines and practices became under the pressure of external repression. The movement could not have survived the persecu-

118

tion of more 'orthodox', or politically acceptable faiths if it had not spoken to the minds and hearts of ordinary people, and satisfied a deep need for individual fulfilment. Too often the reports that have reached us on gnostic sexual practices reflect only the horror of the casual observer who has not deemed it necessary to probe deeply into their meaning, but is content to ascribe them to the exercise of uninhibited passion, and a purposeful flouting of public morals. There may have been an element of truth in their accusations: sexual passion was certainly involved, and it could be, as we have observed, a periodic release of repressed emotions in an entirely unnatural, self-restrictive, cultic situation. Again, many law-defying sects did, indeed, flout the established code as a gesture of defiance against a world order they considered to be totally corrupt—an attitude not without its modern parallels in extremist political circles. But now, as never before, we are able to see gnosticism in its proper historical perspective, and to find its roots deep in the oldest strata of Israelite thought, curiously combined with elements from Iran and even farther east. We shall, therefore, seek not to condemn, but to understand.

8

The Love Feast

In the New Testament rare reference is made to a festival called the Agape, or Love Feast (Jude v 12; and possibly II Peter 2^{13}), which, it appeared, certain nonconformist groups had made the occasion for 'carousals' and other pleasure-seeking activities. The Syriac translators, at any rate, associated the Agape with ceremonies for the comforting of the dead, and this accords well with the meaning of the Greek word *agapao*, 'love'. It is used by the classical tragedians for affection for the departed, and in the Bible specifically for the spiritual relationship between man and God, while in the Greek version of the Old Testament it can render the Hebrew word for 'entice, allure'.

The Agape appears to have involved a common meal and was clearly a more significant occasion than a mere tea-party where all vowed eternal friendship with one another. We may reasonably suppose that its purpose was to establish communion between the suppliant and his God, like the Essene 'Messianic Banquet'. This, in its ideal form, was a ritual meal at which the Messiahs themselves would be present as representatives of God. As in the Eucharist, bread and wine were consumed by all present, having first been blessed by the presiding officer:

[This is the order of the ses]sion of the men of repute [who are called] to meet for the Council of the Community. When the

[Priest-] Messiah shall summon (?) them, he shall come at the
head of the whole Congregation of Israel with all the priests, [the
elders, sons] of Aaron, [invited] to the meeting as men of repute.
And they shall sit [before him, each man] according to his rank.
And then [the Mess]iah of Israel shall [take his place], and the
chiefs of the [clans of Israel] shall sit before him, [each] in the
order of his dignity, according to [his station] in their camps and
marches. And before them shall sit all the heads of [the family of
the congre]gation, and the wise men of [the holy Congregation],
each in the order of his dignity.

And when they are gathered together at the common table to
eat and [to drink] new wine, and the communion table is laid out
for eating and the new wine [mixed] for drinking, let no man
extend his hand over the first-fruits of bread and wine before the
Priest (i.e., the Priestly Messiah); for he will bless the first-fruits
of bread and wine, and will [stretch forth] his hand over the bread
first. Thereafter, the Messiah of Israel (i.e., the lay Messiah, the
Prince) will stretch forth his hand over the bread, and all the
Congregation of the Community [will give blessings], each according to his dignity.

It is according to this prescription that they shall proceed at
every ritual Meal at which at least ten men are gathered together.
(The Rule of the Congregation, Col. II)

The last paragraph clearly assumes that the rite could be
performed in anticipation of the final Banquet by a small
quorum of members of the Order. However the ritual may have
developed in form and meaning within Essene circles, it apparently took on a very special invocatory function in later times
when the elements became God's own Substance, his 'body'
and 'blood', through which partakers might introduce into
their own bodies the divine Light. Since the martyred Messiah,
or Christ, had himself been representative of that Light on
earth, sent from the Pleroma to redeem mankind, the cele-
brants were invoking the spirit of the dead in the Agape, as the
Syriac commentators fully appreciated.

The gnostics, as we have seen, identified semen and menstrual blood with the divine Substance in as powerful a form as
it was possible to find on earth, and we are thus not unduly

121

surprised to find that among many of their number these life-giving elements were made an essential part of the common meal. One account from a fourth-century bishop describes in suitably shocked tones the ritual as performed by a group called the Phibionites:

> The shameless ones have sexual intercourse, and I am truly abashed to say what scandalous things they practise . . . Following coitus in uninhibited lust, they proceed to blaspheme Heaven itself. The man and woman take the ejaculated sperm in their hands, step forward, raise their eyes aloft, and with the defilement still on their hands, offer up prayers . . . They present to Him who is essentially the Father of us all, what lies in their palms, saying, 'We offer unto Thee this gift, the Body of the Messiah.' They then proceed to eat it in their infamous ritual, saying, 'This is the Body of Christ, and this is the *Pascha* [ie, the Passover Meal] through which our bodies suffer and are made to acknowledge the Passion of Christ.' They behave similarly with a woman's menstrual blood: they collect from her the monthly blood of impurity, take it, eat it in a common meal, and say, 'This is Christ's blood.'

Like the Essenes, these gnostics interpreted the biblical visionary's monthly fruiting tree alongside the miraculous stream from the Temple with the Tree of Life, but identified the 'fruit' with female menses:

> When they read in the apocryphal writings [Revelation 22²]: 'I saw a tree which bears twelve fruits in a year, and he said to me, "That is the Tree of Life," they interpret this allegorically to mean a woman's menstrual discharge.

The ecclesiastical chronicler had even more horrifying matters to relate:

> They do not allow children to be conceived during intercourse. They indulge in their pernicious customs not to beget offspring, but for pleasure, for the devil toys with them and makes a mockery of mortal creation. Although they allow their sexual pleasure

122

to reach a climax, they save their impure seminal ejaculation before it can flow into the womb and beget children, and eat the abomination themselves. If, however, one of them allows the semen to penetrate the womb so that the woman becomes pregnant, listen to what else they do which is even more shocking. If they can reach the embryo with their fingers, they tear it out, take the dead foetus, pound it in a mortar with a pestle, and flavour it with honey, pepper, and other herbs, and with anointing oil, to avoid being sick. Then they come together, these devotees of a cult of pigs and dogs, and each of them takes a morsel of the pounded embryo. And having consumed this cannibal feast, they pray to God: 'The Archon of Desire has not deceived us; we have collected our brother's sin.' Apparently they believe this to be the perfect Passover meal.

Eating human flesh was a common accusation levelled against Christian groups by outsiders, just as it was against medieval witches. As in similar instances in the Old Testament, where reference is made to fertility rites involving the god Molech, the stories probably derive from a misunderstanding of the word 'seed', which can in many languages, including our own, mean both 'semen' and 'children' (Jeremiah 32[35]; II Kings 23[10]; cp. Leviticus 18[21–23]).

A few more details of this gnostic Agape ritual emerge from the same ecclesiastical source:

When, still in the grip of this frenzy, they reassemble, they smear their hands with their shamefully ejaculated semen and, rising, lift their polluted hands in prayer, standing completely naked, as if thus to demonstrate their sincerity before God. Both men and women pamper their bodies day and night, anointing themselves, bathing, feasting, and sleeping together after indulging in their drinking parties. They despise those who fast, and say that fasting is an offence since it was ordained by the Archon who created the world. One should eat to keep up the body's strength so that it can give of its fruit when required.

(Epiphanius, *Panarion*, 26)

However distasteful the uncomprehending outsider may

find the gnostics' practice of *coitus interruptus* and anointing
their bodies with sperm, it had a long tradition in Canaanite
religion. The semen of the fertility god could be seen spurting
as rain from heaven during an orgasmic thunderstorm; in
concentrated form it appeared in certain powerful plants like
the Mandrake, or Holy Plant, identified in many cultures with
the sacred fungus, *Amanita muscaria*, or in the aromatic gums
and resins that formed part of the traditional unctions of priests
and kings. Such functionaries thus became 'holy', that is,
separated to the god's service, being smeared, or 'anointed'
with his divine Substance. They were therefore called 'the
anointed ones', that is, 'messiahs', or 'christs', more specifically
in the Old Testament, 'those anointed with Jehovah/Yahweh'
(I Samuel 26[11]; Psalms 2[2]). In all probability, we should see here
the origin of the name given popularly to the latter-day Essenes,
'Christians', that is, those who had been 'smeared' or 'anointed'. By rubbing on this divine unction, whether obtained, like
some gnostics, from their own bodies, or from certain special
herbs or plants, they believed they were donning the panoply of
God.

Since this divine essence, the Light of the Pleroma, was also
the source of the Knowledge of God, the *gnosis*, anyone thus
anointed was granted special insight, as the New Testament
says:

> . . . you have been anointed by the Holy One and have knowl-
> edge of all things . . . the anointing which you received from him
> abides in you, and you have no need that anyone should teach
> you; as his chrism teaches you about everything, and is true, and
> is no lie, just as it has taught you, abide in him.
>
> (I John 2[20, 27])

For the true gnostic, this ritual was not, as its detractors liked
to maintain, a piece of sexual perversion, but a step towards his
goal of spiritual enlightenment. If, furthermore, he mixed with
this life-force the ingredients of the traditional Jewish anointing
fluid, aromatic oils like myrrh, cinnamon, and cassia, the vol-
atile substance in the heat of an enclosed oracular chamber

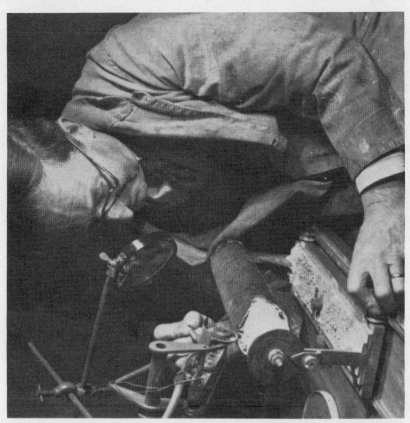

Plate 10 (left) The author examines the copper (treasure) scroll; *Plate 11 (right)* The late Professor H. Wright Baker cutting the copper scroll at the Manchester College of Science and Technology (U.M.I.S.T.)

Plate 12 (above) The Essene Hall of Congregation in the setting sun

Plate 13 (below) A small cistern, possibly a baptistery, in the Essene Monastery, Qumran

Plate 14 (above) The Monastery Scriptorium, Qumran

Plate 15 (below) Inkwells and plaster tables found in the Essene Scriptorium, Qumran

Plate 16 (above) 4Q Therapeia

Plate 17 (below) 4Q Therapeia; infra-red photograph (43.407), copyright Palestine Archaeological Museum, Jerusalem, reproduced by arrangement (ref. PAM 218 of 25/viii/65)

would contribute to that delusion of omniscience through their intoxicating effect. Again, the fumes from the sacred incense of the chapel, if made to the biblical formula, would assist the process of hypnosis:

> sweet spices, stacte, and onycha, and galbanum, sweet spices with pure frankincense . . .
>
> (Exodus 30[34])

Doubtless it was the effects of this combination that led the second-century Alexandrian Bishop Clement to speak of the 'frenzy of a lying soothsayer', his oracles merely an 'intoxication produced by the reeking fumes of sacrifice' (*Homilies* III, 13).

Knowledge and healing were merely two aspects of the same life-force. Gnostic Essenes, a descriptive phrase which incorporates both functions, 'knowing' and 'healing', symbolised and effected their calling through their anointing. Thus the epistle-writer James in the New Testament suggests that anyone of the community who was sick should call the elders to anoint him with oil in the name of the Master (5[14]). The Twelve are pictured as driving out demons and anointing the sick with oil (Mark 6[13]). Healing by unction persisted in the Church until the twelfth century, and the anointing of the dying, a relic of this practice, has remained a custom among Roman Catholics to this day.

In the process of separating out from living beings the spark of Light, the Manichaean Elect had a special role to play. They were those of the Order who had attained a spiritual pre-eminence, and were believed to be particularly hallowed vessels for the collection and return to its source of the imprisoned Good in created matter. Less favoured members were expected to give them every assistance, and might be led through their *gnosis* to the throne of heavenly grace, but they could never hope to emulate the spiritual endowment of the Elect.

Outsiders charged the Elect with taking advantage of their special position to seduce female members in their homes. As well as asking them to donate their menses for ritual purposes,

129

it was said that they prevailed upon them to allow sexual congress to procure semen. In return, the Elect offered the women the opportunity to accompany them through the heavenly spheres, at each ejaculation uttering the secret names and passwords by which they could pass on to the next stage.

Saint Augustine (4th–5th century), in his synopsis of the entire Manichaean system (*de haeresibus ad Quodvultdeum*, 46), refers to an investigation which took place in Carthage, when certain female Manichaeans were 'persuaded' to confess their crimes:

> A maiden named Margarita brought this vicious scandal to the public attention when she said that through this illegal mystery cult she had been ravished while still below the age of twelve. Thereupon he [the tribune Ursus] managed, not without difficulty, to persuade a certain Eusebia, a seemingly chaste female Manichaean, to confess that she had suffered the same experience for the same reasons. On examination, it was afterwards confirmed that, in the course of the disgraceful crime, ground meal was sprinkled underneath the copulating pair to absorb the semen so that it could be mixed and consumed . . . One of them admitted that those who practise such acts are really called Catharists . . . but all derive from one single founder, and are all in general Manichaeans.

The Catharian movement (from the Greek *Katharoi*, 'Pure Ones') must have been remarkably long-lived, as it still flourished in western Europe in the twelfth and thirteenth centuries. Their dualistic philosophy marks them out as gnostics, and it seems that their heresies caused the Church at that time quite as much trouble as they had done earlier. They are associated with various sects, and in the Balkans were known as *Bogomils*, or *Bougres*, that is, Bulgarians, a nation thereafter stigmatised by that aspect of Catharism which seems to have achieved special notoriety, that is, buggery (Old French *bougre*, 'heretic; sodomite').

Not surprisingly, the ascetic Manichaean Elect did not always find it necessary to use women to obtain their semen; the same result, without the risk of causing pregnancy, could be

130

achieved with a male partner. Again, the practice of ritual sodomy was not new; the Old Testament speaks of cultic priests whose sexual function was the equivalent of the 'sacred prostitute' and were known, presumably through their manner of copulation, as 'dogs'. Ancient Sumerian has a term for a particular type of priest which in other contexts means 'womb', and which has a semantic equivalent meaning, literally, 'penis-anus'.

The dedication of 'seed', that is, sperm, to local fertility gods like Molech was specifically forbidden in the Jewish Law, and, significantly, the injunction is followed by similar warnings against committing buggery. The passage continues: 'and neither shall any woman have sexual relations with a beast; it is a perversion' (Leviticus 18^{21-23}). Here it was not the cultic practice of restoring to the god his own Substance that was at fault so much as the waste of seed and frustrating the natural process. In those days the world was still good, the creation of a beneficent deity who had commanded men and animals to be fruitful and multiply. Jehovah was best served by implanting the seed where it might bring forth young, even though the first-fruits, the choicest of the produce, must then be restored to the god in sacrifice (Leviticus 23^{9-14}).

In an account of the beliefs and practices of the gnostic sect known as the 'Serpent People', or Ophites (from the Greek *ophis*, 'serpent'), left to us by the third-century Church Father, Origen, we have a further snippet of information about the semen-anointing ritual. Apparently, the leading participant, called the 'Father', applied the chrism, or 'seal' as it was known, to one described as the 'son' or 'youth'. He thereupon affirmed: 'I have been anointed with the white chrism from the Tree of Life' (*Contra Celsum* VI, 27).

This further reference to the 'Tree of Life' is interesting and has also to be connected with a gnostic interpretation of the first Psalm, noted by Epiphanius, where the passage:

He is like a tree planted by streams of water,
    that yields its fruit in its season,
    and its leaf does not wither (v 3)

131

is said to refer to 'seminal ejaculation in pleasure', and 'the leaf does not wither', to mean 'we do not let it fall on the ground, but we eat it ourselves' (*Panarion* 26, 8). We have, therefore, both the menstrual blood and the semen of the gnostic rites connected with the Tree of Life which, as we saw, was understood in Essene circles to be the 'many-fruited tree' on which the Master had been crucified.

The blood and water motif also appears in the gnosticising Fourth Gospel myth of the crucified Jesus:

> One of the soldiers pierced his side with a spear, and at once there came out blood and water.
>
> (John 19[34])

Possibly a similar theme is to be seen behind the curious story contained in a gnostic work entitled 'Questions of Mary (Magdalen)', noted again by Epiphanius:

> Jesus gave them a revelation when he took them with him up the mountain. He prayed, and then took a woman out of his side and began to have sexual intercourse with her. He caught his ejaculated semen in order to demonstrate that such behaviour was necessary for us to live.

In the same work, the saying of Jesus, 'What if you were to see the Son of Man ascending where he was before?' (John 6[62]), is interpreted:

> that is when you see ejaculated semen restored to its Source.

The Gospel stories that have come down to us in the New Testament canon are, of course, only a small part of the mythical literature circulating in the various messianist sects which proliferated after the disruption of the Essene central administration in AD 68. It is clear that the so-called Great Church early on purged the stories of elements it considered unsuitable, or which would hinder the movement's acceptance by the authorities, Jewish and Roman, who threatened its survival. John's mystical interpretation of the Jesus myth was presumably deemed inoffensive enough to circulate freely, despite its clear gnostic bias, and its even clearer lack of interest in making the story read like history. (See Appendix 2.)

The prime function of the Manichaean Elect was, as has been said, to separate out the divine Light from the material dross in which it had been incarcerated. This applied as much to vegetable matter as to living animals. Thus it was thought that the digestive processes were an essential part of this sacred duty. The living spark of the Good remained in the body and the rest passed out with the excreta. But whereas with lesser mortals the Good thus rescued was merely entrapped once more in any offspring they might engender, the Elect took care not to beget offspring, and so they built up a store of this divine Substance within themselves. They thus became more and more the Children of Light, as the Essenes called themselves, of the same Substance as their heavenly Father.

The dietary regulations of some gnostics forbade the eating of meat because it was thought that in the death of those animals the spark of life and Light had been extinguished and the carcass therefore contained nothing that was of any spiritual benefit to the eater. Life persisted, however, in vegetable matter, and could thus be absorbed into the system. The only restriction here, however, was that the life-force was so precious that its disruption in the act of plucking the root, and thus 'killing' the plant, was forbidden to one of the Elect. He had therefore to rely upon the rest of the community to supply his needs. Their guilt incurred in the gathering was absolved in that it had been done in the service of the Elect, 'so that the divine Substance purified in their bodies obtained pardon for those by whom it is presented for purification', as Augustine reports in his treatise on Manichaeism.

The Dead Sea Scrolls refer a number of times to the 'Purity of the Many' to which all novices aspired, but which they were permitted to approach only after some years of instruction by the elders, and examination in Council. Some scholars have long maintained that this 'Purity' was a sacred meal reserved for the advanced members of the Order, and we should probably associate it with the gnostic rite of purification by eating, separating the Good from matter, from which they obtained the name of Catharists, 'Purifiers'.

The process through which the Elect offered back their accumulated life-force to the divine Source has some particular interest:

> Everything of Light, refined from matter wherever it exists, is restored to the Kingdom of God as the ultimate source of its emanation, by the sun and the moon. These vessels are similarly made of pure divine Substance.
>
> (Augustine, *de haeresibus*, 46, 2)

The way these channels of divine grace were used is recounted by another source of information, a neo-Platonist called Alexander of Lycopolis, writing in about AD 300. Apparently, the Manichaeans saw in the continual waxing and waning of the sun and moon the reception and transmission by those heavenly luminaries of the divine Substance:

> During the periods when the moon is waxing, it receives the power separated from matter, and throughout that time becomes filled with it; but when it is full, it passes it up to the sun as it wanes. The sun in turn transmits it to God. When this has happened, it again receives a further increase in Spirit from the next full moon, and having absorbed it, similarly permits it to reach God; and so the process continues automatically.
>
> (*Against the Dogma of Mani*, 5)

Thus, we are told, the Manichaeans honour the sun and moon, but 'not as deities, rather as channels through which one may attain to God'. Saint Augustine adds, in this respect:

> They offer prayers to the sun during the day, according to its position in the sky, and to the moon at night, when it is visible; should it fail to appear, they stand in a posture of prayer, facing the north, on the setting sun's path of return to the east.
>
> (*id*. 46, 6)

134

Now, perhaps, we can better understand why the Essenes, according to Josephus, were careful lest the rays of the sun should fall upon their excrement after evacuation, 'wrapping their mantle about them, that they may not offend the rays of the deity' (*War* II viii 5 § 148). For them, the sun and moon were 'divine' in that they were periodically filled with, and duly transmitted, the stream of God's Substance as they received it from their earthly vessels, the Elect.

Among the papyrus fragments from the Partridge Cave there is a liturgical document which includes a prayer offered at sunrise, and the psalmist of the Hymns Scroll pays similar respect to the movements of the heavenly bodies:

> Bowing down in prayer I will pray for grace,
>   from season to season unceasingly;
> when light emerges from [its dwelling-place]
> and when the day finishes its course
>   in accordance with the laws of the Great Light in heaven . . .
>
> (Col. XII)

The Community Rule lays it down that the Master

> . . . shall bless Him [with the offering] of the lips at the times ordained by Him: at the beginning of the dominion of light, during its circuit and when it is gathered to its appointed place; at the beginning of the watches of darkness when He opens its treasure and places it aloft, and also during its course as it retreats before the light; when the stars shine forth from the Holy Abode, when they are withdrawn to the dwelling-place of glory; at the regulation of the seasons by the days of the new moon, both on their circuits and their intervening days. When they (the new moons) are renewed, they become great for the Holy of Holies, and a sign for the opening of His eternal mercies.
>
> (Cols. IX–X)

Epiphanius speaks of a Jewish sect called Ossaeans, clearly the Essenes, as emigrating during the disastrous revolt against the Romans to the east bank of the Dead Sea and into Transjordan. They later became known as the Sampsaeans, a name in

135

which it is not difficult to see the Aramaic word for 'sun', *shimsha*'. So, by the fourth century at least, this reverence for the sun would appear to have earned for the Essenes' successors the name of the 'Sun-people'.

To summarise, then: the gnostics expressed their world-renouncing ideas in myths and rituals. Their aim was to separate the divine spark, the Light, or Good, from the dross of the material world in which, through the process of creation, it had become entrapped. Until that divine Substance could be returned to the Fullness, or Pleroma, from which it had come, the millennium could not dawn. Those who had been especially favoured by God with an unusually high degree of spiritual illumination, the Elect, were the chosen vessels through whom Light was channelled back to heaven. They had to avoid procreating offspring, and thus imprisoning more Light in corrupt flesh, but their seed was powerfully endowed with that divine Substance and was a means of imparting grace to their followers, and of offering back to God His own. Female 'seed', thought in those times to be represented by menstrual blood, was similarly imbued with the Good, and both elements formed an essential part of the sacred meal of the gnostic Agape celebrations, their Eucharist.

The semen of the Elect also served in the initiatory rites of 'baptism', and its application by smearing, or anointing, probably gave the latter-day Essenes their most common designation, 'Christians', the 'anointed ones'. In their digestive processes, also, the Elect fulfilled their pupose of separating the entrapped Light from corrupting matter, so that the very process of eating was a sacred rite, and earned for them and their successors the name of Catharists, 'Purifiers'.

The accumulated store of Light they thus acquired was returned to God through the sun and moon, whose 'waxing and waning' was reckoned to denote their filling and emptying, as they passed on to the Pleroma the accumulations of the divine Substance offered to them through gnostic ministrations. This addressing of the sun in their rituals won some gnostics the name of Sampsaeans, 'Sun-people'.

9

The Noble Lie

'I wonder if we could contrive the noble lie that would in itself carry conviction to our whole community.'

(Plato, *Republic* Bk. III 414)

'Mythology is what grown-ups believe, folk-lore is what they tell their children, and religion is both.'

(Cedric Whitman, letter to Edward Tripp, 1969)

The gnostics loved a good story. Their world-renouncing philosophy dealt in intangibles, and such abstract ideas are not easily conveyed in words. Mythology therefore played a large part in their teachings, and since the gnostics themselves bridged a number of different cultural worlds, they could draw upon a rich store of myths and legends to illustrate their philosophical speculations.

The gnostics were, above all, individualists; self-discovery and self-fulfilment were everything. They felt themselves unfettered by the conventions of ordinary men, and in conduct this led to extreme libertinism on the one hand, and a debilitating asceticism on the other. In their teaching, their mentors were similarly unconstrained, and this freedom resulted in a bewildering array of doctrines and interpretations of scriptural texts and popular myths. We have seen something of the latitude permitted to the Essene commentator in his interpretation of biblical passages, to the extent even of changing the words to suit his purpose, let alone spinning out of the text meanings that could never have been intended by the original writer. Later gnostics, unrestrained by any central authority after the fall of the Essene centre in AD 68, felt even freer in their use—or misuse—of ancient writings and mythologies. They produced a wealth of imaginative legends, only a few of which have survived independently, but more appear in the works of their ecclesiastical opponents.

We have to appreciate that there are problems in trying to sort out the various characters in the gnostic myths and what they are intended to represent. This is true of most mythologies, but the messianist gnostics were famed for their lack of uniformity: the same character can embody a number of different ideas on different occasions. Bishop Irenaeus of Lyons (*c.* 180) was mainly concerned with trying to bring order into the Church, but despaired of the chaotic situation presented by the gnostic factions. He liked uniformity above all, and complains in his writings of the heretics' love for variety and novelty. His aim was to direct the central stream of the movement's teaching back into the Judaistic mould, with one God, creator of all, redeeming a wayward mankind through His fatherly love. He might act through his 'two hands'—the Son and the Holy Spirit—but His essential unity was not impaired. It was thus possible to devise a theological system which was cohesive, and, given the basic tenets, more or less rational and credible in a sceptical world.

The gnostics were less optimistic about created matter and reasoned that since the world was obviously corrupt, to continue to believe in the Jewish creator-God forced one on to the horns of a dilemma: either God was Himself evil, or He was incompetent. They preferred the dualistic solution they had inherited from the East. There were, in fact, two gods: one the creator, and evil; the other, good, whose Substance—Light and Knowledge—could only be mediated to the material world through a series of Redeemers who would lead man's soul out of the morass. Such divine mediators were at least translatable into human terms, since their function was to communicate with ordinary men and women, and they had thus to assume mortal guise. As they were entering the world of the flesh, they must be expected to behave in a human fashion, and be tempted on all sides as man himself. In portraying these day-to-day situations, the gnostic myth-maker could let his imagination run wild and utilise his biblical proof-texts with even greater freedom.

Irenaeus led the way in making one cycle of these myths, relating to the activities of a latter-day Joshua/Jesus and his fishermen disciples, a canon of authority in matters of teaching and practice for his Church. This party eventually came to dominate the whole messianist movement and their canon of selected stories and sayings, the New Testament Gospels and Acts, became the exclusive source of information for all believers. Those elements that had been excluded, including the more occult teachings such as appear in Clement's recently discovered 'secret gospel', were locked away for the use of the Church's inner circle, and the remainder either consigned to the Apocrypha or destroyed during the anti-gnostic purges which marked the Great Church's rise to power.

This massive depletion in the faith's store of tales in favour of the single authorised cycle had a number of most unfortunate consequences, not the least of which being a distorted view of the origins of the movement, and of the religio-political situation obtaining in Roman Palestine before AD 70. For the canonisation of the Joshua/Jesus legends focused so much popular piety and theological speculation on its central figure, that it became essential to historicise the myth, and successive generations of a largely non-Jewish Church were led to believe as fact the absurdly anachronistic and slanderously inaccurate picture painted in the Gospels of Jewish institutions in a Roman-dominated Palestine of the first century. Before long, pious pilgrims were scouring the Holy Land for relics of the Nazarene Master's life on earth, and erecting shrines to commemorate his activities and death in the most improbable places.

The gnostic rival factions were equally conversant with the Joshua/Jesus stories, but they did not succumb to the temptation of appealing to them as the ultimate source of religious authority; like St Paul, they had no great theological interest in the day-to-day activities of their chief character or his companions, apart from the underlying theme of man's redemption. It would never have occurred to them to build a church over the supposed location of the Master's crucifixion, although placing it solemnly on the site of an existing temple dedicated to a pagan love goddess might have appealed to their sense of humour.

Of more interest than the Joshua/Jesus stories to at least one major section of the gnostic movement was a cycle of legends concerning a certain 'Samaritan' magician called Simon and his female companion Helen. Simon actually makes a brief appearance in the extension of the Gospels relating to the supposed activities of the disciples after the Crucifixion. In the eighth chapter of the book of Acts, Simon's conversion and baptism to the Faith is reported, along with that of many of his fellow-citizens. When news of this extraordinary event reached Jerusalem, the apostles despatched two of their number to complete the Samaritan's initiation with the Holy Spirit, the 'Gift of God'. Simon envied their power of transmitting the divine Light by the rite of laying-on of hands, and offered to buy the secret for money to add to his own magical repertoire. His offer was angrily rejected by Peter who sharply rebuked his presumption and advised him to pray for forgiveness, 'for your heart is not right before God . . . I see that you are in the gall of bitterness and in the bond of iniquity' (Acts 8 [9-24]).

Since Simon Magus was held in such esteem by a large section of the opposition, it was natural enough for the Church Fathers to fasten upon him as the source of the 'heresies' which so threatened the unity of the movement in the early centuries. The discreditable incident recorded in the book of Acts reflects this antagonism of the Church. For the gnostics, Simon was the representation in myth of divine Light made flesh. They portrayed him as coming to the Jews as the Son, to the Samari-

140

tans as the Father, and to the gentiles as the Holy Spirit (Iren-aeus, *Against Heresies*, I 23 1). They probably no more believed in an historical Simon than they did in a Nazarene Jesus of the first century, but again, the 'orthodox' faction's historicisation of New Testament mythology, including Simon Magus, has for centuries distorted our understanding of the origins of the gnostic movement, forcing a ridiculous truncation upon a long-term religious development over centuries. Only within the last few decades have scholars begun to appreciate the existence of a 'Jewish gnosticism' long pre-dating the turn of the era, and this new perspective is in a large measure due to the discoveries by the Dead Sea and at Nag Hammadi in Egypt.

The early Church theologian Origen (third century) reports that the Simonians 'never confess Jesus as the Son of God, but they say that Simon was the Power of God', a claim reflected in the story in Acts: 'this man is that Power of God which is called Great' (Acts 8[10]). That elevated estimate of their semi-divine hero did not stop the gnostics circulating a fund of stories about Simon and his mistress Helen, and, of course, this encouraged their opponents to add many more, mostly scurrilous, and to distort those already widely known to suit their anti-Simonian propaganda. At this distance, we have to try to sort out the more original elements of these tales, and to trace their prob-able source and purpose. The exercise will be useful if only to illustrate the way in which many of the New Testament stories of Jesus were fabricated.

Our earliest patristic source of information on Simon is that of Justin Martyr (*c.* 150; *Apol.* I 26 56; *Dial.* 120). He tells us that Simon came from the Samaritan village of Gitta, and that he went to Rome in the time of Claudius Caesar (AD 41–54). Elsewhere we learn that his father was called Antonius, his mother Rachel, and that he was educated in Alexandria, and skilled in the wisdom of the Greeks, and in magic (Clement, *Homilies* Bk II). His female companion, Helen, he had rescued from her life as a prostitute in a brothel, having convinced her that he was the First God, and that she, in her former glory, had been his First Thought. In aeons past, she had sprung from his

141

mind and, knowing the divine intention, had created the angels and archangels, who in turn made the earth and its inhabitants, including man. She was otherwise known as Wisdom (*Sophia*) or the Holy Spirit.

Helen receives much attention in gnostic mythology and seems, at least in some quarters, to have received honours scarcely less than those accorded Simon himself. She was regarded as the Mother of all mankind, and given the title of *Kuria*, Lady. Unfortunately, having been involved in the creation of matter, she had found herself entrapped in its corrupting toils and could not return unaided to her Father's heavenly dwelling. Compelled to assume mortal form, she passed through many incarnations, including that of the famous Helen of Troy on whose account the Trojan war was fought. After this Greek experience, Helen was manifested in various human guises, each more humiliating than the last, until she ended up in a brothel in Tyre.

Her Father, seeing her plight, realised that he could only save her by descending to earth himself. To do so he must needs pass through the heavenly spheres controlled by the principalities and powers, and to accomplish this safely, he had to assume the identity of each. On reaching earth, he took upon himself mortal form and entered fully into human experience. He became all things to all men, and allowed himself to be called by whatever name men liked to choose.

Thus the Supreme Deity achieved his purpose and saved Helen from the corrupting power of creation. In doing so, he showed those mortals who were able and willing to listen to his words how to follow his example, and pass unhindered through the heavens guarded by demonic powers. They learnt the secret of freeing their souls from the cloying grip of matter, and let them soar aloft to merge with the Fullness from which they had come. First they must know themselves, and express their true nature through their faith in the Redeemer. Thenceforth they could afford to reject the world and its values, since, in God as seen in Simon, they had been offered salvation by grace, not earned by their own efforts, but freely given to those who had

142

the Knowledge of God. This was the true *gnosis*, and for those who had attained its blessed state, there was no further need of the Law, and they could spurn social conventions.

This libertarian attitude is reflected in the Simon/Helen mythology, and has its parallels in the relaxed posture adopted by Joshua/Jesus in the Gospel stories towards Pharisaic teachings and social customs of that time. In that cycle, of course, Helen's place is taken by Mary Magdalene.

One of the titles given Simon in gnostic literature is 'the Standing One', or, as we might better render the name, having regard to its probable Semitic origin, 'the Pillar' (see below, Chapter Twelve). It is in association with the first of the so-called 'Pillars' of the Church, St Peter, that Simon appears in a number of stories recounting his adventures in Italy. The two antagonists are locked in mortal combat for the faith of their respective followers, and one is reminded of the schisms which apparently took place within the Essene movement. The Scrolls speak of several factions, known characteristically by biblical names, such as the House of Absalom, the House of Peleg ('Division'), and the House of Judah. Some New Testament scholars, on the other hand, have seen in the Simon *versus* Peter confrontation a reminiscence of the Cephas *versus* Paul controversy mentioned in the Epistle to the Galatians (2^{11}), and have tried to identify Paul with the mythical Simon. In fact, as we now know, the title Cephas is an Essene official designation, and its application to the mythical Peter of the Gospels as a kind of nickname is occasioned by no more than a play on words (see below, p 208).

The story of the Simon–Peter controversy appears in our patristic sources simply as a medium for denigrating the gnostic opposition and their supposed leader Simon Magus, and is in line with the defamatory account in Acts. The various versions agree that in Rome Simon attracted many to his side with his magic, against which Peter was obliged to pit his own powers. A list of Simon's miracles includes making statues come to life, wrapping himself in fire without being burnt, making bread out of stones, changing himself into a serpent, or

143

into a goat, showing two faces, opening and shutting doors without touching them, making robot-like vessels to wait upon him in his house, and, above all, flying in the air.

Simon's reputation for flying is a persistent theme in these stories. In a third-century Syriac work we read:

> But when we [the apostles] scattered to the twelve parts of all the world to preach the Word, then Satan acted and disturbed the people to send after us false apostles for the refutation of the Word. And he sent out from the people one whose name was Cleobius [said elsewhere to have led a party of gnostics], and joined him to Simon, and also others after them. They of the house of Simon followed me, Peter, and came to corrupt the Word. And when Simon was in Rome, he disturbed the Church greatly, and turned many away. And he showed himself as though flying . . . And once I went and saw him flying in the air. Then I arose and said, 'By the power of the name of Jesus I cut away thy powers.' And he fell and broke his ankle. And then many forsook him but others who were worthy of him, remained with him. And thus was established the Simonian heresy.
>
> (*Didascalia* VI 9)

Eusebius (*c* 324) speaks of a confrontation with Peter first in Judaea:

> Forthwith Simon was smitten in the eyes of his mind by a divine and wonderful light, and when he had first been convicted in Judaea by the Apostle Peter of the evil deeds he had committed, he departed in flight on a great journey over the sea from the East to the West, thinking in this way only that he would be able to live as he wished.
>
> (*Historia Ecclesiastica* II 13, 14)

A source closer to its gnostic origins is the *Acts of Peter and Paul*. It reports that after Paul had left Rome, Simon caused a stir in Aricia where he had worked many miracles and called himself the Great Power of God. He received a summons from on high: 'Thou art God in Italy, the Saviour of the Romans; come quickly to Rome.' He promised to arrive the next day at

144

the seventh hour, flying through the air towards the city gate. At that time smoke was seen approaching the city, and suddenly Simon appeared in its midst. The brethren were in a state of sudden consternation because Paul was away, and since they had been left with none to comfort them, most of them defected. Peter was bidden by Christ to go to Rome to rescue the hard-pressed believers, and, in a series of contests, he successfully countered Simon's magic with his own.

However, Simon persisted in trying to deceive the people but as no one then believed him, he announced that he was going to return to God.

> Men of Rome, [he said] do you think that Peter has shown himself stronger than I, and has overcome me? And do you follow him? You are deceived. Tomorrow, leaving you impious and godless men, I will fly to God, whose Power I am, having been weakened. Even though you may have fallen, I am the Standing One, and I go to the Father. I will say to Him, 'I am the Standing One, Thy Son, whom they wished to overthrow; but having refused to agree with them, I have come to Thee.' The people came together to see Simon fly, and he appeared soaring over the city. But Peter prayed, and Simon fell and broke his leg in three places. The people then stoned him, and he was carried away to die.

In a fourth-century source, a rather more dramatic version of the flying incident describes it thus:

> They had seen the chariot of Simon Magus and the four flaming horses scattered by the mouth of Peter, and disappearing in the name of Christ.

On this occasion also, Peter's intervention resulted in Simon's breaking his legs in the fall, and then, worn out by tortures and humiliation, Simon had himself thrown from the summit of a lofty mountain (Arnobius, *contra Gentes* II 12).

The chariot is an interesting elaboration of the flying motif, recalling the mystic contemplation of the divine chariot of Ezekiel we meet first in the Scrolls and thereafter in later Judaism (see above, p 98ff). We may presume that gnosticism continued the Essene tradition in this respect, and probably featured a transfigured Simon ascending to glory in the fiery chariot, like the prophet Elijah (II Kings 2$^{11-12}$).

Simon's flying exploits have their parallel in the Joshua/Jesus cycle, in the story of the Master's being tempted to cast himself down from the Temple pinnacle (Matthew 4$^{5-7}$). The accident engineered by Peter was presumably inspired in part by the opposition's aim to contrast their Saviour's assurance that the angels would bear him up, 'lest you strike your foot against a stone'. Simon's broken legs would disqualify him for the propitiatory role of the paschal lamb, again in contrast with Jesus, whose legs were not broken on the Cross, 'that the Scripture might be fulfilled: "Not a bone of him shall be broken"' (John 19^{33,36}).

The placing of the flying contest and its tragic outcome may have owed something to the classical legend of Icarus, the young man whose attempts to fly to the sun ended in disaster when the wax of his wings melted in its rays. Suetonius tells us that at the games initiated by the emperor Nero (AD 37–68) some brave soul tried to imitate the legendary hero, with similar results. The apocryphal *Acts of Peter and Paul* probably has this in mind when it places the Simon–Peter confrontation in Rome in Nero's days, and elaborates on the flying story. In order to counteract the successes achieved by the preaching of Peter and Paul, the Jews and priests in Rome urge Simon to confront Peter. Simon is summoned before Nero, and by his miracles he manages to convince the emperor that he is divine. Nero then calls upon Peter and Paul to appear before him, and to debate the issue in his royal presence. The contest is first one of words, in which Peter produces a letter from Pontius Pilate about Jesus. Then the protagonists turn to magic. Each challenges the other to read his mind. Peter blesses and breaks a loaf of bread, and has it prepared to give to some dogs which Simon is about to unleash against him, thus proving that he had foreknowledge of Simon's intentions. Simon then begins his flying act, and Peter counters the move by praying, 'I adjure you, angels of Satan, who bear him in the air in order to deceive the hearts of unbelievers, by God the creator of all, and by Jesus Christ . . . drop him!' Simon falls and dies, and Nero puts Peter and Paul into prison. However, recalling that Simon had once appeared to raise himself from the dead three days after he had been killed, the emperor keeps his body to see if he will repeat the miracle.

This recurrent flying motif in the Simon legends must illustrate some important aspect of gnostic belief. The initiate knew that to achieve salvation he had to find a way of releasing his imprisoned soul from his body and let it find its way to heaven, like a bird freed from its cage. So Josephus records of the Essene gnostics of an earlier generation:

> For it is a fixed belief of theirs that the body is corruptible and its constituent matter impermanent, but that the soul is immortal and imperishable. Emanating from the finest ether, these souls become entangled, as it were, in the prison-house of the body, to which they are dragged down by a sort of natural spell; but when once they arc released from the bonds of the flesh, then, as though liberated from long servitude, they rejoice and are borne aloft.
>
> (*War* II viii 11 § 154–55)

A sense of flying is also the common experience of those who enter a trance state, however induced, and women report a similar sensation of floating in sexual orgasm. It is one of the purposes of mythology to express such experiences in story form, and so we find flying, whether on witches' phallic broomsticks, or on carpets, or on animals, a common theme in folktales the world over.

A common effect of the use of hallucinatory agents is said to be the sensation of flying over vast distances. It is significant that witches often claimed that their ability to fly was due to some special ointment that they had first smeared over their naked bodies. A sixteenth-century Inquisitor, Henry Boguet, reports:

147

Some rub themselves with a certain ointment, and others use none. There are also some who are not witches, but after anointing themselves do not fail to fly up through the chimney and to be carried away as if they were witches.

(An Examen of Witches, 1590, tr. E A. Ashwin, 1929, p.44)

We have earlier noted the narcotic effects of the biblical anointing-oils, and of incense, and one is reminded of Ezekiel who was 'lifted up by the Spirit between earth and heaven' and brought 'in the visions of God' to Jerusalem from his place of exile in Mesopotamia. The Prophet Muhammad was similarly conveyed by night to the divine Presence where he communed with Allah face to face:

Glory be to Him who journeyed by night with His servant from the Sacred Mosque [that is, the Ka'aba at Mecca] to the Furthest Mosque [that is, the Temple at Jerusalem] around which we have bestowed blessing, that we might show him some of our signs . . .

(Qur'an 17.1)

Professor A. J. Clark has examined three of the cited formulae for the 'flying ointments' of the medieval witches, and notes that one of them contains aconite and belladonna (Deadly Nightshade), which could induce both excitement and irregular heart action. He says that the latter symptom in a person falling asleep 'produces the well-known sensation of falling through space, and it seems quite possible that the combination of a delirifacient like belladonna with a drug producing irregular heart action like aconite, might produce the sensation of flying' (Appendix in Margaret Murray's *Witch-cult in Western Europe*, 1921).

We need not doubt that these herbs and many hallucinatory drugs would have been included in any Essene and gnostic pharmacopoeia, and formed part of the stock-in-trade of the itinerant Magi, the great drug-pedlars of the ancient world.

Interesting and illuminating as are such practical realities underlying gnostic and New Testament mythology, they do not really penetrate to the basic sources. In origin this whole messianist movement was Jewish, however far its ideas may have strayed from the severely monotheistic basis of biblical theology. In our appraisal of the Dead Sea Scrolls we have noted how the Essenes' interpretation of history was founded on a pattern set by Israel's past, as recorded in the Bible. What was to happen in the Last Days would be a repetition of past events: another Exodus from slavery, another desert-wandering, and another glorious entry into the Promised Land. Similarly, their understanding of God's will for the world had already been revealed to Moses and to the prophets; all that man needed to know was contained in the Bible. The function of their teachers was essentially to reinterpret for their age the writings that had come down to them. Every word of Scripture was inspired, its source the Mind of God. Those whose task it was to study the Word must be similarly endowed with divine wisdom, so that their understanding of the sacred text would be no less authoritative for their time.

We have seen something of how the Essene biblical commentators treated the text, and anyone who has studied Jewish exegesis in the Talmud and Mishnah will be well aware to what lengths these old rabbinic scholars felt free to elaborate on single words and phrases to justify decisions relating to doctrine and conduct. They were no less uninhibited in their weaving of folk-tales from proper names and single words used in a variety of meanings, being assisted in this punning by the orthographic deficiencies of the Bible text. Hebrew, like most other Semitic languages of an early period, was written with consonants only; the indication of vowel sounds by means of signs written above or below the letters was a comparatively late invention. The sense required was usually conveyed sufficiently by vocal tradition and there was surprisingly little room for misunderstanding within a connected passage. However, removed from their context, unvowelled words could be interpreted in many different ways; the Hebrew consonants for 'word', for example, can mean 'plague' or 'pasture', as well as the various verbal forms of the associated root 'speak'. So an imaginative myth-maker could fabricate his stories from a few such unvocalised words, introducing such vowels as might offer a new twist to the narrative, or an allusion to some other passage of Scripture.

It may seem to the modern western reader a trifling conceit to spin out words and phrases, and to play with puns, in order to concoct stories about divine heroes or heroines, whether they be Simon, Helen, or Jesus of Nazareth. The purpose, however, was serious. First, to be able to tie a myth into Scripture gave that story authority, since every word of the Bible was reckoned inspired and capable of illustrating divine truth. Second, stories thus contrived enhanced the dramatic presentation of its underlying message, and thus its memorability. It has to be remembered that these myths were primarily for telling, not reading. The teaching they enshrine was best remembered as part of a dramatic narrative, and their authors would have insisted that it in no way detracts from that message's validity that the tales are fiction and not fact, a lesson which has still to be learnt by those well-intentioned enthusiasts who waste time and energy trying to 'prove the Bible true'. The western reader must dismiss from his mind questions of historical veracity—did such-and-such an incident actually take place, or did so-and-so really exist?—and simply appreciate the story as a piece of dramatic art, allowing its overall impact on the emotions to produce the attitude of mind the myth-maker intended.

Thus, when we seek a common origin for the myths about, say, Simon Magus and Helen, and Jesus and Mary Magdalene, we should not be deterred by looking at the end-product and remarking their differences: Simon flew in the air, but Jesus refused to launch himself from the brow of the hill; Simon came from Samaria and found Helen in Tyre, Jesus lived in Nazareth and preached in Judaea, and so on. We have first to look at the messianist factions which produced the story-cycles in a realistic cultural and religious perspective, and then try to find the biblical texts from which the various stories are almost certainly derived.

150

There are problems, of course. In the first place we are dealing with second-hand material in both cases: the gnostics' myths have come down to us mainly through the medium of their opponents, fighting for the unity of the movement and, perhaps, for their lives; the New Testament narratives are written in Greek, yet purport to tell of Jews in first-century Palestine, presumably speaking a Semitic language, Aramaic, and steeped in biblical tradition and native folk-lore. If some of the Gospel stories were ever expressed in Semitic form, they have been smoothed into their present narrative fluidity by their translation into a syntactically more pliable Greek, and to us today by centuries of familiarity in western cultures. The more we strive to keep our modern versions of the Bible up-to-date with successive translations into the vernacular, the further we leave behind the halting, formal Semitic structures of the original linguistic milieu. Thus, for instance, when the Dead Sea Scrolls were first found and their texts translated for popular reading for comparison with far more familiar New Testament sayings, the supposed similarities often seemed to non-specialist readers hardly discernible, or even at all credible.

As has been frequently urged throughout these pages, to understand Christian origins we have to put ourselves back in the time and place of the Essenes and their immediate gnostic successors, and try to look at their traditions and expectations through their eyes. Above all, they were a People of the Book, and the clues to the origins of their mythology lie in the Book itself.

10

Tyre, Once Proud City

Happily, the main biblical source for the Simon–Helen stories is self-evident. The clue lies in the place where our heroine pursued her ancient trade, Tyre. The prophet Ezekiel (26–28) has a long tirade against the city, in the course of which it is portrayed as a fine ship doomed to destruction. Isaiah (23) utters a similar oracle against Tyre, while in the forty-fifth Psalm, the city is personified as a princess paying court with gifts to the messianic king, a 'christ' anointed by God above his fellows. Out of these three passages much of the Simon–Helen mythology has been spun, and, since they are laudatory in their praise of the fine city, as well as condemnatory for its part in Israel's downfall, both the gnostics and their enemies in the Church found here grist to their respective mills. Doubtless there were far more stories circulating among the gnostic communities about Simon and Helen than have been preserved by their enemies, and we may assume that more use was made of the messianic allusions in the forty-fifth Psalm than would have survived the Great Church's censorship. In fact it seems likely that already in earlier Essene times the subject of this Psalm had been referred to the Teacher of Righteousness, to judge from one very fragmentary commentary from the Scroll caves (4Q 171 IV 23–27).

First we have to appreciate that to the Old Testament pro-

phets and psalmist, Tyre epitomises all that was considered
most desirable in pagan eyes; she was the model of beauty and
wisdom:

> O Tyre, you have said,
>   'I am perfect in beauty!'
> Your borders are in the heart of the seas;
>   your builders made perfect your beauty . . .

(Ezekiel 27³⁻⁴)

> Because your heart is proud,
>   and you have said, 'I am god,
> I sit in the seat of the gods,
>   in the heart of the seas,'
> yet you are but a man, and no god,
>   though you consider yourself as wise as a god—
> you are indeed wiser than Daniel;
>   no secret is hidden from you;
> by your wisdom and your understanding
>   you have gained power for yourself,
> and have gathered gold and silver
>   into your treasuries;
> by your great wisdom in trade
>   you have increased your power,
> and your heart has become proud in your power—
> therefore thus says the Lord God:
>   'Because you consider yourself
>   as wise as a god,
> therefore, behold, I will bring strangers upon you,
>   the most terrible of the nations;
> and they shall draw their swords against the beauty of your wis-
>   dom,
>   and defile your splendour.
> They shall thrust you down into the Pit,
>   and you shall die the death of the slain
>   in the heart of the seas.
> Will you still say, "I am a god,"
>   in the hands of those who wound you,
> though you are but a man, and no god?' . . .

(Ezekiel 28²⁻⁹)

Son of man, raise a lamentation over the king of Tyre,
   and say to him, Thus says the Lord God:
You were the signet of perfection,
      full of wisdom
      and perfect in beauty.
You were in Eden, the Garden of God;
      every precious stone was your covering,
      carnelian, topaz, and jasper.
      chrysolite, beryl, and onyx,
      sapphire, carbuncle, and emerald;
and wrought in gold were your settings
      and your engravings.
On the day that you were created
      they were prepared.
With an anointed guardian cherub I placed you;
      you were on the holy mountain of God;
in the midst of the stones of fire you walked.
You were blameless in your ways
      from the day that you were created
      till iniquity was found in you.
In the abundance of your trade
      you were filled with violence, and you sinned;
so I cast you as a profane thing from the mountain of God,
      and the guardian cherub drove you out
      from the midst of the stones of fire.
Your heart was proud because of your beauty;
      you corrupted your wisdom for the sake of your splendour.
I cast you to the ground;
      I exposed you before kings,
      to feast their eyes on you . . .

(Ezekiel 28[12–17])

It is clear that the biblical prophet is himself drawing upon a rich source of early Canaanite mythology concerning Tyre. In particular, the reference to being 'wiser than Daniel', a Canaanite hero whose wisdom is fabled in the Bronze Age literature of ancient Ugarit in Syria, shows that the sea-port must once have been a centre of a Daniel cult. This fabled character is mentioned along with Noah and Job as a person of excellence in Ezekiel 14[14, 20], and in the apocryphal works of Jubilees and

154

Enoch, favourite reading of the Essenes, Daniel appears as one of the fallen angels. According to Jubilees, Enoch married his daughter, fittingly, since in the list of fallen angels, Daniel is accorded the seventh position, as Enoch is seventh in the list of pre-Flood patriarchs (Genesis 5).

The very ancient myth of the rebellious angels who fell—or were pushed—from heaven and begat a race of giants on earth when they lusted after mortal women, is only hinted at in the Bible, as we saw earlier:

> When men began to multiply on the face of the ground, and daughters were born unto them, the sons of God [that is, the angels] saw that the daughters of men were fair; and they took to wife such of them as they chose. Then the Lord said, 'My spirit shall not abide in man for ever, for he is flesh, but his days shall be a hundred and twenty years.' The Nephilim [that is, the Rephaim, 'those fallen from heaven', see above, p 63], were on the earth in those days, and also afterward, when the sons of God came in to the daughters of men, and they bore children to them. These were the mighty men that were of old, the men of renown.
>
> (Genesis 6$^{1-4}$)

The story was much more developed in Essene-gnostic circles, since it seemed to provide an answer to the perennial question: whence came evil into the world? The solution assumed by this story was that it came when Wisdom, through the medium of angelic treachery, imparted enough knowledge to man for it to become 'a dangerous thing'. The Simon–Helen cycle develops much the same theme, identifying Helen as Wisdom, imparting the power of creation to ill-intentioned angels, who in turn made the world and its creatures. The biblical oracle against Tyre, and the widespread tradition that the fallen angels first descended on Mount Hermon in nearby Lebanon, implies that Tyre and its immediate hinterland, rich from its sea-borne trade, was considered more heavily endowed with divine wisdom than anywhere else; it was, indeed, the veritable 'Garden of God', the seat of all Knowledge, the Phoenician 'Eden':

155

With an anointed guardian cherub I placed you;
you were on the holy mountain of God.

(Ezekiel 28[14])

The old myth went on to relate that as punishment for their betraying the secrets of heaven, the rebellious angels were condemned to be imprisoned in the Pit of hell-fire which, as we saw earlier, was thought to burn under the Dead Sea Rift Valley (see above, Chapter Four). So, in the eyes of the prophet, once proud Tyre would be similarly punished for her arrogance:

They shall thrust you down into the Pit.

(Ezekiel 28[8])

The Ezekiel oracle seems to combine the old fallen-angels myth with the biblical account of the expulsion of Adam and Eve from Paradise:

so I cast you as a profane thing from the mountain of God,
and the guardian cherub drove you out
from the midst of the stones of fire,

(Ezekiel 28[16])

to be compared with:

He drove out man; and at the east of the Garden of Eden he placed the cherubim, and a flaming sword which turned every way, to guard the way to the Tree of Life.

(Genesis 3[24])

The gnostics found in Tyre's degradation biblical testimony to their heroine's exile from her heavenly home. Furthermore, the concept of a divine being renouncing celestial glory to effect a rescue mission in the underworld was a common feature of long-established Canaanite fertility religions, and associated with the cult of Astarte, the Queen of Heaven, biblical Ashtoreth (I Kings 11[5, 33] etc), Mesopotamian Ishtar. She had been a local goddess of Tyre and Sidon, and a central feature of her mythology was that each year, when the summer's sun had

156

burnt away the vegetation from the fields, she journeyed under the earth to seek her lost lover/son, the god of fertility, Tammuz. When the spring rains revived the soil's fruitfulness, the return of the pair was celebrated throughout the Mediterranean world.

An ancient Sumerian version of the myth tells us that the Queen of Heaven, Innanna, the moon-goddess, abandoned heaven and descended to the nether world. There she passed through seven gates, the equivalent of the seven heavens through which the soul must rise to God, and at each she was divested of some item of her regalia until she arrived naked before her judges. She was condemned to death, and for three days and nights her corpse hung upon a stake. Finally, the heavenly Father, missing the presence of the celestial mistress, had the water and food of life sprinkled upon her corpse. She revived, and rose from the underworld to occupy new temples as their rightful patroness.

The Babylonian Ishtar is made to enact the same role in a Mesopotamian version of the myth. She, too, goes down to the land of darkness. At seven gates she is progressively stripped of her finery, and is then subjected to extreme humiliation. The supreme god, seeing that all sexual activity had ceased on earth, creates a eunuch who descends to rescue Ishtar. He sprinkles over her the water of life, and, reclothed, she returns to earth and restores its fertility.

In Greek mythology, a similar tale centres on Persephone/Kore, who was lured to the underworld by her uncle Pluto, and had to be rescued by her mother Demeter. In Egypt the fertility goddess is the native Isis, sometimes identified, like Helen, with Athena, and, like the Sumerian Innanna, connected with the moon. Helen was also occasionally called *Luna*, 'Moon'. Furthermore, Isis, according to Plutarch, represented divine Wisdom, *Sophia*, and the creator of all things. In mythology, Isis, like Helen, had once served as a prostitute in Tyre.

The Therapeutae, Egyptian gnostic successors of the Palestinian Essenes, claimed Isis among their patrons. She was reckoned to cure the sick and to bring the dead to life, and she bore the title 'Mother of God'. Until the exaltation of the Blessed Virgin Mary in Christian mythology, Isis held pride of place as the representation of the maternal principle, and it is not always easy to distinguish between them in early cultic figurines of mother and child.

We have already seen how the roots of Essenism and its gnostic successors lay deep in Palestinian soil. We are not therefore surprised to detect in their religion strong affinities with the old fertility cults of their homeland, as in the identification of the Substance of God, the source of all creation, with human seed. The gnostic rituals which so horrified the uninitiated, like the eating of semen and menstrual blood in the sacred Agape feast, and the anointing of the body with ejaculated sperm, probably went back thousands of years in the folk-religion of the Near East. However much prophetic movements in Israel sought to purge the religion of Jehovah/Yahweh of these agricultural cult-practices, and kings like Josiah tried to rid the Temple precincts of reminders of such illicit worship (II Kings 22–23), the day-to-day needs of ordinary people were too closely tied to the fertility of their fields and livestock to separate them from the old loyalties. And the strongest of these was, and still is in the Mediterranean lands, to the Mother Goddess, protector of the womb and of the growing seed, whether she be called Isis, Astarte, Helen, Venus, or the Virgin Mary. We may analyse the myths, detect their various strands, identify their characters portrayed under a host of names and guises, but when all is done, religion is an exercise of the emotions, and the few basic needs that fuel their fires are common to all men.

The gnostics appreciated this multi-faceted nature of their faith and did not devote themselves to rapt contemplation of every aspect of their incarnate Redeemer's mortal existence. The saving mission of the Essene Teacher had been primarily effected by his death on the Tree, for by faith in that propitiatory act the believer could achieve immortality and conquer death. Other details of his career were of little concern. After all, he had died in 88 BC, and a century and a half later his followers had been dispersed from their home by the Dead

158

Sea. Social and political conditions had completely changed since the Teacher's day, and the fall of the Temple in AD 70 had further disrupted Jewish life and apocalyptic expectations. It was true that the Teacher had experienced many trials and temptations in his lifetime, and had been faced with dissension within his own party as well as violent opposition from without. He had borne the prime responsibility for organising and administering a community of his followers in the trying conditions of the Dead Sea valley, and was the spiritual leader for the whole Essene movement throughout Palestine and probably the entire Mediterranean area. But for the gnostics of two centuries later, and more, these events were long past. It was sufficient that they had preserved the Master's words in oral tradition, perhaps even copies of the writings themselves; but, above all, they had the assurance of his continuing love in their religious experience.

Their myths, then, of Helen and Simon are not locked into any one period of history; Helen appeared in many forms, Simon came as all things to all people. He was not supposed to represent the life-history of the Essene Teacher. The one important theme underlying the stories was simply that God had communicated with His Chosen People through a succession of witnesses—prophets, priests, and preachers—and in the fullness of time He had sent His own self to dwell among men and suffer the humiliation of mortality. Through him, devotees could find their way back to heaven. The precise manner of their spiritual pilgrimage, its rituals and prayers, must differ with the time and place of each individual and his community, so to dwell too much upon a single incarnation of the deity, or to try to emulate his manner of living in a completely changed social situation, would achieve nothing but frustration and disillusionment. We may even infer that the very incredibility and triviality of so many of the Simon–Helen stories were purposely designed to dissuade believers from indulging in profitless hero-worship, or aspirations to the 'imitation of Christ'.

The Joshua/Jesus cycle was of another order. This was intended to be credible; it was a piece of propaganda to deflect

159

from the nascent movement the suspicion and hatred of the Roman civic authorities. It brought the Essene 'Joshua/Jesus' more or less up-to-date, and placed him in the historical circumstances of the first century, naming names, citing places and authorities, and, above all, giving this Jewish prophet such an improbable pro-Roman stance as might warm the hearts of those gentile agents into whose hands the Gospels might quite easily fall.

That was not the cycle's only purpose, of course. Embedded in the stories were mystic passwords, cultic titles and functions, moral attitudes and other teachings vital to the functioning of a sect in imminent danger of being persecuted out of existence, and lacking, since the destruction of the Dead Sea monastery, a cultic and doctrinal centre for the regulation of the faith. The cycle failed in the first object: the few pagan references we have to the Christians in the first century are scurrilous enough; the second fell foul of an ecclesiastical authority bent upon historicising the stories to establish their own claims to leadership through a supposedly unbroken apostolic succession. The real significance of titles like 'Cephas' or the 'Sons of Thunder/Boanerges' was lost when they were taken at their face value and trivialised into mere nicknames. The relevance of clever pieces of pseudo-exegesis such as that associating an incantatory phrase like 'Eloi, eloi, lama sabachtani' with the twenty-second Psalm, (Mark 15[34], etc) disappeared in the hands of literalists who ever since have been wondering how on earth to equate this strange 'Aramaic' rendering with the biblical Hebrew from which it is supposed to have been derived.

The gnostics knew of the Joshua/Jesus cycle, of course, and in a far more extensive corpus than the comparatively sparse selection which was eventually allowed to survive for popular circulation among the faithful. Other stories of Jesus are preserved in the Apocrypha, while more come to light periodically in new finds, like Clement's 'secret gospel' and the Nag Hammadi Coptic papyri. But, as far as we know, the gnostics never fell into the trap of taking the stories seriously; they appreciated the dangers of placing too much emphasis upon the central characters of the myth and thereby diverting attention from its main theme, the saving of men's souls. They insisted on the primacy of the Message, not the Man; the Nativity was not allowed to outshine the Crucifixion. There is no Bethlehem Star and Stable in the Pauline correspondence, no Cana conjuring tricks with water and wine, no fig-tree cursing in Bethany; just Christ, crucified. Paul does not date the Teacher's martyrdom with a time and place; perhaps it might have saved the world much tragic misunderstanding and bloodshed had he done so. But he was not to know that those he sought to lead to God through the redemptive passion of an incarnate Redeemer would one day devote their spiritual energies to sending armies to fight for spurious relics of his earthly life, nor, indeed, to devoting time, skill, and money in debating seriously the authenticity of a piece of soiled linen as the shroud that had enwrapped his body.

So, for the gnostics, Simon and Helen appeared in many different forms and were called by a variety of names. The message of hope they proclaimed to mankind was the same, but the medium and manner of expression were adapted to suit the audience and the time.

The Alexandrian gnostics were well acquainted with those Greek philosophies which spoke of Ideal Forms existing outside the mortal sphere and of which their earthly representations were but shadows of reality. Thus the incarnations of the godhead, in Helen and Simon, were 'phantoms' (*eidola*), shapes or images in the mind; the substance remained in heaven. The Semitic equivalent of this word, *tsir, tsur(ah)*, 'image', was sufficiently close in appearance and sound to the name of the city Tyre (*tsor*), for the gnostic exegetes of the oracles on that city to find here a scriptural testimony to the validity of their speculations. Furthermore, the concept was capable of wider application over the whole field of divine and human relationships, with biblical support.

A psalmist, speaking of the perishability of material possessions and of flesh itself, says:

This is the fate of those who have foolish confidence,
   the end of those who are pleased with their portion.
Like sheep they are appointed for Sheol;
   Death shall be their shepherd;
straight to the grave they descend,
   and their form [*tsur*] shall waste away;
Sheol shall be their home.
But God will ransom my soul from the power of Sheol for he will
   receive me.

(Psalm 49[13-15])

Away in his Mesopotamian exile, the prophet Ezekiel saw in his imagination the ideal Temple, and is bidden to recount to his fellow exiles the 'form [*tsurah*] of the House' that he envisaged. Similarly, the New Testament apocalyptist sees in a vision 'the holy city, new Jerusalem, coming down from God, prepared as a bride adorned for her husband' (Revelation 21[2, 10]; see below, p 173ff). The New Jerusalem, the Church, is thus the Form, or the projection of the Mind of God, as Helen, the 'First Thought', is the projection of spiritual reality in the material sphere. The early Church theologians were wrestling with such ideas and phrases in their attempts to understand the incarnation of the Messiah, which the writer of the Fourth Gospel expresses in the concept of the materialisation of the Logos, the Word:

In the beginning was the Word, and the Word was with God, and the Word was God. He was in the beginning with God; all things were made through him, and without him was not anything made that was made. In him was life, and the life was the light of men . . . And the Word became flesh and dwelt among us, full of grace and truth; we have beheld his glory, glory as of the only Son of the Father . . . And from his fulness we have all received, grace upon grace . . .

(John 1[1-16])

A gnostic mythologist might have changed the personal pronouns to suit a feminine Wisdom/Helen, but would otherwise have found here an adequate expression of his concept of

162

the incarnation of the creative Principle. The Essenes similarly believed in the pre-existence of all creation in the Mind of God:

By Thy wisdom [all things exist from] eternity,
    and before creating them Thou knowest all their works for ever
        and ever.
[Nothing] is done [without Thee]
    and nothing is known apart from Thy good will . . .
Thou hast formed every spirit
    and [. . .] the order for all their deeds . . .

Thou hast created the earth by Thy power
    and the seas and the deeps [by Thy might].
Thou hast fashioned all their [deni]zens
    according to Thy wisdom,
and hast ordained all that is in them
    according to Thy will.
[And] to the spirit of man
    which Thou hast formed in the world
[Thou hast given authority . . .]
    for days everlasting, and for unending generations . . .

Thou hast allotted their duty
    to all their generations,
and judgement in their appointed seasons [. . .]
their visitation for reward as well as their afflictions;
    Thou hast allotted it to all their offspring
    to the measure of endless generations,
    and years to eternity . . .
In the wisdom of Thy knowledge
    Thou didst establish their destiny before ever they existed.
All things [happen] according to [Thy will],
    and without Thee nothing is done . . .

What can I say that is not foreknown,
    and what can I publish that is not foretold?
All things are graven before Thee
    on tablets of Remembrance
    for everlasting ages,
and for the numbered cycles
    of years everlasting
    in all their seasons;

163

they are not hidden or absent from Thy presence . . .

It is Thou who hast created breath for the tongue
    and Thou knowest its words;
Thou didst establish the fruit of the lips
    before ever they were formed . . .

(Hymns, Col. I)

I know through the understanding that comes from Thee
    that [righteousness] is not in the hand of flesh,
that man [is not master] of his way,
    and that it is not in mortals to direct their step.
I know that the inclination of every spirit
    is in Thy hand;
Thou didst establish all its [deeds] before ever creating it,
    and how can man change Thy words?
Thou alone didst [create] the just
    and establish him from the womb
    for the time of favour appointed,
that he might hearken to Thy Covenant
    and walk in all [Thy ways],
and that Thou mightest [. . .] over him
    in the abundance of Thy compassion,
and relieve his straitened soul to eternal salvation,
    to perpetual and unfailing peace.
Thou wilt raise his glory
    above mortality.

But the wicked thou didst create
    for the [time] of Thy [wrath],
and Thou didst vow them from the womb
    for the Day of Massacre . . .
Thou hast ordained for them great judgements
    before the eyes of all Thy creatures,
to be a sign [. . .],
    that all may know Thy glory and Thy power . . .

(Hymns, Col. XV)

Everything that happens in this mortal sphere, then, was for
the Essene and his gnostic successors the projection of the Mind
and Intention of God. Where human frailty—or the evil designs
of demonic powers—corrupts that image, a barrier is raised be-

164

tween God and man that prevents his being revealed as a son of God. The aim of the gnostic mystic was to achieve for himself a perfect reflection of his heavenly Form through which he might establish his original kinship with his Father. As St Paul writes:

> For all who are led by the Spirit of God are the sons of God . . . you have received the spirit of sonship. When we cry, 'Abba, Father!' it is the Spirit bearing witness with our spirit that we are the children of God . . .
>
> (Romans 8$^{14-16}$)

The role of the Holy Spirit is that of a mediating influence, whose absorption by the believer through faith effects that identity of himself with the Fulness from which he came. Whether the manifestation of that Spirit was expressed mythically as Simon, Helen, or Jesus/Joshua, the devotee believed that God had, at some point in history—it mattered little exactly when—divested himself of his glory, or as St Paul would say, 'emptied Himself' of His divinity, substituted for the 'form of God' the 'form of a servant' (Philippians 2$^{5-7}$), and showed man the way to regain his former 'image' of sonship:

> For those whom he foreknew he also predestined to be conformed to the image of his Son, in order that he might be the first-born among many brethren
>
> (Romans 8^{29})

As the degree of God's self-abasement involved pain and humiliation, the marks of mortality, so the believer, too, must suffer to achieve eternal life. St Paul expresses his own experience and hope thus:

> For his sake I have suffered the loss of all things, and count them as refuse, in order that I may gain Christ and be found in him, not having a righteousness of my own, based on law, but that which is through faith in Christ, the righteousness from God that depends on faith; that I may know him and the power of his resurrection, and may share his sufferings, becoming like him in

165

his death, that if possible I may attain the resurrection from the dead.

(Philippians 3^{8–11})

The Essene Scrolls commentator on the famous biblical text,

The righteous shall live by faith

(Habakkuk 2⁴)

is feeling his way towards Paul's theological position in his exegesis:

Interpreted, this concerns all those who observe the Law in the House of Judah, whom God will deliver from the Hall of Judgement because of their suffering and because of their faith in the Teacher of Righteousness

(see above, p 102)

11

Helen, the Harlot of Tyre, and Light of the World

Many other aspects of the Simon–Helen image could be teased by the gnostic exegetes from the oracles on Tyre. The ascription to Simon of 'that power of God which is called Great' in the story about him recounted in the book of Acts has its scriptural justification in such passages as:

> by your wisdom and understanding
>   you have gained power for yourself . . .
> by your great wisdom and trade
>   you have increased your power

$$\text{(Ezekiel } 28^{4,\ 5})$$

A characteristic play on words here also provided a name for Simon's mother, Rachel (meaning, properly, 'ewe'), from a similarly sounding Hebrew word *rachal*, 'to trade'. That theme was developed in the New Testament story when Simon is made to offer money for the priceless gift of the Holy Spirit, and earned him thereafter the dubious honour of having his name associated with financial inducement to ecclesiastical preferment, 'simony'.

Helen's connection with Tyrian trade was rather more venal.

Her image as a Tyrian prostitute is based largely on the conclusion of Isaiah's version of the oracle against the proud city:

> At the end of seventy years, it will happen to Tyre as in the Song of the Harlot:
> 'Take a harp,
> go about the city,
> O forgotten harlot!
> Make sweet melody,
> sing many songs,
> that you may be remembered.'
>
> At the end of seventy years, the Lord will visit Tyre, and she will return to her hire, and will play the harlot with all the kingdoms of the world upon the face of the earth. Her merchandise and her hire will be dedicated to the Lord; it will not be stored or hoarded, but her merchandise will supply abundant food and fine clothing for those who dwell before the Lord.
>
> (Isaiah 23[15–18])

In the Joshua/Jesus cycle of stories, the hero also is represented as accompanied by loose women and treating them as friends. Mary Magdalene is the best-known of these, and a good deal of extra-biblical speculation has centred upon her and her relationship with Jesus. In formal terms she is the equivalent of Helen, but in the Gospel narratives she plays a far less important role than her gnostic sister. As a literary creation, she probably owes much to the same kind of imaginative treatment of the Tyre oracles as many of the Helen stories. For instance, her name, Magdalene, as has long been recognised, is a Greek rendering of a Semitic word meaning 'hairdresser', whose root means 'to braid, entwine', used of various materials, including hair. The profession was apparently not rated very high in the social scale, and women practising the art were considered ladies of easy virtue. Mary's epithet may have something to do with a detail of the forty-fifth Psalm in which the Christ-king's 'queen', the Tyrian princess, is described as decked in 'gold-braided robes', that is, finding in the Hebrew word for 'braid' an allusion to the synonymous root in

168

Magdalene's name. Be that as it may, the underlying conception of her previous harlotry, like Helen's, finds a more significant source, not only in the description of the Tyrian city as a whore, but in the term used for the Anointed's regal bride.

The word used in the Hebrew text for 'queen' is a rare one, with a basic meaning of 'rape, ravish'. Later Jewish scribes thought the word too obscene to be read aloud in the synagogues, and at each place where the verb occurs in the text they require a euphemism, 'lie with', to be substituted, as we might mumble, 'er—sleep with' on encountering in reading aloud the vulgar four-letter word for 'copulate'. It may well be, then, that the psalmist's use of this special word for 'queen' here, in a passage concerned with the king's ritual anointing, carries with it an allusion to cultic prostitution.

The old fertility religions of Canaan, to which we have already drawn attention in connection with Helen's Mesopotamian and Egyptian associations (see above, p 156ff), ranked the so-called sacred prostitute high among the temple entourage. She represented the power of creation and played an important role in those sexual ceremonies designed to encourage the fertility of the natural world. Her spiritual successors among the gnostics were those female devotees who served the Elect in procuring their semen and offering their menses for the Agape feasts. As scriptural support for their 'prostitution' they could cite the Isaiah oracle's assertion that the harlot's hire of Tyre 'will be dedicated to the Lord' (23[18]): her self-sacrifice was for man's salvation.

So once more we have tried to look behind the story and isolate the much more important theme underlying the myth. That, in effect, is the motivation of all serious study of ancient mythology. Unhappily, where piety has dulled the edges of critical research, examination of the New Testament stories has too often contented itself with trivial details of the narratives themselves, or with imaginative elaborations of the received traditions, all of which merely confuses rather than clarifies the essential issues.

Helen's name is not derived from any one example of biblical

169

exegesis, but signifies a piece of imagery which is far-reaching and important. The Greek word *helene* means 'torch' and in the story of that most famous Helen of history, on whose account the Trojan war was reputedly fought, the connection is explicit in the tradition that she signalled to the Greek ships waiting offshore by waving a torch from a Trojan tower. Another version of the incident has it that while the Trojans slept, exhausted from their night of revelry, Helen lay awake, and a bright light blazed above her chamber, to be repeated out at sea by a fire-basket of pine-wood chips which Agamemnon lit as a signal to his fleet.

The fourth-century Epiphanius dwells upon this incident as illustrating Helen's gnostic role in the enlightenment of mankind:

> Through its shining, as I said, he signified the display of light from above . . . As the Phrygians, by dragging in the wooden horse, ignorantly brought on their own destruction, so the gentiles, that is, men apart from my *gnosis*, produce perdition for themselves . . .

Helen, then, symbolises Light as divine Knowledge, the true *gnosis*. Her role on earth was to lead men through the darkness of created matter back to God. The imagery of the Torch of Wisdom and of Light and Fire as the projection of the Word of God is widespread and powerful, and has its roots deep in Old Testament mythology. In the Exodus story, in particular, the wandering tribes under Moses are led by a pillar of cloud in the daytime, and a pillar of fire by night (Nehemiah 9^{12}). The original conception is of a smoking torch whose column of smoke could be seen in daylight, and whose glow lit the way ahead in times of darkness. When, at Horeb/Sinai, Jehovah appeared before his people to reveal to them the Law through Moses, he showed himself in volcanic fire:

> And you came near and stood at the foot of the mountain, while the mountain burned with fire to the heart of heaven, wrapped in darkness, cloud, and gloom. Then the Lord spoke to you out of

the midst of the fire; you heard the sound of words, but saw no form; there was only a voice.

(Deuteronomy 4^{11-12})

Isaiah (4^5) envisaged a time when Jehovah would cover 'the whole site of Mount Zion and her assemblies, a cloud by day, and smoke and the shining of a flaming fire by night' just as he demonstrated his protective and revealing presence to the Israelites around the Tabernacle in the wilderness.

In the apocryphal Wisdom of Solomon, this guiding light is specifically identified with Wisdom herself:

she became unto them a covering in the daytime; and a flame of stars through the night.

(10^{17})

To be filled with divine inspiration was to radiate light. After Moses had encountered Jehovah on Sinai and received the revelation of the Law, 'his face shone because he had been talking with God' (Exodus 34^{29}). Similarly, in the Transfiguration of Jesus, 'his face shone like the sun and his garments became as white as light' (Matthew 17^2). The literary model used here by the New Testament mythologist is that of a previous Joshua/Jesus, the high priest of the restored Jewish community after the Exile. In a vision, the prophet Zechariah sees him standing before the angel of the Lord, clothed in filthy garments:

And the angel said to those who were standing with him, 'Remove the filthy garments from him . . . Let them put a clean turban on his head . . .'

(3^{3-5})

Like the Joshua/Jesus of the New Testament story, in clothes 'glistening, intensely white, as no fuller on earth could bleach them' (Mark 9^3), the high priest is then revealed as a 'Helen', that is, a burning torch, 'a brand plucked from the fire' (v.2). The New Testament apocalyptist, using the same literary

171

source, incorporates in his vision of the Son of Man the seven-branched candlestick of the Zechariah oracle with the transfigured Christ of the Gospels:

> I see, and behold, a lampstand all of gold, with a bowl on the top of it, and seven lamps on it, with seven lips on each of the lamps . . .
>
> (Zechariah 4²)

> I saw seven golden lampstands, and in the midst of the lampstands, one like a son of man . . . his head and his hair were white as white wool, white as snow; his eyes were like a flame of fire . . . and his face was like the sun shining in full strength.
>
> (Revelation 1¹²⁻¹⁶)

Before the heavenly throne in Zechariah's vision there burned 'seven torches of fire, which are the seven spirits of God' (4⁵), or, as the gnostics would say in their mythological terms, seven 'Helens'.

Helen is associated in classical mythology, like her twin brothers the terrible Dioskuroi, Castor and Pollux, with tongues of fire, a phosphorescence seen by sailors dancing upon a ship's yard-arm at sea. Saint Paul's Alexandrian ship, which, like his probably quite fictitious travels around the eastern Mediterranean, owes something in its composition to the Tyrian trading-ship oracles, was marked with the sign of Helen's Twin Brothers (Acts 28¹¹). The ship bearing the missionary of True Knowledge, the *gnosis*, is thus a symbol of Wisdom, as elsewhere in patristic literature the Church is portrayed as a ship, her sails filled with the Holy Spirit. Her 'ensign' displays the sign of the Twins, the flickering fire which also descended upon the heads of those disciples who received the Holy Ghost at Pentecost:

> When the day of Pentecost had come, they were all together in one place. And suddenly a sound came from heaven like the rush of a mighty wind, and it filled all the house where they were sitting. And there appeared to them tongues as of fire, distributed and resting on each one of them. And they were all filled with

172

the Holy Spirit and began to speak in other tongues, as the Spirit gave them utterance.

(Acts 2$^{1-4}$)

In the union of Simon with Helen, we have a mythological expression of the concept of Wisdom as the 'bride' of God, paralleled in the New Testament by the Church as the 'bride' of Christ (Revelation 21^9; see above, p 162). As before their separation they had been one, so now they are rejoined as one flesh, one Substance.

Similarly, in the Wisdom of Solomon, the king seeks Wisdom as his bride:

> Her I loved and sought out from my youth, and I sought to take her for my bride. And I became enamoured with her beauty. She proclaimed her noble birth in that it is given her to live with God, and the Sovereign Lord of all who love her . . . perceiving that I could not possess (Wisdom) except God gave her to me . . . I pleaded with the Lord and besought Him . . . 'Give me Wisdom, her that sitteth by Thee on the throne.'
>
> (Chapters VIII–IX)

Helen, the emanation of God, was credited (or blamed) in gnostic myth with creation, as is Wisdom in the same apocryphal work:

> O God . . . who madest all things by Thy World, and by Thy Wisdom hast formed man.
>
> (9^1)

Word and Wisdom are here synonymous as the author of creation; Philo of Alexandria and the writer of the Fourth Gospel called it Logos, Word (John 1^1), as we have seen, and the gnostics named her Helen, the Torch.

In the New Testament, also, we have another figure associated with the Word of God which, if it were not for the familiarising effect of ecclesiastical tradition and iconography, would surely strike the modern reader as absurdly incon-

173

gruous. In the Fourth Gospel and the Apocalypse, Christ is called the Lamb:

> The next day he [John the Baptist] saw Jesus coming towards him, and said, 'Behold the Lamb of God, who takes away the sin of the world.'

$$(1^{29})$$

The resultant imagery developed in the Apocalypse strains the imagination even more than some of the bizarre situations presented by the Simon–Helen mythology. We see the 'Lamb' standing by the throne of God, 'as though he had been slain, with seven horns and seven eyes' (5^6); he appears as a wrathful judge from whom 'the kings of the earth and the great men and generals, and the rich and the strong, and everyone, slave and free' hide in fear (6^{15-16}); he maintains a register of the Elect in the 'Book of Life' (13^8, 21^{27}); with Moses he provides the angels with their song of praise to God Almighty (15^3); he is a shepherd who guides the victims of the Great Tribulation to 'springs of living water' (7^{17}).

Translated back into a Semitic context, the origin of this imagery is plain: it is simply an ingenious piece of word-play, relating Aramaic *'imera*', 'Lamb', with the Hebrew *'imerah*, 'word'. The mythologist thus usefully combines the sacrificial aspect of Christ's earthly role as the Passover lamb, sacrificed for the sins of the people ('Behold the Lamb of God who takes away the sins of the world'), with his pre-existent nature as the Creative Principle, the Logos, Word, seated at the right hand of God.

When the Lamb, as the risen Joshua/Jesus, seeks the hand of the Church in wedlock, we have the Apocalypse restating the Simon–Helen myth of the reunification of Wisdom with the godhead:

> Then came one of the seven angels . . . and spoke to me, saying, 'Come, I will show you the Bride, the wife of the Lamb.' And in the Spirit he carried me away to a great, high mountain, and showed me the holy city of Jerusalem, coming down out of heaven from God.

$$(\text{Revelation } 21^{9-10})$$

Let us rejoice and exult and give him the glory,
    for the marriage of the Lamb has come,
    and his Bride has made herself ready;
it was granted to her to be clothed with fine linen, bright and
        pure:
for the 'fine linen' is the righteous deeds of the saints.
    And the angel said to me, 'Write this: Blessed
are those who are invited to the marriage supper of the
Lamb.'

                                     (Revelation 19^{7-9})

When, elsewhere, the apocalyptist envisages the heavenly choir of 'white-robed' Essenes who had passed through the Great Tribulation of persecution, he sees their celestial state as a renewal of an earthly existence at the feet of their Teacher, now glorified as the Lamb of God, that is, the risen Word:

Then one of the elders addressed me, saying, 'Who are these, clothed in white robes, and whence have they come?' I said to him, 'Sir, you know.' And he said to me, 'These are they who have come out of the great tribulation; they have washed their robes in the blood of the Lamb.
    Therefore are they before the throne of God,
    and serve him day and night within his temple;
    and he who sits upon the throne will shelter them with his
        presence.
    They shall hunger no more, neither thirst any more;
    the sun shall not strike them, nor any scorching heat.
For the Lamb in the midst of the throne will be their shepherd,
    and he will guide them to springs of living water;
    and God will wipe away every tear from their eyes.

                                     (Revelation 7^{13-17})

It was as a source of 'living waters' that the Teacher had portrayed himself in his hymn:

Thou hast lodged me beside a fountain of running waters in a
        waterless land,
    and by a spring in a parched land,
    and by channels that irrigate a garden [of delight in the
        wilderness] . . .

175

But Thou, O my God, hast put into my mouth
   as showers of early rain for all [those who thirst]
   and a spring of living waters . . .
               (Hymns, Col. VIII; see above, Chapter Three)

We have already seen how the Essenes applied to themselves and their desert sanctuary the prophecy about the 'river of life' running eastwards from the Temple threshold, to bring life and healing to the desert of 'eastern Galilee' about the Dead Sea. This striking image is applied in the Apocalypse to the future Community, the New Jerusalem, purged of all the sin and infidelity that had previously barred the Children of Light from its ministrations, and now made worthy of the presence of God and His Lamb, in the company of the Elect. The Wisdom of God would irradiate the whole city.

   . . . and night shall be no more; for they need no light of lamp or sun, for the Lord God will be their light
                      (Revelation 22^5)

   . . . its lamp is the Lamb. By its light shall the nations walk . . .
                      (Revelation 21$^{23-24}$)

We have thus returned to Helen, the 'torch', now portrayed as the Lamb, the 'lamp', symbolising Light as divine Knowledge, illuminating the path back to God. Our study has shown once more that it is not the story-line that is important in any true myth, but the underlying theme that it is meant to represent. Above all, in respect of the New Testament stories about Joshua/Jesus, it should have made us beware of taking them at their face value, least of all as accurate records of contemporary events and people. By running together similarly-based myths from the gnostic story-book, we have tried to show that in all there is a common fount of inspiration, with a long history of theological development. At the end of the day we may feel that we have lost the historical Jesus of the Gospels, but discovered—or rediscovered—a timeless revelation of the divine purpose.

176

12

The Day-spring from on High

As we saw earlier, one of Simon's titles was the 'Standing One' (Greek *estos*); see above, p 143). If we follow our usual practice of seeking the Semitic original of the name, the result opens up a whole series of correspondences in the area of our study. The Greek term is clearly a translation of the Semitic word for 'pillar' (*'ammud* in Hebrew, of the verbal root *'amad*, 'stand'). That designation is significant because St Paul refers to the three leaders of the Jerusalem community as 'Pillars', as if it were a recognised honorific title:

> James, and Cephas, and John, who were reputed to be pillars.
> (Galatians 2⁹)

We have to assume that to be a Pillar of the messianist movement implied more than an architectural feature, metaphorically supporting the roof of a house; for Simon to have borne the name, inherited, his followers maintained, from his predecessor John the Baptist and someone called Dositheus, it must have had some particular cultic significance in the Order.

Certainly, there is a wealth of scriptural allusion to 'pillars' on which to draw, particularly in the story of the desert wanderings of the Exodus story, noted in the previous chapter:

And the Lord went before them by day in a pillar of cloud to lead
them along the way, and by night in a pillar of fire to give them
light, that they might travel by day and night; the pillar of cloud
by day and the pillar of cloud by night did not depart from before
the people.

(Exodus 13$^{21-22}$)

When Moses entered the tent, the pillar of cloud would descend
and stand at the door of the tent, and the Lord would speak with
Moses. And when all the people saw the pillar of cloud standing
at the door of the tent, all the people would rise up and worship,
every man at his tent door. Thus the Lord used to speak to Moses
face to face, as a man speaks to his friend . . .

(Exodus 33$^{9-11}$)

The psalmists record that God

spoke to them in a pillar of cloud

(Psalm 99^7)

in the daytime he led them with a cloud,
    and all the night with a fiery light.

(Psalm 78^{14})

When, on their return from the Exile, the Jewish leader Ezra
led his people in prayer, he, too, records those events in history
through which the nation received the revelation of God's purpose:

By a pillar of cloud thou didst lead them in the day, and by a
pillar of fire in the night to light for them the way in which they
should go . . .

. . . thou in thy great mercies didst not forsake them in the wilderness; the pillar of cloud which led them in the way did not
depart from them by day, nor the pillar of fire by night which
lighted for them the way by which they should go . . .

(Nehemiah 9$^{12, 19}$)

178

Naturally enough, later writers saw in this 'pillar of cloud' the very fount of revelation, the seat of Wisdom herself. The author of the apocryphal work Ecclesiasticus (Ben Sira) has her say:

> In the high places did I fix my abode, and my throne was in the pillar of cloud.
>
> (Ecclesiasticus 24⁴)

Similarly, the writer of the Wisdom of Solomon identifies Wisdom with the pillars:

> she became unto them a covering in the daytime,
> and a flame (light) of stars through the night.
>
> (10¹⁷)

In the biblical book of Proverbs, speaking of Wisdom as God's helper in the work of creation, the writer says that she

> Built her house, she has set up her seven pillars.
>
> (9¹)

This may refer to the seven planets, or possibly to the days of the week, each of which was heralded by the appearance of an important constellation, the Morning-star, Venus.

At this point we enter into another and, for our purpose, crucial range of significance for the Pillar of Wisdom. For one of the titles of the Morning-star in Hebrew is 'Pillar of the Dawn'. It was regarded with great awe by the ancients, and invested with miraculous powers. This is the 'Day-spring from on high' which John the Baptist's father, Zechariah, promised would

> give light to those who sit in darkness and in the shadow of death.
>
> (Luke 1⁷⁸⁻⁷⁹)

In ancient Babylon, a royal cult had apparently identified the ruling monarch with the Morning-star, for the prophet Isaiah promises his downfall:

How are you fallen from heaven,
O Day-star, son of the Dawn!

$$(14^{12})$$

In the New Testament, however, it is Jesus, the Davidic Messiah, who is the 'bright Morning-star' (Revelation 22^{16}), and the author of the second epistle of Peter advises his readers to treasure in their hearts the record of God's witness in the Transfiguration of His Son,

as a lamp shining in a dark place, until the day dawns and the Morning-star rises in your hearts,

$$(1^{19})$$

connecting the harbinger of dawn with the Torch of divine illumination noted in the previous chapter.

To have the 'Day-spring' in one's heart is to be blessed with the power of Christ:

He who conquers and keeps my works until the end I will give him power over the nations . . . even as I myself have received power from my Father; and I will give him the Morning-star.

(Revelation $2^{26\text{-}28}$)

It is clear, then, that in such circles, the Pillar of Dawn, the luminary of the morning and evening skies, was equated with Wisdom, and so with the 'pillar of cloud' and the 'pillar of fire' which led the Israelites through the desert. It was thus a very suitable title to give the leaders of the messianic community, whether actually present, like James, Cephas, and John, or past—real or mythical—like Dositheus, Simon, or John, the so-called 'Baptist'. They were those who, above all others, had the power of the Morning-star in their hearts, and were accordingly illumined with the mystic *gnosis*, the Knowledge of God. They had been vouchsafed the gift of the Holy Spirit.

Now, having identified the true significance of the honorific title Pillar, we can penetrate to the real meaning of John the Baptist's epithet, and, incidentally, of the descriptive title

180

accorded the so-called Haemerobaptists, 'Day-bathers' (from the Greek *haemera* 'day', *baptizo* 'dip, bathe; baptise'), a mysterious sect of Jewish-Christians who flourished in the early centuries of our era.

Whether these 'pseudo-Christians', as the Haemerobaptists were regarded by the Church Fathers, ever practised ritual baptism or not, or whether John the Baptist—if he ever existed—was thus distinguished outside the Joshua/Jesus and gnostic myths, has very little relevance to the real meaning of their names. For 'baptise' in both instances is nothing but a play on, or a misunderstanding of, the Semitic word underlying the Greek. The verb for 'dip, baptise' in the spoken dialect of Palestine, Aramaic, is *'amad*, exactly similar in form to the root of the Hebrew for 'stand' and 'pillar', *'amad*, noted above. So, almost certainly, what lay behind the unremarkable title 'Day-bathers', or 'Day-baptists', was the more meaningful 'Pillars of the Dawn, or Day', the Hebrew name of the Morning-star, Venus. They were, in fact, believers who claimed they had received the promised 'Day-spring' in their hearts. Similarly, the charismatic figure who is portrayed in the Gospels as preceding the Messiah, and who figures in gnostic mythology as one of the movement's founding fathers, was John the Pillar ('Baptist'). As the Morning-star precedes the sun, and the pillar of smoke went before the pillar of fire to guide the Israelites like a torch in the wilderness, so John prepared the way for the Christ:

There was a man sent from God, whose name was John. He came for a testimony, to bear witness to the light, that all might believe through him. He was not the light, but came to bear witness to the light . . .

And this is the testimony of John . . . 'I am the voice of one crying in the wilderness, Make straight the way of the Lord . . .'

(John 1[6-8]; [19-23])

When we look further into ideas of the time about the powers possessed by the Morning-star, a number of other facets of gnostic belief and practice become more comprehensible. Writing in the first century of our era, Pliny the Elder recounts some of the common folklore concerning the planet Venus, the Daystar:

> Before the sun revolves a very large star named Venus, which varies in course alternately, and whose alternative names in themselves indicate its rivalry with the sun and moon—when in advance and rising before dawn, it received the name Lucifer, as being another sun and bringing the dawn whereas when it shines after sunset it is named Vesper, as prolonging the daylight, or as being a deputy for the moon . . . Further, it surpasses all the other stars in magnitude, and is so brilliant that alone among the stars it casts a shadow by its rays. Consequently there is great competition to give it a name, some having called it Juno, others Isis, others Mother of the gods . . .
>
> (*Natural History* II 36–37)

This wonderful star was supreme in its generative power. When, as a lesser 'sun', it slipped from the connubial bower before its master, it came dripping with the divine semen. The sun, yawning and stretching its blazing path across the sky, would burn away the fragrant drops that its forerunner had scattered, but, until then, they would remain as dew on the face of the ground, the most powerful conceptual fluid of Nature. So again Pliny:

> Its influence is the cause of the birth of all things upon earth; at both its risings it scatters a genital dew with which it not only fills the conceptual organs of the earth, but also stimulates those of all animals.
>
> (*Natural History* II 38)

Even the sea creatures were affected by this miraculous sperm. Pearls were 'born' within the shell by the direct influence of the dew; well might Aphrodite have been portrayed sailing ashore on the coast of Cyprus in such a 'womb' of the sea bed. Again Pliny:

The source and breeding-ground of pearls are shells not much differing from oyster-shells. These, we are told, when stimulated by the generative season of the year, gape open, as it were, and are filled with a dewy pregnance, and consequently when heavy are delivered, and the offspring of the shells are pearls that correspond to the quality of the dew received.

(*Natural History* IX 107)

Of more interest to the Essene and Therapeutae physicians was the idea that dew produced the more powerful drugs:

After the rising of each star, but particularly the principle stars, or of a rainbow, if rain does not follow but the dew is warmed by the rays of the sun . . . drugs (*medicamenta*) are produced, heavenly gifts for the eyes, ulcers, and internal organs. And if this substance is kept when the dog-star is rising, and if, as often happens, the rise of Venus or Jupiter or Mercury falls on the same day, its sweetness and potency for recalling mortals' ills from death is equal to the Nectar of the gods.

(*Natural History* XI 37)

We can now begin to understand better why the Therapeutae were said to rise before the dawn to offer their prayers. It was not, as has been commonly assumed, to worship the rising sun, but to beseech of its forerunner, the Morning-star, the gift of divine understanding in their hearts. They prayed for a 'fair day, and for truth and a clear judgement in their vision' (see above, p 111).

We saw earlier that the gnostic Agape meal, and the anointing, or secret 'baptism', involved the use of human semen (see above, Chapter Eight). The seed of their Elect, purified through their total dedication to God's service, was the nearest to God's own Substance that they could achieve. In the natural world its equivalent was the morning dew, the gift of the Morning-star. We may suppose that part of the Therapeutae's morning ritual was to take this 'genital dew' and anoint their eyes and bodies 'for truth and clear judgement'.

Spittle was similarly regarded as a semen-substitute by the

ancients, and some similar ritual probably underlies the story of Jesus healing the blind man by making a poultice of clay and spittle to place upon his eyes, testifying to his role in the world as the 'Light' (John 9⁵).

The belief that dew was vested with special generative powers is witnessed in the Old Testament in passages of particular interest to the messianist. When the Israelites awoke in the desert after an evening of filling their bellies with quail flesh, it was to discover that the 'spermal emission' of the dew had left behind it manna, the 'bread of heaven' (Exodus 16¹³ᶠᶠ). The Fourth Gospel has Jesus relate himself to this heavenly food:

> I am the bread of life. Your fathers ate the manna in the wilderness, and they died. This is the bread which comes down from heaven, that a man may eat of it and not die . . . I am the living bread which came down from heaven . . . the bread which I shall give for the life of the world is my flesh.
>
> (John 6⁴⁸⁻⁵¹)

Dew, it was thought, could revive even the dead:

> Thy dead shall live, their bodies shall arise. O dwellers in the dust, awake and sing! For your dew is the dew of herbs [or luminaries, that is, the stars], and you will let it fall upon the land of the Shades [Rephaim].
>
> (Isaiah 26¹⁹)

Above all, the biblical exegete could find in the messianic Psalms testimony to his belief that God had begotten His Anointed, the Christ, and had done so through the genital dew scattered by the Morning-star:

> He said to me, Thou art my son, today I have begotten thee,
>
> (Psalm 2⁷)

and, again,

> from the womb of the dawn, (in) dew I have begotten thee,

184

read by the Greek translators as:

> from the womb of the Morning-star I have begotten thee.
>
> (Psalm 110³)

Both of these Psalms are quoted in the New Testament to support the claims of Joshua/Jesus to his messianic office. We may reasonably suppose that the myth of the Virgin's conception of the Christ-child through the Holy Spirit (Luke 1) owes something to the idea of the divine seed being implanted into the womb of Mother-earth and 'of all animals' through the action of the Morning-star.

Certainly both the New Testament and the Dead Sea Scrolls support a widespread belief that the coming of the Messiah was to be heralded by the appearance of a special star prophesied by Balaam in the Old Testament:

> A star shall come forth out of Jacob,
>   and a sceptre shall arise out of Israel.
>
> (Numbers 24¹⁷)

In the Essene documents the Star is equated with the so-called Interpreter of the Law who took his people into exile. On his return he would appear as the priestly Messiah, in company with the 'Shoot of David', the warrior Prince. The Star passage also appears among the messianic 'proof-texts' of Joshua's Blessing and Curse, written on the parchment sheet from the Partridge Cave (see above, p 79). We noted that the context of the quotations indicates their relevance to the Teacher of Righteousness himself, as the 'second Joshua', and it is therefore of special interest that the same Star quotation was applied to the gnostic leader, Dositheus, the supposed successor to John the Baptist and predecessor to Simon Magus.

There are other clear connections between this Dositheus and the Essenes. Convergent testimonies from fourth-century and medieval witnesses describe the followers of Dositheus as adherents of a strict Jewish sect which arose in Maccabean times. They were said to have rejected the orthodox Jewish

185

calendar and its religious festivals in favour of one based on a month of thirty days, reckoned by the moon. The Essenes probably originated as a result of pietist reaction to Maccabean excesses, and one of their distinctive teachings was certainly that relating to their adherence to a lunar calendar of a thirty-day month, in consequence of which they would not participate in the Jerusalem cultus. We also learn that the Dositheans were gathered 'in the vicinity of Jerusalem', which might be said to apply to the Dead Sea area, some twenty miles to the east; and, with obvious Essene parallels, they were said at one time to have been persecuted by a Jewish high priest.

Dositheus, like his reputed predecessor John the Baptist, was said to have 'thirty disciples'. This may well have some allusion to the thirty days of the Dosithean/Essene calendar, if, like the Haemerobaptists, properly 'Pillars of the Dawn', the thirty were called 'Pillars' and their number accorded with the risings of the Morning-star to be expected in a lunar month of thirty days.

As late as the sixth century some controversy raged among Samaritans on whether the famous prophecy in the Bible about the coming of a Prophet 'like Moses' referred to Joshua, son of Nun, or to Dositheus:

I will raise up for them a prophet like you from among their brethren; and I will put my words in his mouth, and he shall speak to them all that I command him. And whoever will not give heed to my words which the prophet shall speak in my name, I myself will require it of him.

(Deuteronomy 18[18–19])

Thus, the gnostic teacher Dositheus was being linked in those sectarian circles with his biblical predecessor Joshua, son of Nun. Furthermore, this text is the first of the messianic testimonia in the Essene document just mentioned, where reference is to the latter-day 'Joshua/Jesus', the Teacher of Righteousness. Interestingly, in view of the reported source of this disputation, the Samaritan community, the Essene version of the biblical text is in a form peculiar to the old version of the books of Moses, the Pentateuch, preserved by the Samaritan sect.

Another tradition recorded of the Dositheans is that they were very careful to avoid pronouncing the divine name Jehóvah/Yahweh, or even its usual surrogate Adonai, 'Lord'. Again, it is of note that the second word of this biblical quotation on the Essene parchment happens to be the divine name, written, as elsewhere in the Scrolls, with just four dots representing the four Hebrew letters of the divine name, a warning to the reader not to pronounce the word.

Finally, Origen, the third-century Church Father, asserts that some of Dositheus's disciples held that he had not really died but, like Enoch, Elisha, and Jesus, had been translated miraculously to heaven. This may well be an indication that the Teacher was thought by his followers to have been taken up to rejoin his Father after his crucifixion. Since the Scrolls already witness to the belief that 'one who teaches righteousness' would reappear in the Last Days, it is not difficult to understand how the idea that the Teacher had ascended to heaven after his martyrdom could have developed. His return in glory at the dawn of the messianic age could be more readily understood if, in the intervening period of expectation, he had assumed his rightful place at God's right hand.

From all these correspondences we may deduce that in the mysterious 'Dositheus' we should see a portrayal in gnostic mythology of the Teacher of Righteousness, and we can understand some of the theological speculation which must have gathered around this 'second Joshua/Jesus' of the Essene community. He was regarded as the Prophet, Priest, and King of the messianic testimonia. He was the Pillar, the 'Standing One', medium of God's Word to man, and present to all who believed in him as the power of the Morning-star, that is, the Holy Spirit.

This latter identification is further substantiated by a close look at his Greek name, Dositheus, meaning 'Gift-of-God', similar to the Semitic name John (Greek *Ioannes*, Hebrew *Yohanan*, 'God-is-gracious', or *Yonathan*, 'God-has-given'). It can be no coincidence that 'Gift-of-God' is precisely the epithet applied most consistently to the Holy Spirit. It is implicit in the story about Simon wanting to purchase the Spirit with money ('you thought you could obtain this gift of God with money'— Acts 8²⁰). The Samaritan woman by Jacob's well is reproved by Jesus for not recognising the 'gift of God' through whom she might have received 'living water' to eternal life (John 4¹⁰). Peter promises his audience at Pentecost that they, too, could receive the 'gift of the Holy Spirit' after baptism (Acts 2³⁸; cp. 10⁴⁵, 11¹⁷). St Paul thanks God for 'His inexpressible gift' (II Corinthians 9¹⁵), and the writer of the epistle to the Hebrews relates heavenly enlightenment with this Gift, the Holy Spirit:

> For it is impossible to restore again to repentance those who have once been enlightened, who have tasted the heavenly gift, and have become partakers of the Holy Spirit.
>
> (Hebrews 6⁴)

The distribution of the Gift is itself a 'sign' of God's grace:

> ... while God also bore witness by signs and wonders and miracles, and by gifts of the Holy Spirit distributed according to his own will.
>
> (Hebrews 2⁴)

The Gift could be conveyed by the laying-on of hands:

> Do not neglect the gift you have, which was given you by prophetic utterance when the elders laid their hands upon you
>
> (II Timothy 4¹⁴)

As in the Simon story, the Jerusalem delegation of the two Pillars, Peter and John, 'laid their hands' on the Samaritan converts and thus imparted to them the Holy Spirit (Acts 8¹⁷). So the writer of the epistle urges his reader 'to rekindle the gift of God that is within you through the laying-on of my hands', so that, being thus recharged, he might demonstrate to the world 'a spirit of power and love and self-control' (II Timothy 1⁶⁻⁷).

In summary, then, the so-called Pillars of the Church are those who are blessed with the power of the Morning-star in their hearts. They have the Gift-of-God, the Holy Spirit, which is divine Wisdom, the true *gnosis*. John 'the Baptist', whether an historical person or not, the mythical Simon and Dositheus are thus all Pillars of the Faith, as are the Haemerobaptists, properly Pillars of the Dawn, or 'Morning-stars'. Most important of all, Dositheus ('Gift-of-God') was but a representation in gnostic mythology of the Essene 'Joshua/Jesus', the Teacher of Righteousness, the real-life personality behind the New Testament Jesus of Nazareth.

13

'Will the *real* Jesus Christ please stand up?'

There is, then, a whole series of related ideas, Old Testament, Essene, gnostic, and New Testament, which form a continuum of developing religious thought. If we look behind the mythology for the underlying strata of shared conceptions we become more and more aware of the common fount of the Judaeo-Christian tradition. Of course, this is not new; the Bible of the early Church was, after all, the Old Testament. What is new, thanks largely to the Dead Sea Scrolls, is our ability now to recognise in the so-called intertestamental period (that is, in the crucial centuries between the most recent books of the Old Testament canon, say Daniel in the second century BC, and the earliest writings of the New Testament, the letters of St Paul) that the Essene movement provided just the right mix of early Canaanite folk-religion, prophetic Yahwism, Babylonian magic, and Iranian dualism to have produced gnostic Christianity. What it could not produce, and never did, was an historical Joshua/Jesus Messiah living in Palestine during the first century AD and bearing any real resemblance to the benign, improbably naïve, not to say downright ignorant, conjurer-prophet that popular imagination has largely created out of the Gospels.

190

Behind the Jesus of western religious tradition there did exist in history an Essene Teacher of Righteousness of a century before. He was a leader of men, but not a magician. He himself was heir to a great prophetic tradition, but he was also an innovator. He led his followers into the desert and with them endured great privations and disappointments, not least with dissidents inside his own community. He believed that the suffering he shared with his people had a propitiatory role in the salvation of Israel, that together they had been 'chosen of grace to atone for the earth', as the Order for the Community has it (VIII 6). He believed he was following in the footsteps of a previous Joshua/Jesus who had led the Israelites into the Promised Land, and, like him, he set out for the men of his Covenant a Way, based upon the Law which had been first revealed to Moses and which must now be reinterpreted to serve the new situation. Because we now have in our hands the literary record of that Way, thanks to the discoveries by the Dead Sea, we can see how that revelation became further adapted under the pressure of socio-political events of the first century to serve people on the fringes of Judaism, or completely outside that dispensation, as an expression of an intensely personal faith.

This was the religion that became characterised as messianism, or 'Christianity', and which, for various reasons, earned the disapproval of contemporary religious and secular authorities. It began, as we can now see, as an amalgam of many different beliefs, from widely scattered parts of the Near East. That very diversity of origins was the strength of its universal appeal, to Jew and gentile, to Roman and to Greek, to rich and poor, master and slave; but it was its organisational weakness. What we call now 'gnostic Christianity' was too many things to too many people to allow a regulative theological control, or to present a cohesive front to other, more established beliefs with strong sacerdotal traditions of doctrinal authority. Without this common front, gnosticism could not serve the needs of a state bureaucracy, nor earn for itself the support of imperialist treasuries and armies to further its evangelism.

One faction of the messianist community did, however, seek

191

such recognition and the security it promised. When, in the early fourth century, the so-called Great Church attained its goal, its internal enemies lay torn and bleeding, or scattered into the heretical wilderness. Their books were burned, their doctrines forsworn, and often intentionally perverted. Its mythology was misrepresented and mocked, but a single figure was wrested from its rich store of imagery and made paramount, even historical. The Joshua/Jesus cycle of stories was pruned of some of the more improbable narratives, given an unrealistic pro-Roman slant, and combined with genuine Essene moral teachings suited more to the sheltered life of a closely knit desert commune than the rough-and-tumble of secular living. It purported to offer to the general reader the real-life history of a Jewish rabbi who, in three short years of a preaching ministry in a hostile Palestinian environment, succeeded in changing the world.

Absurd though the myth was in its historical and religious pretensions, and sadly misleading in its presentation of contemporary Judaism, its stories contained such elements of truth and reflections of deep religious sentiment, combined with a fluency of style and an illusory simplicity of content, as to procure a sympathetic and ready audience in the gentile world. Its protagonists, the Great Church, eventually won the day and its hierarchy ensured that for the future the writings of the canonical New Testament should be invested with supreme and incontrovertible authority as sources of doctrine and history.

Now, two thousand years later, we have to try to break through this artificial barrier of self-imposed infallibility, and to reconstruct the world of conflicting ideas of the early centuries, and the mainspring from which they derived their animation. The Scrolls from the Dead Sea help; the anti-heretical writings of the Church Fathers offer some information on their opponents' ideas, however distorted and biased. But above all, we are now largely freed from the constraints of ecclesiastical bigotry and obscurantism that have for so long hindered objective research.

All the same, the evidence is sparse enough. The New

192

Testament is still our main witness, and we cannot afford to neglect the Gospel narratives, however lacking they may be in chronological consistency or unsupportable in matters of fact, historical, geographical, topographical, sociological, political, philological, or religious. What we must do in any re-examination of their evidence is to dismiss from our minds twenty centuries of accumulated exegetical and pietistic tradition, and consign our fondest images of flaxen-haired, blue-eyed shepherds calling sheep, knocking on doors, patting small children on the head, hanging on crosses, or lying limp and lifeless in a mother's arms, to the realm of the fanciful, where they belong. The popularity of such creations in the western world says more for the ignorance and pious credulity of the average western Christian and his susceptibility to ecclesiastical persuasion than for their realism.

In the Gospels we are dealing with highly complex creations, offering several levels of interpretation. They have been woven from many strands of tradition such as we have seen are contained in the gnostic stories, and they often involve the kinds of unrestrained exegesis of biblical texts evidenced in the Essene scrolls. Embedded in these narratives are scraps of real history, fleeting glimpses of actual persons and events. Proper names may be reckoned the least authentic elements, although 'nicknames' often conceal official titles or secret catchwords; but only madmen would commit to writing and free distribution the actual identities of people and places involved in the movement's activities. The secret police of the imperial power were actively seeking out cells of dissidents in that hot-bed of potential revolt, and Christian communities were regarded, probably rightly, with extreme suspicion. There were still close links between some factions of Essenism and the Zealots, for whom messianism was synonymous with the establishment of a Jewish state in Palestine.

Even where the Gospel stories do reflect details of the period following the fall of the Temple in AD 70, it is unlikely that we should be able to recognise their provenance, since we are all too ignorant of the history of that time to be able to relate such

193

incidents and persons to their context. Our main interests must lie in an earlier period, when Essenic messianism was in the making. If the New Testament narratives can tell us anything about those times, particularly about the fate of the Teacher and his followers' developing ideas of the Master's role, then its witness cannot be neglected. That, indeed, should be the main purpose and direction of all New Testament research from now on, rather than fruitless attempts at justifying its aberrations and inconsistencies as if it really were an historical record.

Above all, we have to remember that the myth of Jesus of Nazareth as recorded in the Gospels was just one of a number of Redeemer mythologies. We have looked at a similar presentation concerning the incarnation of the godhead as Simon and his companion Helen. We have seen how religious ideas underlying those characters are very clearly common to the more 'gnostic' parts of the New Testament, particularly many of the Pauline writings and the Johannine works, including the Fourth Gospel and the Apocalypse. These may be regarded as the more 'authentic', that is, more directly evolved, parts of the corpus. It is, incidentally, some indication of the revolution in scholars' understanding of Christianity's true origins that the Johannine compositions, for so long considered the latest of the New Testament documents, and least representative of 'primitive Jewish-Christianity', are now generally agreed, thanks to the witness of the Scrolls, to stem from the very heart of the messianist movement. It is significant also, as has already been pointed out above, that Paul and the compiler of the Fourth Gospel show the least interest in details of the 'historical' Christ and his mortal career; they are far more concerned with the import of his incarnation as the Son of God, and of his atoning death for the salvation of the world.

The fact is that we should have been more ready to accept the essentially unhistorical nature of the Jesus stories had we only the witness of these works. Misled by the seeming historicity of the so-called Synoptic ('single-viewed') tradition represented by the first three Gospels, scholars have been more interested in setting the chronological and other

194

inconsistencies of John against the records of Matthew, Mark, and Luke, or, more speculatively, against the supposed witness of the lost source of all three. Nevertheless, the one historic event which is fundamental to St Paul's understanding of messianist theology was the crucifixion of the Teacher, and John's witness is similarly oriented towards the Cross. When he has the forerunner, John the Baptist, proclaim: 'Behold the Lamb of God, who takes away the sin of the world!', he relates the Incarnation to the Cross as but two aspects of God's one redemptive purpose.

We have seen how the ingredients of this messianist theology are already being formulated in the Scrolls and related intertestamental literature. It is also clear that their development along Pauline lines could only have come about through socio-political pressures operating on the community, and Judaism generally, over the whole period between the Testaments. Any shorter chronology makes no sense at all, least of all the truncation of such deliberation and its acceptance between the supposed death of the Teacher in AD 30 and the first of the Epistles, hardly more than a decade later. We may suppose that the crucifixion of the Teacher of Righteousness in about 88 BC sharpened Essene speculation that had already long been centred upon the Suffering Servant concept of Old Testament prophecy and the propitiatory role of the true Israel in the world. Political events gradually forced upon the theologians a realisation of the hopelessness of the old world-dominating messianism of post-exilic Judaism. The way was then open for a more spiritual conception of the Kingdom of God, and, combined with a growing pessimism over the material world, this gradually gave rise to the extreme anti-materialism of the gnostics, and their concentration on achieving personal salvation through mystic contemplation. But again, this was not new in itself; its roots lay in the Old Testament and received further nourishment in the alien soil of Iranian dualism, the opposition of the cosmic forces of Good and Evil, God and Satan, the influence of which is so clearly marked

195

in Essene writings. Like all apparent innovations in human thought, there was behind Essene gnosticism and its saviour-theology a deep hinterland of philosophic exploration. The crucifixion of the Teacher concentrated one channel of thought and directed it upon a single historical event, but the tide of speculation had long been flowing. Nevertheless, the event was a necessary part of its explicit formulation as doctrine; the Essenes and their spiritual successors could find assurance of God's redeeming love in that single act. It did not need a date in human history, nor even a step-by-step account of the events preceding and following the drama of the Cross. Such details might occupy the imagination of the myth-makers, but for the believer the redemptive sacrifice was timeless.

However, for us who love to see history enacted before our eyes, and to assess its play in terms of human relationships, such Pauline unconcern with the details of the crucifixion of the Teacher has been unsatisfying. Hence we have turned eagerly to the compelling fascination of the Gospel drama of Golgotha, and we 'purge our emotions with pity and terror' every Easter-tide.

Now, however, we can no longer disguise from ourselves the obvious fallacies in the Gospel story and its chronology, and must place the martyrdom of the Teacher more than a century earlier. How disruptive this more realistic appreciation of history need be for Christian faith and witness we might consider later, but for the moment our concern must be to glean, if possible, some core of fact from the New Testament narrative that might illumine our understanding of the dramatic events of 88 BC.

We saw in Chapter Five that the probable site of the Teacher's crucifixion was Gilgal, by ancient Jericho and, in the pseudo-topography of the Essenes, adjacent to the city of refuge, Shechem. It was there that the first Joshua/Jesus saw his vision of the angel (Joshua 5^{15}), by the Teacher's Oak. We suggested that it was upon this sacred monument that the 'second Joshua/Jesus' was put to death at the behest of the Wicked Priest, Alexander Jannaeus.

196

Looking across at the New Testament story of Golgotha, we can now appreciate how this actual event formed the basis of the Gospel myth. The Greek translators of the Deuteronomy passage cited earlier (11³⁰) transcribed the placename Gilgal as *Golgol*, as does Eusebius in his work on sacred topography (253.89), and this word is very similar in sound to the Semitic *gulgoleth* (Hebrew), *gulgulta'* (Aramaic), 'skull', which the New Testament writers loosely render Golgotha. Whether there really was in Jerusalem a 'place of a skull' (Mark 15²²) with some particular local association with public executions we cannot know, for there is no other contemporary record of such a location or topographical feature. One suspects, however, that the 'skull' reference has some quite other allusion.

The story of the confrontation of the Teacher, Jesus, by a 'crowd . . . from the chief priests' (Mark 14⁴³) on the Mount of Olives is almost certainly derived in part from a text to which we have already referred:

> As robbers lie in wait for a man, a company of priests on the way to Shechem, they murder, they commit a villainy.
>
> (Hosea 6⁹)

By means of a characteristic piece of Essene exegesis, the myth-makers have read the Hebrew words for 'man' and 'robbers' together as a collective phrase, 'one of a robber band', and interpret it:

> as a company of priests lie in wait for a robber . . .

which then calls forth a question from Jesus:

> Have you come out as against a robber . . .?
>
> (Mark 14⁴⁸)

Here and there it is possible to see in the biblical exegesis flashes of a wry, bitter humour, even in the description of such tragic events as this prelude to the Teacher's death. It may well be that the name Golgotha, 'Skull', owes something to this kind of wit. After all, we have to remember that the story recounted in the Gospels is almost pure fiction; its purpose was quite other than to depict the real events that had taken place in very different circumstances a century or more previously. Pathos is there, certainly, and intended by the narrators, but the details, and particularly the place-names and the names of the chief characters, are often deliberate inventions. It is here in general that we should look for the more covert allusions in the Gospel narratives. In this instance, we may suspect that the clue lies again in the 'robber' of the Hosea text. If one were to ask the ordinary Jew of the first century (or, indeed, honest citizens of almost any other time) who were the greatest robbers of all, he would probably have answered without hesitation, 'Why, the publicans, tax-collectors, of course!'

The Hebrew word for 'poll-tax' is the same as that for 'skull', *gulgoleth*, and is so used in the Bible; in late Hebrew and Aramaic it actually has the specific meaning of a capitation tax gathered on behalf of the Roman government. So by directing the mind of the knowledgeable reader to this politically sensitive interpretation of 'robbers', as those who collected the poll-tax for the hated Roman provincial government, the exegete incorporates into the story of the crucifixion a covert piece of anti-Roman propaganda, while still finding his necessary scriptural authority in the Hosea text. Again, one has to remember the circumstances in which these stories of Joshua/Jesus were promulgated. The Romans were the main enemy; the orthodox Jewish establishment ran them a close second. Nothing was ever going to persuade the Jewish authorities to accept the messianists and their blasphemous estimate of the Creator; there was always a hope that the less comprehending Roman administrators might be prepared to write the movement off as a weird but comparatively harmless religious cult, and leave them alone. In fact, as has been said, the hope proved futile, and those of the Faith were persecuted unmercifully from both sides. Nevertheless, the Gospels stand as a monument to the ingenuity of the myth-makers in promulgating their teachings under the very nose of the enemy in such a way as to incorporate sly asides like the 'poll-tax' reference in the name of the accursed hill on which their Teacher died, while at the same

198

time piously absolving the Pilates of their world from any blame in the affair.

Similarly, in another, apparently less sinister, context, a despised publican Quisling is given pride of place as one eager to hear the Master's words, and is rewarded with an assurance of salvation. It will be recalled that, in this tale, a rich tax-collector named Zacchaeus of Jericho wanted to see Jesus, but could not do so in the crowd of eager sightseers because of his small stature:

> So he ran on ahead and climbed up into a sycamore tree to see him, for he was to pass that way.
>
> (Luke 19)

In this case, by an ingenious piece of exegesis using the same Hosea text, the Essene myth-makers have produced the framework of a story which has amused and captivated audiences for two millenia, and which will no doubt continue to do so, for its ostensible message is one of hope for sinners: no one, not even collectors of the Inland Revenue department, are beyond salvation. The commentators have taken the first words of the text in the previously determined sense:

> as a man of the Robbers lies in wait on the road to Shechem, a crowd . . .

from which they have spun out the story. The small stature of Zacchaeus finds its textual justification in a playful reading of the place-name Shechem. The proper meaning of this word is 'shoulder', used topographically to indicate a hillside or ridge. It is ordinarily used in connection with personal stature, normally of tall people like Saul (I Samuel 9²), but here as a short man unable to see over the heads of the crowd, being only of 'shoulder-height'. Similarly, from the place-name Shechem comes the intriguing little botanical detail that he climbed into a 'sycamore tree'. The significance of this gratuitous note becomes clear when we look at the Greek name of the tree, *sukomorea*, properly the 'fig-mulberry' (that is, *sukon-moron*). The

199

story-tellers have taken the first part of the compound name, *suko-m* from 'Shechem', and the second part from the name of the famous tree at Shechem/Gilgal, the 'Tree of the Teacher', or *Moreh*. Thus, behind the simple tale of a short-statured tax-man clambering into a sycamore tree to obtain a better view of Jesus, we have an important allusion to the sacred monument at Gilgal on which the Essene Master was left hanging by his executioners. In the words of the Sibylline Oracle already quoted:

> There shall come from the sky a certain exalted man who spreads his hands on the many-fruited tree, the noblest of Hebrews . . . (see above, p 82)

Confirmation of this connection with the Essene Teacher comes from the name given to the publican, Zacchaeus. It is the Greek form of the Aramaic word *zakkai* meaning 'righteous, innocent', a piece of bitter irony when applied to a member of this most detested profession among Jewish collaborators, but having a very special relevance to the Master's title, the Righteous Teacher, or, as it is more commonly rendered, the Teacher of Righteousness.

It has to be emphasised that in this kind of exegetical treatment of biblical texts, and its imaginative elaboration of single words and phrases into totally unrelated stories, we are not dealing with *allegory*, the portrayal of one subject under the guise of another. Obviously, Zacchaeus the publican does not represent the crucified Teacher; the town of Shechem was not a sycamore tree. But by word-play and literary allusion it is possible to find a reference to the one from the other, and, in the eyes of the ancient commentators, still obtain for their myths some scriptural support.

We need not doubt that, at the time when these stories were promulgated, there would still be in each messianist cell one or two Jewish teachers well versed in the Hebrew Scriptures, who would uncover the stories' inner meanings for the rest of the company. Later, when these interpreters died, or fell away from

200

their allegiance to the movement, the various literary allusions would be lost, leaving only the face-value of the stories to amuse, comfort, and often perplex their readers, or to be asserted by an authoritarian Church as representing doctrine and historical fact.

The question must arise in the mind of most modern Christian readers how far the uncovering of the many layers of meaning in the New Testament records detracts from the religious value of their traditional interpretation. The answer, in many cases, would probably be very little. The promulgation of the Joshua/Jesus myth had many purposes, as we have seen. One was certainly to convey to the scattered and hard-pressed messianist communities reminders of their secret teachings and rituals, pass-words, cultic titles, details of community organisation, and the like. The blatantly pro-Roman propaganda of many of the 'surface' narratives is not to be taken seriously, of course. In the circumstances obtaining in those days such tender regard for the imperialist power was hardly more than a sick joke, and had a first-century rabbi dared to shrug off a burning political issue of the day like the punitive tax system with a gentle 'render unto Caesar . . .' kind of response, he would have earned himself a Zealot dagger in his back inside three minutes, let alone three years of open ministry.

On the other hand, the high-toned moral teaching with which people today, Christian and non-Christian, equate the Faith, is probably authentic and, in its substance, early Essene in inspiration. However, the Teacher's contemporary followers would certainly not have extended their fraternal love, necessary for survival in the Secacah-type of closed community, to the world at large. They might learn to love their enemy and restrain their self-assertion for the sake of harmony under the stressful conditions of a joint ascetic existence, but they would have considered it a dereliction of duty not to hate sinners, that is, those who were not of their high calling, or who had rejected the Law as they interpreted it. That included Jews outside their circle, let alone gentiles who were altogether beyond the pale. Their antagonism was not a personal vindictiveness, or even an

201

emotional attitude, it was rather a theological position directed at the Jewish establishment who had failed in their duty to remain free of outside involvement with the gentile world, but had opted for some degree of collaboration with the occupying forces for the sake of political expediency. Above all, the Essene was taught to hate with all his heart the powers of Darkness which had cosmically contrived this rebellion against God by His own Chosen People.

After the disruption of the Jewish Revolt of AD 66–70, and the scattering of the Essene communities, a much broader-based movement took the place of the old closed establishments of Palestinian Essenism. It incorporated Jews and gentiles, Romans and Greeks, slaves and freemen. The salvation they all sought was a personal experience, offered by God freely through His grace, and not as a reward for obedience to the Jewish Law, and it was therefore open to all men. They looked back to the incarnation of a Redeemer who taught mankind the way back to the Fulness of God, and if, as time went on, he showed less and less resemblance to the real-life Essene Teacher of the Dead Sea community, and their ideas of salvation became far removed from the old messianic dream, the myths their story-tellers spun for the faithful could present the Saviour in a variety of different guises to suit every need in every time and place.

The biblical injunction to 'love thy neighbour as thyself' (Leviticus 19[18]) could, in those circumstances, be adapted to a more universal application, in theory if not in practice. Believers were no longer constrained by the Jewish Law or its exclusivity of obligations and promises. Indeed, some gnostics denied the need to be subject to any law at all, since any man-made institution could only be temporary and tainted with the corruption of all creation. Love, by which alone man's soul could be drawn to God, and through which like-minded believers might find harmony in their spiritual striving, was paramount. For God is love, and it is this Substance that man's soul shares with the divine.

Love, in the New Testament, is essentially a mystical quality,

202

not necessarily translated into practical morality. Again, it would have saved the Church a great deal of unnecessary theological hair-splitting, and confusion in its ethical teaching, if it had recognised the real nature of the Gospel myth it asserted was historical fact, and of the teachings it forced into the mould of a guide to day-to-day living. It was neither, even though there are elements of reality in its narratives, and of sublime moral sentiment in the sayings of the Master. Only when the multi-faceted nature of the New Testament writings is fully appreciated can we profit from those aspects that are relevant for our time, and feel free to discard those which are outmoded, or were never intended to be taken at their face value.

14
'And on this Rock . . .'

Between the first Joshua, son of Nun, and the Essene Teacher of Righteousness, the Bible knows of another Joshua, son of Jehozadak. His grandfather Seriah had been high priest at the time of the capture of Jerusalem in 586 BC, but had been executed by the Assyrian Nebuchadnezzar, and his son Jehozadak was carried captive to Babylon, where Joshua was probably born (II Kings 25^{18-21}; I Chronicles 6^{15}). After the Restoration, Joshua, as high priest, along with Zerubbabel, as governor, directed affairs at Jerusalem (Haggai 1; Zechariah 3). Joshua took a leading part in the erection of the altar of burnt-offering and laying the foundations of the new temple which was to replace the one destroyed by the Assyrian invaders.

Our present interest in this other Joshua/Jesus, the son of Jehozadak, is that he, and the lay administrator of the restored community, were regarded as messiahs. The prophet of the Restoration, Zechariah, refers to them as 'the anointed ones, who stand by the Lord of the whole earth' (4^{14}). Furthermore, the Essenes and their messianist·successors viewed several aspects of the leader's work, as seen through the visionary's eyes, as directly applicable to their own situation.

In leading the caravan of returned refugees back to Palestine after their exile in Mesopotamia, Joshua and Zerubbabel were re-enacting the roles of Joshua, son of Nun, and his companion

204

Eleazar, who led the Israelites across the Jordan when first the Chosen People entered the Holy Land. Bearing in mind the cyclical view of history held by the Essenes, it would have seemed fitting that the nation's leader in both cases should have been called Joshua/Jesus, meaning 'Yahweh/Jehovah saves'. So the book of Ecclesiasticus eulogises Joshua, son of Nun, as

> formed to be according to his name—a 'great salvation' for His chosen, to take vengeance upon the enemy, and to give an inheritance to Israel
>
> (46^1)

as the angel commanded Joseph, the Virgin Mary's espoused husband, to

> call his name Jesus, for he will save his people from their sins.
>
> (Matthew 1^{21})

Further reason for thinking of Joshua, son of Jehozadak, as Messiah, could be found by readers of the Greek Scriptures from the translators' rendering of a passage in Jeremiah's prophecy relating to a messianic scion of the House of David, a 'righteous Branch, or Shoot':

> I will raise up for David a righteous Branch, and he shall reign as king and deal wisely, and shall execute judgement and righteousness in the land. And this is the name by which he shall be called: 'Yahweh is (our) Righteousness.'
>
> (23^5)

The Greek translators transcribe this title as if it were a proper name, Yozedek, 'Yahweh-is-righteousness', the equivalent of the Hebrew name of Joshua's father, Jehozadak. Zechariah himself takes up the messianic theme from Jeremiah:

> Take from them silver and gold, and make a crown, and set it upon the head of Joshua, the son of Jehozadak, the high priest; and say to him, Thus says the Lord of Hosts: Behold the man whose name is the Branch . . .
>
> (6^{11-12})

205

We noted earlier how, in Zechariah's vision, he saw Joshua, 'a brand plucked from the fire' (3^2), stripped of his filthy garments and reclothed to shine, like the transfigured Jesus of the Gospels, as one possessed of the Spirit (see above, p 171). There follows the vision of the golden lampstands with seven lamps representing the seven 'eyes of the Lord which range through the whole earth' (4^{10}). This same imagery is borrowed by the New Testament apocalyptist to portray Jesus standing in the midst of seven golden lampstands, 'his head and his hair white as white wool, white as snow; his eyes were like a flame of fire, his feet like burnished bronze . . . and his face was like the sun shining in full strength'

(Revelation 1¹²⁻¹⁶).

Joshua, son of Jehozadak, is promised access to the councils of heaven if he fulfils his priestly function in the restored temple:

> And the angel of the Lord enjoined Joshua, Thus says the Lord of hosts: if you will walk in my ways and keep my charge, then you shall rule my house and have charge of my courts, and I will give you the right of access to those who are standing here.
>
> (Zechariah 3⁶⁻⁷)

That same privilege was claimed for the Essenes:

> And He has given to them (the Elect) an inheritance in the lot of the Holy Ones (the heavenly angels); and with the Sons of Heaven He has associated their assembly for a communal Council. Their assembly will be in the Holy Abode as an eternal Planting, during every epoch that may dawn.
>
> (Community Rule XI 7-9)

If, then, the earlier and later Essenes found in the Joshua/Jesus of the Restoration a prefiguration of their Teacher and Christ, so also they saw in the restored Israel the pattern for their own fellowship of the Elect. Zechariah envisaged Joshua's little company of returned exiles as a seven-faced Stone or Rock, and the New Testament takes over this figure to represent the missionary Church. The key passage in the prophetic oracle is:

> for behold, upon the Stone which I have set before Joshua, upon a single stone with seven facets [literally 'eyes'], I will engrave its inscription . . .

$$(3^9)$$

We find the idea of 'seven facets' echoed in the Scrolls, where a Psalm commentary speaks of the community consisting of 'seven divisions of the (returned) exiles of Israel'. Another scroll which deals with the great apocalyptic war against the forces of Darkness in the Last Days says that the army of the Sons of Light would be arranged in 'seven formations' (IX 4). The seven-fold division of Israel has its biblical precedent in the first Joshua's allocation of the conquered territories to the seven tribes 'whose inheritance had not yet been apportioned' (Joshua 18²).

The New Testament book of Revelation speaks of the 'seven churches that are in Asia', and combines the seven 'eyes' or facets of the Stone, the seven lampstands, being 'the eyes of the Lord, which range through the whole earth', with the 'seven eyes of the Lamb [that is, as we saw, Wisdom, the Word] of God', which are 'the seven spirits of God sent out unto all the earth' (5⁶). Each of the seven churches, bearing witness to the Word of God in the world, is under the care of a guardian angel, representing the seven planets, similarly ranging the heavens (1²⁰).

More familiar is the use made of this prophecy in the well-known saying in Matthew's Gospel about Peter as the Stone or Rock upon which the Church would be founded. Following on his acknowledgement that Jesus was indeed 'the Christ, the son of the living God', the Teacher congratulates the apostle, and says:

> . . . you are Peter [Greek *Petros*], and on this Rock [Greek *petra*] I will build my Church, and the gates of Hades shall not prevail against it. I will give you the keys of the kingdom of heaven, and

whatever you bind on earth shall be bound in heaven, and whatever you loose on earth shall be loosed in heaven.

(Matthew 16[18-19])

The play on the Greek words here, between *Petros* and *petra*, is obvious, and needs no further comment. The hidden play on Peter's title Cephas (John 1[42]) with the Aramaic word for 'stone', *kepha'*, points to another level of interpretation on which a small parchment scrap from the Partridge Cave, published here in the Appendix for the first time, throws a welcome new light. We shall look at this deeper level of understanding later (see below, p 211ff).

Peter's confession about Joshua/Jesus being the expected Christ, or Messiah, is in fulfilment of the promise made in the Zechariah oracle:

Hear now, O Joshua the high priest, you and your friends who sit before you, for they are men of good omen [or portents], for I am about to introduce my Servant, the Branch . . .

(3[8])

We have already seen that the Branch or Shoot of David was a title given to the coming Messiah. An Essene commentary on a text from the book of Samuel refers God's promise to David's scion that He would be 'his father, and he shall be my son' (II Samuel 7[14]; see above, p 103), to this Branch of David who, it says, 'will arise with the Interpreter of the Law' in the Last Days. Thus, Peter's confession that the Joshua/Jesus who stood before him was 'the Christ, the son of the living God' was in line with Essene expectations, and showed Peter to be a 'man of good omen' whose perspicacity had grasped the truth of the prophecy's fulfilment.

The prophet Isaiah also speaks of his followers as 'signs and portents in Israel' given him by God (8[18]), and the same phrase is used by the Essene Teacher of Righteousness to describe his disciples:

Thou hast made me a father to the sons of grace, and as a foster-father to the men of portent

(Hymns Col. VII; see above, p 103)

208

The secrecy enjoined upon the disciples by Jesus in the Matthew story stems from that same Isaiah prophecy:

Bind up the testimony, seal the preaching among my disciples
(8[16]; see above, p 79)

Then he strictly charged the disciples to tell no one that he was the Christ.

(Matthew 16[20])

A very great deal of interest has centred upon this story about Peter, his confession, and the keys of the Kingdom, not least because it has served as a proof-text to support the claims of the Roman Catholic Church to ecclesiastical primacy. Since it was believed that Peter had been the first Bishop of Rome, it followed that all those dignitaries who succeeded him to that office could similarly claim to share in Jesus's commendation of Peter's witness and his appointment as 'the Rock' on which the whole Church was founded.

It is no part of this present work to enter into the controversy over the apostolic succession, for, as by now must be clear, there is probably no historical basis to the incident recorded in the Gospel, nor indeed any reason to believe that there ever was one person called Simon Peter who held office in the messianist movement. We are much more concerned to know whence the various ingredients of the tale derived, and what was the real significance of this apostle's name and titles.

First, the forename Simon, common enough in the New Testament stories, is probably no more than a realisation in name form of the description given the followers of Joshua/Jesus and Isaiah as 'signs and portents'. The Greek name *Simon* looks very much like a play on another Greek word meaning 'sign', *semeion*. Be that as it may, much more interesting from our point of view is the 'nickname' given the first apostle by Jesus, Cephas:

One of the two who heard John speak, and followed him, was Andrew, Simon Peter's brother. He first found his brother

209

Simon, and said to him, We have found the Messiah (which means Christ). He brought him to Jesus. Jesus looked at him, and said, So you are Simon, the son of Jonah? You shall be called Cephas (which means Peter)

(John 1$^{40-42}$)

It is commonly accepted that there is here a concealed play on the Aramaic word for 'stone', *kepha*', hence the (strictly inaccurate) note by the Evangelist: 'which means Peter (*Petros*)'. But this now turns out to be only half the story. Far more significant is that the title Cephas, by which alone, incidentally, St Paul seems to know the leader of the Jerusalem community (the rare appearance in the epistles of the name Peter is generally held to be intrusive) was not a playful nickname given to one individual, but an Essene office of a very special nature. We read in the Scrolls of a number of such appointments, like Overseer, Inspector, and Instructor, day-to-day titles which were common enough to occasion no particular comment from outsiders. But, as has been said before, the Essenes did not commit their more esoteric activities to writing in a way that was open to every prying eye, for theirs was a closed society. A number of their texts were written in code, and elsewhere only the broadest hints are given to the casual reader of more cabalistic doctrines. It is to be expected, then, that titles related to the occult aspects of Essenism should be treated with reserve.

The Essenes were, by name and reputation, 'Physicians' (see above, p 12), and it would not be surprising if many of their secrets had to do with the healing arts. We have to remember that in those days healing was a religious exercise, since all sickness was attributed to the possession of the patient by demons. To recognise the cause of an illness was to unmask the offending spirit, and, by naming him, banish him from the body and mind of the afflicted person. There are plenty of instances of such exorcism recorded in the New Testament myth, the best known perhaps being that of the man with the unclean spirit who dwelt among the tombs in the country of the Gerasenes (Mark 5). Jesus commanded the demon to leave the man, and asked: 'What is your name?' The spirit replied that it was

210

'Legion' and asked that rather than be left to roam the world homeless, he should be given some other creature's body to possess.

The special gift of insight by which the physician might recognise the 'unclean spirit' also enabled him to prognosticate the course of the disease and its most efficacious treatment and likely outcome.

The stories we have in the New Testament myth reflect this special power, not only in Jesus himself, but specifically in Peter, demonstrating his role of inquirer, prognosticator, and healer. These tales, as we may now recognise, have as one of their main purposes the elucidation of the special title Cephas within the society. It appears in the heading of a short report from the Secacah library. The scrap of parchment on which it is written appears to be complete, and it takes its place among a number of 'secular' writings found in the Partridge Cave along with the more easily recognisable religious scrolls. Such few day-to-day documents remind us that the community by the Dead Sea was composed of real people who needed to supply themselves with food, keep their settlement buildings in repair, and heal their sick. This report seems to be a clinical record of treatments given by one of the commune's general practitioners, named Omriel. While the details are difficult to decipher, the general purport is clear, listing the names of patients, their ailments, and treatment provided. Of particular interest, apart from the official's title, is that the subjects of this particular physician's ministrations were 'guests'.

We know that the Essenes were so organised in their many urban communities to allow members to pass freely from place to place, assured always of finding rest and refreshment wherever there was a fellowship of believers to whom they might make themselves known. We might assume that the monastic centre of the Order at Secacah was a place of pilgrimage to which Essenes from elsewhere would come for instruction and spiritual refreshment, but it now appears from this document that it also served as a 'hospital' where the sick could receive treatment at expert hands.

The title of the official to whom (or possibly, by whom) the report was made is written in a somewhat disguised form, *Caiaphas*, transliterated into Hebrew letters from the Greek name familiar to us from the story of Jesus's arraignment before the supreme Jewish council, the Sanhedrin (John 11[49], 18[13ff, 24, 28]; Matthew 26[3, 57]; etc). Some texts of the New Testament transcribe the name *Caiphas*, and it now appears that the form *Cephas*, applied to the first apostle, was either a dialectal version of this variant, or adapted to fit the allusion to the Stone (Aramaic *kepha'*) as the foundation of the Church. In any case, there can be little doubt now that Caiaphas/Caiphas and Cephas are, in origin and meaning, one and the same, 'Investigator', 'Prognosticator'. It is a very special designation of one who is credited with particular insight and the gift of prophecy.

In fact, it has long been suggested that the name of the Sanhedrin's Caiaphas had this significance and derivation, and attention has been drawn to those stories in the New Testament myth in which this so-called 'high priest' acts as a prophet and interrogator:

> But one of them, Caiaphas, who was high priest that year, said to them, 'You know nothing at all; you do not understand that it is expedient for you that one man should die for the people, and that the whole nation should not perish.' He did not say this of his own accord, but being high priest that year he prophesied that Jesus should die for the nation.
>
> (John 11[49–51])

Much confusion has been caused by the term 'high priest' being applied to Caiaphas while Annas was still in that office (Luke 3[2]). In fact, it would seem that the name was given to an official of the hierarchy whose main task was to act as an Investigator, or Inquisitor, for the purpose of determining the religious credentials of messianic pretenders:

> The high priest then questioned Jesus about his disciples and his teaching . . .
>
> (John 18[19])

212

Within the Essene movement, the function of the Caiaphas/Cephas would seem to have been comparable with the Overseer of the community who was responsible for the welfare and spiritual direction of his flock. Scholars were quick to point out the resemblances between the pastoral and teaching functions of the Overseer and the Christian Bishop. He was required to interview all who sought permission to enter the sect, and to teach the Rule of the Community to all judged worthy of initiation. He not only acted as novice-master, but for the whole community was the final arbiter in matters of faith and conduct. In the words of one important scroll:

> He shall instruct the Congregation in the works of God . . . recount before them the events of eternity . . . love them as a father loves his children, bring back those of them who have strayed, like a shepherd his flock . . . He shall loosen all the fetters which bind them, that there be none in his congregation oppressed and broken. Everyone that enters his congregation he shall examine about his actions and his understanding, his strength, his courage, and his property, and shall assign him his place in the lot of Light. Let no member of the camp have authority to admit a person to the congregation against the camp Overseer's decision.
>
> (Damascus Document, Col. XIII)

The same document also makes it clear that if there has to be any trade with outsiders, it should be reported to the Overseer:

> Let no man make a partnership for trading purposes without informing the camp Overseer.

Similarly, any work or trading that is done for an outsider has to be paid for in cash. Clearly these rules could only relate to Essene 'camps', or urban settlements, more involved with the outside world than the monastic community by the Dead Sea, but the idea of reporting dealings with visitors, even other Essenes on pilgrimage receiving treatment in the Secacah clinic, may well lie behind the Partridge Cave parchment.

213

Josephus, the historian, in his description of the Essene organisation, says that 'they elect officers to attend to the interests of the community, the special services of each officer being determined by the whole body' (*War* II viii 3 § 123). It would appear that each establishment would have one overall Overseer, the 'Bishop' of the community, but that in a major Essene centre like Secacah, matters relating to the practice of medicine with all that this occult art involved, investigatory, therapeutic, and prognosticatory, came under the special care of the Caiaphas/Cephas.

The stories we have in the New Testament feature Peter as undertaking the more general functions of an Essene Overseer, combined with the specialised role of a Caiaphas/Cephas, examiner and physician. In the story of the acknowledgement of Jesus's messianic status, 'thou art the Christ', Peter acts like the high priest's inquisitor, pronouncing on the religious credentials of a pretender to that high office. On the other hand, when Jesus appoints him a 'binder and looser' of men's sins, he intends Peter to assume the function of an Essene Overseer who 'shall loosen all the fetters which bind them, that there be none in his congregation oppressed and broken'.

In the Scrolls, the Overseer has the responsibility for hearing complaints and adjudicating disputes between brethren:

> Every sin which a man commits against the Law, and which his companion witnesses, he being alone, if it is a capital matter he shall report it to the Overseer, rebuking him in his presence, and the Overseer shall record it against him in case he should commit it again before one man, and he should report it to the Overseer once more. Should he repeat it and be taken in the act before one man, his case shall be complete.
>
> And if there are two (witnesses), each testifying to a different matter, the man shall be excluded from the Purity provided that they are trustworthy, and that each informs the Overseer on the day that they witnessed (the offence). In matters of property, they shall accept two trustworthy witnesses and shall exclude (the culprit) from the Purity on the word of one witness alone.
>
> (Damascus Document, Col. IX)

And whoever has anything to say with regard to any suit or judgement, let him say it to the Overseer.

(Col. XIV)

Where the dispute is a personal disagreement, it was important to contain the matter to those primarily concerned, urging the principle that 'a soft answer turneth away wrath':

They shall rebuke one another in truth, humility, and charity. Let no man address his companion in anger, or ill-temper, or obduracy, or with envy prompted by the spirit of wickedness. Let him not hate him in the wickedness of an uncircumcised heart, but let him rebuke him on the very same day lest he incur guilt because of him. And, furthermore, let no man accuse his companion before the Congregation without having first admonished him in the presence of witnesses.

(Community Rule, Cols. V–VI)

So precisely the New Testament has the Teacher Jesus instruct his disciples:

If your brother sins against you, go and tell him his fault, between you and him alone. If he listens to you, you have gained your brother. If he does not listen, take one or two others along with you, that every word may be confirmed by the evidence of two or three witnesses. If he refuses to listen to them, tell it to the church; and if he refuses to listen even to the church, let him be to you as a gentile and a tax-collector

(Matthew 18$^{15-17}$)

—than which, despite the eager Zacchaeus in the Teacher's Tree, no human being could be lower.

That passage in the Gospel is followed by the 'binding and loosing' authority given to Peter otherwise in the Confession narrative, and it is Peter who is concerned to ascertain from Jesus further details on the extent to which one brother may be expected to forgive another (v 21).

As holder of the 'keys of the Kingdom', Peter is authorised, like the Essene Overseer, to 'admit a person to the congregation', and to 'assign him his place in the lot of Light'. After the self-destruction of the offending Judas, Peter organises the election of his successor: 'and they cast lots for them, and the lot fell on Matthias' (Acts 1^{26}).

The Overseer is required to act as a shepherd to his flock, loving them 'as a father loves his children', and Jesus similarly urges Peter to 'feed my lambs' and 'tend my sheep' (John 21^{15,16})

On a more mundane level, the Overseer of Property, the Bursar of the community, has charge of finances and regulates the acceptance and registration of personal property surrendered to the common fund by initiates. This money is returned if, after examination, the candidates fail to qualify for full membership of the Order. We may suppose that the Bursar is one of the more specialised offices held under the general direction of the congregation's superintending Overseer, but it is Peter again in the New Testament account who enacts the role in the salutary tale of Ananias and Sapphira. It will be recalled that 'they kept back some of the proceeds' of sale of property, 'and brought only a part and laid it at the apostles' feet'. Peter rebuked the pair for their deceit, and in effect condemns them both to death (Acts 5$^{1-11}$).

The urban Essenes also had a poor-fund:

> They shall place the earnings of at least two days out of every month into the hands of the Overseer and the Judges, and from it they shall give to the orphans, and succour the poor and needy, the aged sick, and the homeless, the captive taken by a foreign people, the virgin with no family, and the maid for whom no man accepts responsibility.
>
> (Damascus Document, Col. XIV)

The New Testament witnesses to a similar arrangement in the Church:

> There was not a needy person among them, for as many as were possessors of lands or houses sold them, and brought the proceeds of what was sold and laid it at the apostles' feet; and distribution was made to each as any had need.
>
> (Acts 5$^{34-35}$)

It seems from the story of Ananias and Sapphira, which follows directly in the narrative, that it is again Peter who has charge of the common fund. Also, it is Peter who speaks for Jesus and his small company when they are approached by the revenue collectors for their contribution to the Temple finances (Matthew 17$^{24-27}$). In point of fact, that incident probably had an ending other than the absurd tale of the shekel in the fish's mouth (v27), whose folkish origin and earthy humour has quite another relevance (see Allegro, *The Sacred Mushroom and the Cross*, p 44ff). As the present writer has shown from a document from the Partridge Cave first published in 1961, the Essenes believed it necessary to pay the half-shekel tribute to the Temple revenues only once in a man's lifetime, contrary to the custom of an annual levy in force in Jerusalem at that time. Doubtless some earlier form of the myth made some allusion to that special sectarian point of view and underlined Essene disagreement in the matter with the Jewish authorities.

The Overseer was required to have 'mastered all the secrets of men and the languages of all their clans' (Damascus Document, Col. XIV). When at Pentecost the Spirit gave the apostles this power of multilingualism, it is again Peter who acts as their spokesman in addressing the mixed assembly (Acts 2). In this sermon recounting the wonders God had performed through His Messiah Jesus, Peter takes on the Overseer's role of mentor to his flock, requiring him to

> instruct the Congregation in the works of God. He shall cause them to consider His mighty deeds and shall recount all the happenings of eternity to them.
>
> (Damascus Document, Col. XIII)

Thus Peter speaks to the company assembled:

> Men of Israel, hear these words: Jesus of Nazareth, a man attested to you by God with mighty works and wonders and signs which God did through him in your midst . . .
>
> (Acts 2^{22})

217

The Fourth Gospel relates a curious remark of Jesus about Peter's old age which can now be explained in the light of his portrayal in the role of the community's Overseer:

Truly, truly, I say to you, when you were young, you girded yourself and walked where you would; but when you are old, you will stretch out your hands, and another will gird you and carry you where you do not wish to go.

(John 21[18])

The Evangelist appends a note to the effect that Jesus was indicating the manner of Peter's death. But this explanation seems hardly justified by what appears, at first sight, to be no more than a casual observation on the helplessness of old age. However, the real significance of the remark becomes apparent when we learn from the Scrolls that the Essene Overseer

shall be from thirty to fifty years old.

(Damascus Document, Col. XIV)

The reason for the early retirement from active duty of this important official is that he needed to be at the very peak of his intellectual abilities. He must be able to command the respect of his flock and not be swayed in matters of order and discipline by his inability to fend for himself, dependant upon the ministrations of his subordinates. A similar age-limit applied also to 'the Priest who enrols the Congregation', who had to be 'from thirty to sixty years old, learned in the Book of Meditation and in all the judgements of the Law so as to pronounce them correctly' (Col. XIV). A fuller explanation of man's failing powers as he grows old is given elsewhere in this document:

No man over sixty shall hold office as Judge of the Congregation, for 'because man sinned, his days have been shortened, and in the heat of His anger against the inhabitants of the earth, God ordained that their understanding should depart even before their days are completed.'

(Col. X)

218

The secondary quotation comes from the apocryphal book of Jubilees (23^{11}), which, as we have seen, was favourite reading of the Essenes. We must presume that the Overseer of the camp needed to be more physically active than a Judge, as well as mentally alert, and so was not expected to be able to give of his best beyond the age of fifty, whereas the Judge could administer the Law satisfactorily for a further ten years. Jesus's observation to Peter on the feebleness of old age is just another instance of the use of myth to impart a piece of regulative instruction in narrative form, in a way that might be better remembered by the audience than if it were merely included in a list of rules such as we have in the Scrolls. The appended note in the text of the Fourth Gospel is clearly intrusive and irrelevant.

The stories about Peter in the New Testament, then, are in general illustrative of the functions of the Essene Overseer and have this as their main purpose. However, his more specialised role of a Cephas, requiring gifts beyond those of the overall administrator of the community, is demonstrated more particularly in the accounts of his healing activities. In the story of the curing of the lame man in 'that gate of the Temple which is called Beautiful', there is a direct allusion to the ability of the Caiaphas/Cephas to discern the spiritual condition of the patient:

And Peter directed his gaze at him, with John, and said, 'Look at us.' And he fixed his attention upon them, expecting to receive something from them . . .

(Acts 3$^{4-5}$)

It was this same perception that enabled Peter to look into the sinful hearts of Ananias and Sapphira when they withheld part of their donation to the common fund. Since it was believed that some past sin was responsible for the corruption of a man's body and his consequent susceptibility to the maleficent influences of demons, it was important for the faith-healer to lay bare the soul of his patient, and then to have the power to pronounce his sins forgiven. The restoration of the sinner to health

219

was proof of the physician's authority to 'loose and bind', such as Jesus granted Peter after the Confession, and as was required of the Essene Overseer:

> to loosen all the fetters which bind them, that there be none in his Congregation oppressed and broken.

Jesus heals the paralytic by forgiving him his sins, affirming that to say 'your sins are forgiven' was, to all intents and purposes, the equivalent of 'rise and walk' (Matthew 9).

Peter demonstrates his healing powers on a paralytic at Lydda by calling upon the all-powerful influence of the risen Jesus, but he is able to restore the saintly Dorcas to life simply by praying at her side and bidding her rise (Acts 9^{32-42}). So powerful was the aura of his presence that, following his discernment of Ananias's false declaration, the luckless miscreant and his wife fell dead, while the sick in Jerusalem's streets had but to fall under Peter's shadow to be cured (Acts 5^{15}).

We may now recognise also in the New Testament myth about Peter another very special title, closely associated in meaning with the occult Caiaphas/Cephas. In the Fourth Gospel, Peter is twice referred to by his patronymic, 'son of Jonah' (Greek *Iona*, sometimes incorrectly rendered 'John'). In Aramaic, the phrase would be *bar-yonah* (*bar*, 'son of'), but scholars have long suspected that the epithet was not a patronymic but rather some form of title. This we can now confirm is almost certainly the case: the word is to be understood as *baryona*, meaning 'divination', the revelation of the seer or recogniser of signs, of a root well-attested in western Semitic where it appears frequently in the form *baru*, 'diviner'. Interestingly, its origins connect it with another word meaning 'physician', directly cognate with the Aramaic root from which, as we saw, the name Essene, 'Physician', is derived. The practice of medicine was fundamentally a matter of recognising signs, not only of physical symptoms, but of the afflicted's spiritual condition, and this was precisely the main function of the Caiaphas/Cephas.

Thus, in this special divinatory sense, the followers of Joshua/Jesus were apprehenders of the 'revelation' or sign, the *baryona*, like the 'men of portent' who sat before Joshua, son of Jehozadak, and the Essene Teacher of Righteousness. They were able to grasp the true *gnosis*, Knowledge of God, revealed to them through their divinely appointed mentor, the messianic Redeemer.

To change the figure, this *baryona* was the 'Peter'-Rock upon which the Church of the Christ was founded. As the Scrolls say of the Essene community:

> It shall be a tried wall, that precious corner-stone whose foundations shall neither rock nor sway in their place,
>
> (Community Rule, Col. VIII)

quoting from Isaiah's prophecy:

> Behold, I am laying in Zion for a foundation
>   a stone, a tested stone,
> a precious corner-stone, a sure foundation.
>
> (28^{16})

The writer of the first epistle of Peter uses the same passage and figure:

> like living stones be yourselves built into a spiritual house, to be a holy priesthood,
>
> (2^5)

and the Essene Teacher of Righteousness extends the metaphor in one of his hymns:

> But I shall be as one who enters a fortified city,
>   as one who seeks refuge behind a high wall
>   awaiting deliverance;
> I will [lean on] Thy truth, O my God.
> For Thou layest the foundations on the Rock,
>   and the cross-beams by a true measure,
>   and the tried stone [. . .] .
>   by a [true] plumb-line,

221

to build a mighty [wall] which shall not sway;
    all who enter therein shall not falter,
for no enemy shall enter,
    since [its doors] shall be armoured gates barring entry;
    and its bars shall be strong and unbreakable.

                                        (Hymns, Col. VI)

A century or two later, the latter-day Essenes would wish to change this figure of the Rock as a refuge of defence to that of a more outward-looking Community of Saints, and a Gospel which would assault even the fastnesses of Hell itself:

on this Rock I will build my Church, and the gates of Hades shall not prevail against it.

15

Know Thyself

'Learn what you are and be such.'

> (Pindar, *Odes*, 5th century BC)

'Man is nothing else but what he makes of himself. Such is the first principle of existentialism.'

> (Jean-Paul Sartre, *Existentialism*, 1947)

The Jews loved God because He made the world; the gnostics loved God because they believed He didn't. The Great Church sought a compromise, and is still searching.

The writer of the Fourth Gospel might seem to have achieved the optimum solution when he wrote:

> For God so loved the world that he gave his only Son, that whoever believes in him should not perish but have eternal life. For God sent the Son into the world, not to condemn the world, but that the world might be saved through him.
>
> (John 3[16-17])

On the other hand, another Johannine work advises its readers:

> Do not love the world or the things in the world. If anyone loves the world, love for the Father is not in him. For all that is in the

life, is not of the Father but is of the world. And the world passes away, and the lust of it; but he who does the will of God abides for ever.

(I John 2$^{15\text{-}17}$)

St Paul believed the world well lost for the faith he had in the crucified Messiah, and longed for a new creation transformed by this saving grace:

Far be it from me to glory except in the cross of our Lord Jesus Christ, by which the world has been crucified to me, and I to the world. For neither circumcision counts for anything, nor uncircumcision, but a new creation.

(Galatians 6$^{14\text{-}15}$)

The fact is that whether the world seems good or bad depends very largely on one's personal situation at the time. Gnostic world-renouncing philosophy was born out of suffering and despair occasioned to a large degree by the political systems that dictated the lives of ordinary people in the Mediterranean world over the turn of the era. The more hopeless the prospect, the dimmer the attraction of material things. In those circumstances the religious man looks either to a cataclysmic reorientation in the world's affairs by a direct intervention from heaven—as the political revolutionary turns to a violent disruption of the social order—or he renounces any interest in things about him and seeks escape and self-fulfilment in some inner mystic experience.

Essenism, as we saw, moved between the last two positions: their messianism changed from a political restructuring of society based upon the hegemony of a Jewish hierarchy in world affairs, to an inner Kingdom of God available to believers of all races who had been elected to their high calling by God.

Nevertheless, the world and its demands could not be so easily discarded. Gnostic attitudes were divided between understanding redemption as a release from normal social conventions, offering complete freedom of thought and behaviour, and seeing it as an escape from desire for the world's pleasures

224

and opportunities, expressed in a life of extreme asceticism.

Adherents to the former group found their mythology in a Helen-type Great Mother who loves mankind and has shared their suffering at the hands of those hostile powers responsible for creating matter and restricting man's freedom for the sake of social order. The ascetics looked to an unknown Father-god whose redemptive purpose for man could only be fulfilled by escape from the snares of fleshly pursuits; they sought to direct their wills upon releasing the divine spark within them that it might merge once more with the Pleroma, or Fulness, from which it came.

The first faction hated the forces that had created the world, and despised the Jews who preached a creator-God and the primacy of the Law; the second tightened the chains of self-discipline about themselves and did their best to ignore creation and minimise its demands upon their bodies, while their souls roamed free.

The so-called Great Church fought its battles against its gnostic opponents within the messianist movement by adopting the Jewish stance of belief in a benign creator-God revealing Himself throughout Israel's history, and formally identifying their Redeemer with the Jewish Messiah. They thus sought to achieve the best of both attitudes; God so loved the world He had created that He thought it worth saving from the corruption that marred its perfection. But the adoption of this Jewish standpoint ran into immediate difficulties. First, it did not offer any satisfying solution to the age-old problem of the existence of evil in this God-created universe, a dilemma that exercised Jewish philosophers no less than pagans. Second, the Church's conception of the Messiah differed so radically from its Jewish prototype as to make it unacceptable to orthodox Jews, and only tolerable to those on the fringe of Judaism at the cost of a considerable dilution of their ethnic and religious exclusivism. The formation of a mythology to meet this situation posed correspondingly complex difficulties. The Essene Teacher of Righteousness on which any 'historic' myth had to be based could have little appeal to a largely gentile audience living in a

225

political and social situation poles apart from the legalistic commune eking out a precarious existence by the shores of the Dead Sea. The fundamentally anti-imperialist attitude of Essenes of the Teacher's time could hardly be expected to appeal to Greek and Roman believers, however persecuted they might be by the local civic and religious authorities. As for the Jews, early Essenes despised their fellow-religionists in Jerusalem, it is true, but for their lack of Jewishness rather than any ethnic exclusiveness.

The result was the promulgation of a myth which was full of compromises and illogicalities. Formally, the Christ/Messiah was based upon the Essene Teacher of Righteousness, and given his type-name 'Joshua/Jesus'. He was thus featured as the fulfilment of Jewish messianic hopes, the 'Branch' of David's royal line, and he followed the pattern of Israel's heroic lawgivers, Joshua son of Nun, and Joshua son of Jehozadak. In the manner of his martyrdom, he conformed to the Teacher's experience, but the full theological development of that propitiatory sacrifice could now be embodied in the myth and its attendant exposition. The words of the Nazarene Jesus reflected many of the teachings of the Essene Master, but were adapted to a more universal outlook and open social order. Embedded in the narrative were some of the more esoteric of Essene doctrines, titles, names, passwords, incantations, and so on, necessary for the maintenance of occult practices, but considered too dangerous for open publication. In the earlier restricted situation, such a risky promulgation of secret lore would not have been necessary, since its transmission was strictly limited to oral teaching and protected from betrayal by awful oaths.

But the overall tenor of the narrative about this latter-day 'Joshua/Jesus' and his followers was quite unrealistic on many counts. Its timetable had been determined according to an eschatological scheme based on an Essene chronology of the 'Last Days'. Whatever versions of the myth were in circulation before AD 70, the fall of the Temple was thereafter pivotal in any estimate of the approach of the millennium, and if the Redeemer's appearance on earth was intended to be a sign of

226

the imminence of that event, then the Joshua/Jesus of the Gospels had to be placed in the immediate run-up to the end of the epoch. More precisely, an important Essene tradition stated that:

> from the day the Teacher of the Community died until the end of all the men of war who had deserted to the Man of Lies there shall pass about forty years.
>
> (Damascus Document, Col. XX 14–15)

The 'about forty years' is a reflection of the 'thirty-eight years' that it took the entire generation of the 'men of war' to perish from the camp during the desert wanderings of the Israelites under Moses, because they had doubted the promise to bring them in safety to the land flowing with milk and honey (Deuteronomy 2^{14}). Reckoning back from the apocalyptic event of the destruction of the Temple, the myth-makers fastened upon AD 30 for the crucifixion of their latter-day Joshua/Jesus, during the procuratorship of Pontius Pilate. The date of the Messiah's birth had then to fall thirty years before that since, as we have seen, it was a rule that the Essene administrative leaders should not be younger than that when they took office. So the Gospel of Luke records

Jesus, when he began his ministry, was about thirty years of age.

(3^{23})

All we know about this period ill-accords with the kind of pro-Roman attitude adopted by this 'low-profile' Messiah of the Gospel myth, or at least with its being tolerated by the fiercely anti-imperialist factions of the Jewish underground movements active at that time, the 'men of war' of the myth-maker chronologists. As has been said, this Nazarene teacher could not have survived three minutes in that tense situation in the capital city, let alone three years.

Even more unrealistic are the details of Jewish institutions and their autonomy under the Roman administration, as has

been often enough pointed out in connection with Jesus's trial
and condemnation, and the part played by the officers of the
Sanhedrin. But in general the portrayal of 'the Jews' as the
main enemy of the little group of Galilean fishermen and their
leader, particularly in the Fourth Gospel, might well make the
unfamiliar reader wonder about the ethnic affiliation of the
story's chief characters if they were not Jews themselves.
Serious studies on the New Testament and its historical situation abound with such instances of incongruity and anach-
ronisms, which cannot all be ascribed to the lapse of time
between the supposed events and their narration in literary
form.

Such aberrations would not have worried most messianist
factions, however. The gnostics did not look for historical accuracy in their myths; they were reckoned to have a far more
serious purpose in the purveying of spiritual truths. What
might have concerned some of them far more was the impression conveyed by many of the stories about the Redeemer
that he seemed at home in the world, and even at times to revel
in its pleasures, not to say extravagances, as when he readily
accepts invitations to dine with rich men in their homes.

In fact, the New Testament presents a kind of compromise
between the old Jewish belief in the creator-God making a
world that He considered 'good' (Genesis 1) and worthy of
redemption, and the less optimistic estimate of gnostic Essenism that creation was evil and worthy only of condemnation.
Both points of view are discernible in the New Testament writings, even within the Pauline corpus where there is a clear shift
of opinion as the expected millennium failed to appear. The history of the Great Church shows the same kind of ambivalence
as it sought to establish its position in the world of power politics, while at the same time appreciating the standpoint of those
believers who spurned the trappings of authority and sought
only the liberty of the spirit. The internal struggle did not end
with the eradication of the gnostic 'heretics' and the establishment of the canon and a uniformity of doctrine. Neither
straitjacket could be completely effective in a movement

founded on the redemption of the individual believer through faith in a personal Saviour. The so-called Apocrypha of non-canonical traditions enjoyed a wide appreciation long after the great councils of the Church had decided which writings were to be considered authoritative for faith and conduct, and which were not. The Reformation when it came was merely the culmination of a spiritual dissatisfaction with authoritarian insensitivity to individual aspirations that had been there from the beginning and were fundamental to the Faith.

More recently, the Church has been bewildered by the multiplicity of demands made upon her resources, and seems unsure whether she should be a soup-kitchen for the underprivileged world, a political agency for social revolution, or should concentrate her energies and limited means on being a medium of divine grace in affairs of the spirit. Along with a growing impatience of doctrinal differences in her ranks, and calls for centralisation of her witness in the world, there persists the need for individuality in worship and an awareness of the insufficiency of traditional forms of religious expression to serve different cultures.

This clamour for a more unified voice in human affairs has also coincided with a growing scepticism of the Church's claims to be the final arbiter in moral judgements. Always by nature conservative in her attitudes, resisting change until even her prelates can no longer withstand the pressures of social progress, the last few decades have seen a technological transformation that has swept away almost overnight the ignorance and superstition which has often served to buttress the Church's moral positions. The invention of the contraceptive pill is a case in point.

Even more serious, the Church's long insistence upon the verbal inspiration, and thus incontrovertibility, of the Scriptures has been forced to give way before the discovery of new documentary evidence, and has been weakened even more through public impatience with barriers of bigotry and obscurantism which have helped for so long to protect the Faith from rational criticism.

229

It is thus only within the last century or so that the insistence of the Great Church upon the historicity of the Joshua/Jesus myth, which played so large a part in the fight to obtain some uniformity of belief and practice in a fragmented movement, has begun to move against the Establishment's best interests. When all men seemed to believe every word of the Gospel stories, the Church's ability to lay claim to 'authentic' relics of the Master's presence on earth, and to build her monuments over the sites he had sanctified by his presence, served to strengthen men's belief in the Church's authority and the truth of her witness. Unlike other eastern faiths, Christianity could 'prove' by such relics the validity of its claim that God had entered history in the person of His Son, and had 'so loved the world' that He had given of His own Substance that He might redeem mankind.

The gnostics may have been sceptical of the Great Church's historical claims, but their dissenting voice was stifled by their defeat in the battle for survival. The question may now be asked, however, did they really lose that struggle? Many died, certainly, their books were burned, and those who managed to escape the persecutions fled into the desert or were forced into fearful concealment. But the individuality they sought in their relationship with God remained an essential part of the Christian religion, not only in the monasteries and anchorites' cells, but in those persistent 'heresies' which have periodically forced their attentions upon the ecclesiastical hierarchy and suffered from its vengeful fury. But the Catharists and the Waldensians of the Middle Ages have no lack of successors in the modern world of so-called 'fringe' Christianity. The present ecumenical movement may achieve some success in the realm of Church administration, but there is little prospect that it will gather together into one spiritual fold all those believers who persist in clinging to their right to 'do their own thing' in belief and practice. For religion, like human love, is at heart an affair of sentiment and personal commitment, a relationship between the believer and his God. At its deepest and most satisfying level there is no room for the priestly intermediary.

Outside the pale of deistic religion, gnosticism has found new expression in the philosophy of existentialism, and has formulated a new mythology. The main thesis of this way of thinking is that man is an individual and has freedom of will to choose for himself. It is a revolt against the determinist philosophy of life which says that our every action and thought is ordered for us by our environment and our social situation and responsibilities. To be himself, man must first know himself. An Arabian gnostic philosopher named Monoimus is cited by the third-century Church Father Hippolytus as saying:

> Abandon the search for God and the creation and other matters of a similar sort. Look for him by taking yourself as the starting point. Learn who it is who within you makes everything his own and says, 'My God, my mind, my thought, my soul, my body.' Learn the sources of sorrow, joy, love, hate. Learn how it happens that one watches without willing, rests without willing, becomes angry without willing, loves without willing. If you carefully investigate these matters you will find him in yourself.
>
> (*Refutation of all Heresies*, VIII 15 1–2)

R. M. Grant, quoting this passage, calls gnosticism 'a passionate subjectivity' (*Gnosticism and Early Christianity*, 1959, p 9), which could well be applied to existentialism. Although Kierkegaard, in the first half of the last century, was primarily concerned with the agonising decisions faced by the intelligent believer in making that necessary leap of blind faith, his assertion that '[the search for] truth is subjectivity' would find support in non-religious existentialist thinking. For Kierkegaard it seemed a terrible responsibility for a Christian to make a choice involving the fate of his immortal soul when his experience is limited to so short a life-span. Unlike moral choices, when a man may decide to act as he would wish other men to do in like circumstances, to make a conscious decision for Christ when he has no means of knowing the outcome of his decision until it is too late, seemed to this Danish philosopher to make our freedom of will a source of anguish. Like the early gnostic, he could not depend on rational 'proof' for the existence

231

of God or the redemption of Christ; truth and knowledge lay within him, and he must make his decision on the basis of that inner perception alone. 'Truth is subjectivity' because everything one does, including the search for objective reality, receives its value from the way in which it is willed and decided by the subject.

Similarly, the existentialist rejects the Hegelian conviction that the world is a rational system, comprehensible through the intelligence in all its parts, since man cannot possibly know enough about its workings from his miserably limited experience in time and space. None of us can know his place, nor have his duty proved to him, but each must take his courage in his hands and choose as best he can.

Kierkegaard's successors in a non-religious context similarly stress the importance of the individual in matters of personal choice, and believe that our individuality is at risk, not nowadays from the need to conform to the demands of Christian 'respectability', but from the inroads made upon the personality by our highly organised technological society. The fullest exponent of this philosophy in our century, Karl Jaspers, speaks of 'transcendence' in terms remarkably reminiscent of the gnostics' 'Unknown God': the very incompleteness of our knowledge and the limitations of our power point to some unknown and unknowable source of being (*Philosophie*, iii, 1932). Unlike the Jewish Talmudist, or 'fundamentalist' Christian, the old-time Bible-thumper, we cannot seek in any traditional revelation a detailed code of rules for conduct; we are in the last resort thrown back upon our own inadequate selves for our authority.

More recent, and better known, is the work of Jean-Paul Sartre, whose 'first principle of existentialism' is quoted at the head of this chapter: 'Man is nothing else but what he makes of himself.' Sartre, like his great Christian predecessor Kierkegaard, was conscious of the agony imposed upon man by free will: 'man is condemned to be free'; his life is an 'ineffective passion'.

The anti-rationalism of the existentialist is a reaction to the

232

over-confidence of the optimists who believe that everything can be explained, and ultimately controlled, by man's reason. The wonderful scientific discoveries of the nineteenth century seemed to promise an unfaltering advance in prosperity and human happiness as part of the newly expounded process of evolution in nature. To a mankind that could invent the steam-engine and lay bare the secrets of the atom, there could be no obstacle to self-fulfilment. The Great War and the subsequent depression checked that optimism, but if the Second World War increased man's scepticism of his moral pre-eminence, the new technology it stimulated, and which in subsequent years has transformed our lives in an Industrial Revolution of far greater significance than anything experienced in the nineteenth century, has increased our awareness of man's power to order his universe. Our young people might well be excused for believing in man's technical omnipotence, even though they might increasingly doubt the competence of our politicians to control its effects. Serious newspapers which would scorn to publish the predictions of Old Moore's Almanack, will unhesitatingly give space to those prophets of our Business Schools from whose hardly less speculative forecasts they will extrapolate some bare percentage figure for the sake of supporting their own gloomy—or exuberant—estimate of the current economic position of the country and its reflection for good or ill on the government in power. Thinking men will treat such predictions more sceptically, and search them carefully for those inevitable factors headed 'Likely Trends', or watch for that deadly particle of qualification, 'if . . .'. They might then turn with more confidence back to Old Moore, or his daily counterpart, the newspaper astrologer.

The gnostic philosphers cared little for the economic state of the world, deeming it but the mischievous plaything of an irresponsible Creator whose purpose was only to corrupt and destroy. The gnostic's existentialist successor simply doubts the forecasts of the statisticians for the reason that he has no confidence in man's ability to judge the actions of free men, now or in the future.

233

This lack of predictability in human actions rules out for him the possibility of ever achieving a social harmony in the world, or perfectibility in man. In this respect, at least, the gnostic was the more optimistic. His hope lay in his own salvation. Through his faith in his Redeemer, whether that be Helen, Simon, or Joshua/Jesus, he believed that the divine spark which is in every man could be released to rejoin the Pleroma from which it emanated. For that hope he was prepared to share the suffering of his Lord, and with his apostolic mentor proudly proclaim that he would 'glory in the Cross . . . by which the world has been crucified to me and I to the world' (Galatians 6^{14}).

APPENDIX 1
4Q Therapeia

The document provisionally named here 4Q Therapeia forms part of the cache discovered in the Fourth Cave, Qumran, in 1952, and purchased subsequently from the Bedouin. It is a small, roughly triangular, piece of leather or parchment, measuring about 77mm wide by between 35mm and 58mm deep. The material is fairly coarse, rough-faced, and there has been some rubbing on the corrugated surface, as well as a few worm-holes. The worst defacement of writing has taken place over the first three lines of script. The document, a sort of 'tag', seems otherwise complete. Skin-colour varies from fawn to dark brown, with a patch of particularly bad staining in the middle of the left-hand side (Plates I and II).

The script may be adjudged fairly late for the Qumran material. The language is an extraordinary mixture of transliterated Greek, Aramaic, and a grammatically irregular Hebrew, giving the inescapable impression of deliberate obscurantism, not entirely unfamiliar in medical writing.

TEXT

TRANSCRIPTION
Conventional symbols are used here for the transliteration of Semitic characters, and the practice of indicating possibilities

and probabilities in the reading of doubtful characters by circles and dots respectively over the letters is that employed in editions of the Qumran texts published in the series *Discoveries in the Judaean Desert of Jordan*. Similarly, as there, a row of three dots within square brackets represents an indeterminate number of missing characters, while a small circle on the line indicates a single missing letter.

1	lk'ps 'ṣgdḥw [. . .] šẙḳl
2	sḥrh 'ỉẙṩ' 'ḳsṅẇṡ tṙṡẙ
3	tyrqwṡ [. . .]' by'₀ [. . .]q
4	šdḥsw mgns mlkyh mnws
5	mḥtyš mqlyḥ mpybšt
6	bġlgws bnwbn bsry gdy
7	dlwy hlkws hrqnws yny w
8	ytr'ytyšyl' zwḥlwlp
8ᵃ	yṭrws ysy
9	'qwl' zkry'l yṅy
10	'ly 'dpy
10ᵃ	'mry'l qp[. . .]

TRANSLATION

¹The report of the Caiaphas (*Qayyᵉphā'*), being an account of ²his rounds of the afflicted (among) the guests: supplies of ³medicines [. . .]

[. . .] swelling [. . .] ⁴which distended him through a kind of flabbiness due to wasting:—⁵a braying of stalks of 'Mephibo-sheth' ⁶in the smegma (found) in the sheaths of the penes of kids.

⁷The ulcer of Hyrcanus Yannai was drawn and ⁸the secretions pertaining to it that were discharging; also for ⁸ᵃPeter Yosai;

⁹Colic – Zachariel Yannai;

¹⁰Eli is witness, dictated by ¹⁰ᵃOmriel, QP (*Qayyᵉphā'*?)

NOTES

Line 1 *l* 'to', or more probably from context, 'by, from', ie *lamedh auctoris*: Gesenius *Hebrew Grammar*²⁸, ed. Kautzsch, tr. A. E. Cowley, 1910 (G-K) § 129ᶜ.

236

k'ps, 'Caiaphas'. The first letter looks more like *beth*, but compare the form of the clear *kaph* in *zkry'l* in 1.9; the upright here has been foreshortened by a crease in the skin, seen clearly in the deformation of the first letter, *'ayin*, of the marginal 1.10[a].

k'ps seems best explained as a transliteration of the Greek name/title Καϊάφας; the medial *'ayin* serving as a vocalic hiatus between the diphthong and the following *a*: cp. *ṭrp'yq'* = τροπαϊακά (S. Krauss *Griechische und lateinische Lehnwörter*, i, 1898, §23 B3; §151; for an equivalent use of *'ayin*, cp. the Arabic sign for *hamza*: W. Wright, *Grammar of the Arabic Language*, i, 1896, p.17[A]).

Transliteration from Greek letters to Semitic is a common feature of this text, but for the practice of a double shift of Semitic to Greek and back to Semitic, cp. *šm'wn* → Σίμων → *symwn*, 'Simon' (Krauss i §106).

For the title *haq-qayyāph* (*qayyᵉphā*), v. M. Par. 3[5] (Maas. 52[a]): Danby *Mishnah*, 1933, p.700 n.7; G. Dalman, *Grammatik des Judisch-Palästinischen Aramaisch*, 1905 (repr. 1960), p.161 n.2; Derenbourg, *Essai sur l'Histoire et la Géographie de la Palestine*, I, 1867, p.215 n.2; E. Schürer, *History of the Jewish People*, II i p.199 n.550; Nestle *Expository Times* x 130; *Zeitschr. f. wissenschaftliche Theologie* 40, 149. Comparison is usually made with the Arabic *qāfa* I and V, 'follow; examine, investigate' (II 'beg': cp. Dozy ii 433), and in particular with the participle, *qā'if*[un], 'prognosticator; physiognomist' (de Lagarde, *Übersicht* 97; cp. Wellhausen *Skizzen* III 152), v. Levy, *Neuhebr. u. Chald. W.B.* iv, 299[b]).

The sense of 'scrutiny' is extended to 'believe to be genuine, trustworthy; find acceptable' as in Accad. *qāpu*, actively to 'entrust someone with something' (I[2] 'entrust, convince') and so to the official designation *qēpu*, 'one appointed, governor, administration' (Bezold *Babyl.-Assyr. Gl.*, 1926, sv. *q'p*, p.241[a]; for form, cp. Von Soden *Grundriss d. Akkadische Grammatik*, 1952, §104[h,j]). Cp. BH *pqd*, 'attend, visit, appoint', and *pāqîd*.

'ṣgdhw, 'his message, report'. Despite the rubbed surface of the

237

skin and part obliteration of the text, the word seems certain. Cp. Pers. *iskudār*, 'courier, postman'; also 'postman's bag' (Stiengass *Pers.-Eng. Dict.* p.59[a]). In Aramaic the word is borrowed as *'yzgd*, *'ys-*, etc.; Syr. *'izgadā'*; *'izgadûthā'*, 'message' (Payne-Smith, *Thesaurus*, 1879–1901 (P-S) 104). The ending here, *-hw*, is presumably an Aram. 3 p.s. masc. suffix.

šykl, 'being an account of': possibly the rel. part. *š(y)* as elsewhere with a form of *kwl* 'measure'.

Line 2   šḥrh, 'his (?) rounds', i.e. BH *šḥr*, 'go around', with an Aram. suffix; cp. BH *saḥar*, 'traffic', and *sᵉḥōrah* 'merchandise'.

'lyṣ', 'afflicted'. The upright of the *lamedh* has been lost in a crack in the skin, and the horizontal has been deflected in the consequent warping. The penultimate letter could be a *pē*, but if the previous letter is correctly read as *yodh*, the space between it and the following sign would leave room for *ṣadē*: cp. this letter immediately above, in 1.1. If the reading is correct, cp. Syr. *'alîṣā'*, 'straitened' (of illness, hunger) (P-S 218)

'ksnws, 'stranger', transliterated from ξένος with the Greek termination; otherwise found as *'ksn'y*, 'stranger, guest, lodger' (Krauss ii (1899) §48; P-S 188).

trsy, 'supplies': the tops of all the letters of this word have been rubbed away. If a true reading, cp. Syr. *trsy* (P-S 4501: Taphel of *rsy*, 'nourish, support, rear'), *thûrᵉsāyā,*' *tharsîthā'*, 'nourishment, supplies' = τροφή (P-S 4502).

Line 3   tyrqws, 'remedies, medicines': cp. Aram. *tyryq*, Syr. *thûrîqā'*, *theryaqē'*, etc. = Θηριακή (Krauss ii §588; P-S 4414, 4429, 4500); prop. Θηριακός, 'concerning venomous beasts', thus 'antidotes' = φάρμακον, 'medicine, drug, remedy'.

by'ₒ: cp. Aram. *bw''*, 'swelling, abcess'.

Line 4   šdḥsw: *dḥs* NH, Aram. 'press, squeeze'; *dᵉḥāsah*, 'squeezing' (on abdomen), Yeb. 42[a].

m-gns, 'from a kind of'; l.w. as in Syr. = γένος 'order, sort, kind'.

mlkyh, for more usual *mlky'*, 'illness, depression', l.w. = μαλακία (Krauss ii §340).

238

m-nws, 'from wasting', *nss*, 'weak, sick'; Syr. *nas, nasîs*, 'infirm, sickly' (P-S 2387ff.); but cp. νόσος, 'sickness, disease' (LXX = *ḥly*).

Line 5 mḥtyš for *mktš, makhtēš*, 'mortar': *ktš*, 'pound, bray', so here 'braying'.

m-qlyḥ, 'of stalks', as in NH *qᵉliḥôth*, usu. NH *qelaḥ*, Aram. *qilḥā'*.

mpybšt, 'Mephibosheth': a folk-name for a drug plant? Perhaps of significance that the biblical Mephibosheth was afflicted with lameness: II Sam. 9¹³.

Line 6 b-glgws, 'milky fluid; smegma ?'; translit. fr. γλάγος (poetic form fr. gen. γάλακτος, nom. γάλα; γλαγάω, 'be milky, juicy'; for use of gen. in forming loan-words, see Krauss i §95).

b-nwbn, erroneously written for *zwbn* ? – *zubbān*, 'sheath of penis' (MBekh, 6⁵: Jastrow *Dict*. i 383: fr. *znb*, 'tail; penis'); otherwise BH *nwb, nyb*, 'fruit' (i.e. 'sappy': G. R. Driver, *Welt d. Orients* i (1950) 406–7).

bsry, 'penes of': Aram. *bsr* = Heb. *bśr*, 'flesh; (euphem.) penis'.

Line 7 dlyw, for *dlwy* ? As elsewhere in this document, there is some confusion between *yodh* and *wāw*: read as pass. part. fr. *dlh*, 'draw', although the verb is prop. used of 'drawing water', ie 'lift up', cp. the phonetically related *tlh*, 'hang'.

hlkws, translit. fr. ἕλκος, 'festering wound, ulcer'; cp. Targ. Aram. *halkᵉšîš*, -*šôš*, 'swelling, bruise, sore': Jastrow 353ᵇ; Krauss ii §229ᵃ = ἕλχωσις, 'ulceration' (in LXX = *šᵉḥîn*, 'boil'; cp. the Qumran 'Prayer of Nabonidus', where the king is cured by a Jewish *gāzîr* of his *šᵉḥîn*: J. T. Milik, *Rev. Bib*. LXIII (1956) 407–15).

hrqnws = Ὑρκανός, 'Hyrcanus' (Krauss ii § 225).

yny – w, ie. 'Yannai' and closely conjoined conj., rather than *ynyy* (= *yn'y*); a customary abbrev. for *Yôḥānān*, 'John'.

Line 8 (w-)ytr'ytyšyl': 'and the secretions pertaining to it';

cp. Syr. *yathîrā'îth, yathîrûthā'*, 'excess' – of the body, i.e. secretions, excrement, etc: P-S 1651f. For *šy = še*, rel. pron., cp. 3Q 15 (the Copper Scroll) IX 14, X 5: Allegro *Treasure of the Copper Scroll*, 1960, pp. 49, 51, 158 n.220, 161 n.234; Milik, *DJD* III pp.294, 295.

zwḥl, 'discharging': *zḥl*, 'run, flow' (NH, Aram.). The following conjunction and start of *lpytrws*, 'for Petros' was written without a break, but the roughness of the skin surface necessitated running over to the next line.

Line 8[a] 'and for Petros (Peter) Yose'; for the name, translit. from Πέτρος, 'Peter', cp. Jer. MKet. III 82[d]: *ywsy br pytrws* (Jastrow 1162[a]).

Line 9 '*qwl*': '*ql*, 'twist', cp. Syr. '*eqālā*', 'griping pain in bowels'. Another possibility here is to read a proper name Aquila, elsewhere written '*qyls*.

The register of lines in this last section is unclear, due mainly to a squeezing up of the overrun of 1.8 and the following words to avoid the rough patch of skin at the bottom of the tag.

zkry'l yny: The middle letter of Zachariel's second name is almost obliterated by a worm-hole.

Line 10 '*d*, 'witness', although the roughly written *daleth* could possibly be read as *resh*, but the skin surface is rough at this point. The following word *py* was written on without an intervening space, but the group may perhaps be read as '*rpw*, 'the back of his neck', despite the clear *yodh* at the end, see above on 1.7.

Line 10[a] shortage of usable skin has forced the scribe to write the signature in the right-hand margin. A narrow strip from the surface of the parchment has removed with it part of the *pē* following *qōph*, and possibly one or two further letters. It is suggested, however, that *qp*, or possibly *qp'*, was intended as a cryptic abbreviation of *Qayyephā'*: see above on *lk'ps* in the first line.

Appendix 2

Recently, a "secret gospel" has come to light which bears interestingly on the anointing ritual discussed in Chapter 8. It was discovered by Professor Morton Smith when reading some old manuscripts in the ancient monastery of Mar Saba in the Judaean Wilderness. In his book *The Secret Gospel* (1974), he records how he recognized the transcript of a hitherto unknown letter from the second-century Church Father Clement of Alexandria. The purpose of the letter was to attack the teachings of one of the most important gnostic groups, the Carpocratians, who flourished at least as early as the second century. In the course of his writing, Clement reveals the contents of what appears to have been an original sequence concerning the young rich man mentioned in Mark's Gospel, and which must have been purged from the version that was allowed to circulate among the faithful. Further references also make it seem that Jesus was understood to have indulged in possibly homosexual practices concerned with a particular form of baptism. These missing elements in the usual form of Mark, although well known apparently in the Church's inner circles, were part of secret traditions not thought suitable for general reading. It seems that Clement's unknown correspondent had been somewhat taken aback to be confronted by "heretics" who knew of a version of Mark which appeared to be genuine, but of which he knew nothing. Clement acknowledges its authenticity and says that it was, indeed, part of an enlarged version of the Second Gospel, written by Mark, who had "left it to the church in Alexandria where it is even now most carefully guarded, being read only to those who are being initiated into the great mysteries." It would seem that some official of the church there had "leaked" its contents to Carpocrates. Nevertheless, Clement warns his reader, "one must never give way, nor . . . should one concede that the secret gospel is by Mark, but should deny it on oath. For," the bishop admits frankly, "not everything that is true needs necessarily to be divulged to all men . . ."

Putting the pieces together, Professor Smith has shown that the story of the raising of Lazarus, found only in the Fourth Gospel, really related to the rich young man whom Jesus had sent away disquieted (Mark 10$^{17-23}$). It was he whom the Master raised from the dead:

> And Jesus, being angered, went off with her into the garden where the tomb was. And straightway, a great cry was heard from the tomb. And going near, Jesus rolled away the stone from the door of the tomb. And straightway, going in where the youth was, he stretched forth his hand. But the youth, looking upon him, loved him, and began to beseech him that he might continue with him. And going out of the tomb, they came into the youth's house, for he was rich. And after six days, Jesus told him what to do. In the evening, the youth came to him, wearing a linen robe over his naked body. And he remained with him that night, for Jesus taught him the mystery of the Kingdom of God. . . .

Clement denies that the phrase "naked man to naked man" was in the original secret gospel, as the Carpocratians had apparently affirmed to the anxious inquirer.

Bearing in mind that only Mark has that curious story about "a young man wearing a linen cloth over his naked body" in the Garden of the Agony (14$^{51-52}$), Smith connects the incident with the earlier nocturnal initiation story of the secret gospel and gives good reason to believe that at least one element of the Church preserved a tradition that the Master "baptized" initiates himself, always at night, and with some kind of erotic ritual. That being so, we may connect the semen-anointing of the gnostics' "Father-son/youth" ceremony with this initiatory

242

"baptism," and suspect that the "water" used was, in fact, the seminal fluid procured during the Elect's sexual activities. As far as the Marcan story of the raising of the dead is concerned, it was used merely to illustrate in mythical terms, possibly for recitation during the ceremony, the life-giving nature of the anointing, or "baptism," liking it to the raising of one spiritually dead into everlasting life.

INDEX

Numbers in *italic* type indicate maps.

245

bar-yonah, baryonah, 220; *see also* Jonah
bastards, 37ff
Belial, 12, 32; *see also* Devil
Belladonna, 148
Bemeselis, 56; *see also* Mesillah
Benjamin, 69
Bethany, 161
Bethlehem, *11*, 30, *71*, 161
Bethshean (Scythopolis), *11*, 72
Bible translations, modern, 151
Biblical exegesis, 18, 37, 47, 79, 137ff, 139,
    149-51, 161, 169ff, 184, 193, 197-201
bigotry, 192, 229
Bishop, 18, 66, 209, 213, 214
blessings and curses, 21, 74, 77, 79
Boanerges ('Sons of Thunder'), 160
Boguet, Henry, 147ff
Bogomils (Bougres, Bulgarians, *bougre* 'heretic',
    buggery), 130
Branch, The, *see* Shoot
bread, and wine, 70, 120ff; of heaven, life, 184
bride (of God, Christ), 105ff, 162, 168ff, 173, 174ff
Bursar (Essene), 216

Caesarea, 20, 32
Caiaphas, Caiphas, 212-14, 220, 236, 237, 240
calendar, 34, 185f
Callirrhoe, 67
camps, 31, 80, 100, 121, 213, 219, 227
Cana, 161
Canaan, 72, 74, 124, 154, 156, 169, 190
cannibalism, 123
canon, biblical, 52, 132ff, 139, 192, 228
Carthage, 130
Cassia, 124
Castor and Pollux (Dioskuroi), 172
Catharists *(Katharoi)*, 130, 134, 230
caves, 10, 18, 23, *25*, 26, 30, 33, 78, 81, 101, 109
cedar, oil of, 78
celibacy, 10, 110, 114-19
Cephas, 143, 160, 177, 209-14, 220, *see also* Caiaphas
Chariot divine, 98ff, 145ff
child, messianic, 49, 92, 185
child-birth, 92
Cherubim, 98ff, 154, 156
China, 114
Chosen People, 32, 45, 159, 202, 205; *see also* Elect
chrism, 131
Christ *(Christos)*, 14, 69, 83, 145, 152, 161, 172, 173,
    174, 180, 181, 207, 208, 210, 214, 231; *see also*
    Anointed
Christian, pre-Christian, designation, 81, 107; ethics,
    192, 201
Christianity (Messianism), 12, 16, 191; uniqueness, 13,
    18, 19
chronology, of Scrolls and New Testament, 14; *see also*
    Paul
Church, early, 12, 13, 14, 15, 16, 18, 66, 123, 129,
    130, 138, 139, 144, 152, 160, 162, 172, 173, 174,
    190, 201, 203, 207-12, 215, 216, 221, 225, 229;
    modern, role of, 229ff
Church Fathers, 140, 181, 192

Church, the Great, 132, 138, 152, 192, 201, 223, 225,
    228, 230
cinnamon, 124
circumcision, 77, 224
cities, of refuge, 80, 196; of the wilderness, 29, 44
Clark, A.J., 148
Claudius Caesar, 141
Clement, Bishop, 129, 139, 141, 160
Cleobius, 144
climate, 10, 21, 22
clinic, Essene, 213ff, 236
coins, 20, 29
coitus interruptus, 122-4
common fund, 216, 219; *see also* poor fund
communal possessions, 12, 16, 27ff
Community, Men of the, 35, 98; Rule, 18, 96, 97ff,
    135, 191, 213, 215, 221
Congregation of Israel, 121
contraception, 122ff, 133, 136, 229
copper (treasure) scroll, 26-30, 33, 75
Coptic papyri, *see* Nag Hammadi
Corinthians, letters to, 83, 99, 188
Covenant, biblical, 48, 68, 77, 80; the New, 20, 36, 49,
    88, 191
Covenanters, 35, 48, 49, 95, 101
Cross, the, 36, 61, 83, 102, 132, 195, 196, 224, 234; *see
    also* Tree
Crucifixion, chronology of, 16, 196, 226, 227; of Jesus,
    14, 132, 140, 161, 195, 226, 227; of Teacher, 36, 40-
    3, 61, 81, 82ff, 85, 101, 132, 158, 161, 187, 195,
    196, 200, 224, 226; practice of, 36, 40, 56, 84
Creation, 78, 104, 169, 179, 223, 225, 228
creator-God(s), 131, 138, 225, 228, 233
cultus, Jewish, 95, 96, 101, 186
cyclical view of history, 30, 45-8, 75, 84, 149, 204ff

Dalmatia, 113
Damascus, 36; document, 77, 213, 214, 217, 218, 227
Daniel, book of, 35, 190
Daniel, the sage, 153-5
Darkness, powers, children of, 12, 32, 69, 96, 111ff,
    202, 207
David, King, 12, 77, 84, 205; scion of House of,
    12, 14, 49, 103, 180, 185, 205, 208; *see also*
    Prince, messianic, Shoot
Dawn, son of, *see* Morning-star
Day-bathers (Haemerobaptists), 181, 183, 189
Day-spring (Day-star), *see* Morning-star
Dead Sea, 9, 10, *11*, 16, 19, 20, 21, *25*, 48, 50-3,
    56, 62, 64, 66, 68, 69, *71*, 83, 101, 110, 135, 156,
    158ff, 176, 186, 226; Scrolls, 9, 10, 17, 20, 23, 30,
    52, 64, 68, 78, 79, 81, 99, 109, 115ff, 135, 141, 151,
    152, 185, 187, 191, 192, 193, 195, 217; editing and
    publication, 15, 19, 24, 26, 29, 151
death, 117, 158, 183
Demeter, 157
Demetrius III (Euchaerus), 36, 39, 56
demons, 12, 15, 66ff, 99, 129, 164, 210ff, 219
desert, 9, 12, 17, 22, 38, 44, 45, 49, 53, 64, 66, 69,
    76, 91, 95, 109, 149, 171, 176, 178, 180, 181, 191,
    227, 230; of Jerusalem, 69; of the Peoples, 68ff
determinism, 233

246

Noah, 45ff, 63, 64f, 70, 108, 154
Numbers, book of, 84, 185

Obedas, King, 39
obscurantism, 192, 231, 237
occult, 95, 212, 226; *see also* secrets
Old Testament, 17, 20, 131, 170, 184, 190, 195
Olives, Mount of, 52, 56, 197
omniscience, 129
omriel, 211, 236
Ophites (*ophis* 'serpent'), *see* Serpent People
Origen, 131, 141, 187
Ossaeans, 135
Overseer, 66, 210, 213-19

Palestine, 9, 10, *11*, 13, 31, 63, 72, 74ff, 94, 113,
    139, 151, 158, 159, 181, 190, 192, 193, 204ff
papyrus, 10, 26, 135
Paradise, 49, 156; *see also* Eden
paralytic, 222
parchment, 10, 17, 23, 26, 185, 187, 208, 235
Partridge Cave (IV), 22ff, 24, *25*, 30, 36, 79, 135,
    185, 208, 211, 213, 217, 235
Passover *(pascha)*, 80, 122ff, 174; *see also* Lamb
Paul, St, chronology, 14, 16, 161, 195; letters,
    teaching, 14, 99, 140, 161, 165ff, 177, 188, 190,
    194, 195, 196, 210, 224, 228, 234; person,
    143, 145, 172
pearls, 182ff
Peleg ('Division'), House of, 143
Pentateuch, 78, 187
Pentecost, 172, 188, 217
People of the Book, 48, 151
Persecution, 139, 174, 175, 192, 198, 226, 230
Persephone/Kore, 157
Persia, *see* Iran
Peter, St *(Petros)*, 117, 143-7, 180, 207-21; letters of,
    120, 221
petra 'stone', 207ff
Petra (Nabatean), 56
Pharisees, 10, 37, 39, 91, 94, 143
pharmacy, pharmacopoeia, 55, 63, 148
Phibionites, 122
Philip, apocryphal gospel of, 117
Philippians, letter to, 165ff
Philo Judaeus, 10, 96, 109-11, 173
physician, 12, 64, 183, 214, 220; *see also* healing
Pilate, Pontius, 146, 199, 227
pillar, 143, 177, 180, 187ff; of fire, cloud, 170,
    177-80, 181; of the Church, 143, 177, 188ff; of the
    Dawn, 179, 180, 181, 186, 189; *see also* Morning-
    star
Pit, 86, 89, 111, 115, 153, 156; *see also* Hell
Plain, the *see* Arabah
Planets, 95, 112, 179, 207
planting, eternal, 53-5, 98
Pleroma, see Fullness
Pliny, the Elder, 10, 31, 182ff
Pluto, 157
political independence, 36, 94ff, 100; theocracy,
    15, 95, 224
Pompey, 94ff

Poor Fund, 216
Poor Ones, 86
power, of God, *see* Simon; temporal, 114, 153, 230
prayer, 21, 96, 111, 122, 134, 135, 159, 178, 183
predestination, 95ff, 102, 163-5, 224; *see also* election
Presbyters, 18
presence, divine, 99, 100, 105, 148
Priest, The, 13, 36, 79, 121, 187, 218
Prince, messianic, 12, 32, 79, 100ff, 111, 152, 168ff,
    185, 187
prognostication, 48, 211
Promised Land, 46, 48, 49, 74ff, 77, 80, 84, 149, 191,
    227
Propaganda, 159
prophecy, art of, 212
Prophet, The (messianic), 79, 186, 187
prophets, biblical, 12, 13, 32, 46, 47, 48, 149,
    152ff, 158, 159, 195
propitiation, 84, 102, 146, 158, 191, 195
prostitute, common, 14, 82, 115ff, 141, 152, 157,
    167ff; *see also* Helen; sacred, 131, 169
Proverbs, book of, 104ff, 116, 179
Psalm 37, commentary on, 42, 82, 113
Psalms, biblical, 69, 104, 131, 152, 160, 161ff,
    168, 178, 184ff, 207
Pure Ones, Purifiers, *see* Catharists
purification, 21, 82, 133ff
Purity of the Many, 133ff, 214

Queen of Heaven, 156ff
Qumran, *11*, *25*, 29, 48, *73*; *see also* Secacah
Qur'an, 148

rachal 'trade', 167
Rachel, Simon's mother, 141, 167
rain, thunderstorm, 21, 118, 124
rapha 'heal', 64
Raphael, 64
rationalism, 232ff
Red Sea, 48, 111
Redeemer (saviour), redemption, 15, 45,
    46, 64, 83, 85, 95, 97, 102, 107ff, 112, 121, 138,
    140, 142, 144, 146, 158, 161, 169, 191, 194, 195,
    196, 199, 202, 205, 221, 224ff, 227, 228, 229, 230,
    232, 234
Repentance, Day of, 78; *see also* end-time
Rephaim, 63ff, 66, 155; *see also* Shades
Restoration, post-Exilic, 204ff
revelation, divine, 96-106, 112, 117, 176, 178, 179,
    232; book of, *see* John, St
revolts, Jewish, 20, 33, 95, 135, 202
Rift Valley, 9, 19, 21, 44, 50, 62, 64, 69, 156
Righteous Ones, 56
river of life, *see* waters, living
robbers, 81, 197ff
Rock, of Church, 206-10, 221; of Restoration, 32,
    206ff
Roman Catholic Church, 129, 209
Romans, 14, 16, 20, 31, 32, 33, 34, 35, 75, 94ff, 101,
    110, 132, 135, 144, 160, 191, 193, 198, 201, 202,
    226, 227; letter to, 165
Rome, 16, 113, 114, 139, 141, 143-7, 209
Rule of the Congregation, 120ff

250

251